AF225158

SHAPING
PATHS

How to Design and Deliver
PRACTICAL Training

By JAMIE DIXON

SHAPING PATHS: How to Design and Deliver PRACTICAL Training

Copyright © 2019 by Jamie Dixon.
All rights reserved.

Published by Jamie Dixon
ISBN-13: 978-1-5272-3685-1

No part of this book may be reproduced in any form or by any means electronically or otherwise, unless permission has been granted by the author and/or publisher, with the exception of brief excerpts for review purposes.

Cover creation by Bogdan Matei

Editing and formatting by Lorraine Reguly from www.WordingWell.com

List of Contents

Why This Book? 9

How to Use this Book 11

Part 1—Training Doesn't Work? 13

- Outcome Focus 14
- Direction 16
- Energy Budget 18
- Intrinsic Motivation 20
- Involvement 22
- Flow 24
- Reflection and Practice 26

7 Training Success Factors Summary 28

Part 2—Mapping the Gap 29

- Performance Gaps 31
- Knowledge Gaps 32
- Skill Gaps 34
- Mindset Gaps 38
- Motivation Gaps 41
- Communication Gaps 46
- Environment Gaps 49

6 Performance Gaps Summary 52

Defining Outcomes 53

- Who Decides? 54
- Why Run This Training? 58
- What Are the Expectations? 60
- How Will This Impact the Business? 62
- What Will Learners Do Differently? 65

5 Key Questions Summary 68

Part 3—Designing for Lasting Impact 69

Researching a Solution 72

- The 4 Key Questions..74
- Steal vs. Copy 77
- Working with Subject Matter Experts..81
- Using Other Sources 84
- Finding the Vital Few...87

Researching a Solution Summary 91

Designing for Application..92

- 3 Conditions for Habit Change 94
- They Will Forget..98
- The Barriers to Recall 99
- Knowledge in the Head and Environment 103
- How Tools Aid Application 106
- Follow the Path of Desire 108
- Design for Context..111
- Reduce the Gap 114
- Mnemonics Aid Recall 115
- Memory through Association 116
- Memory through Chunking...119
- Memory through Logical Sequence 122
- Memory through Visualisation 123

Designing for Application Summary..125

Designing for Emotion 126

- Three Levels of Emotional Design 129
- Making a Strong First Impression 132
- What Do You Remind Me Of? 134
- Expectations and Satisfaction..139
- Using Rewards..141
- Make it Meaningful 144
- Adding Joy 146

- Surprise! 147
- Mystery 148
- Gamification 149
- Elevating Status 153
- A Sense of Belonging 155

Designing for Emotion Summary 157

Part 4—The Five Elements of Delivery 158

Priming 160
- The Drivers of Social Behaviour—SCARF 162
- Generating Interest 170
- Making a Strong First Impression 172
- Building Rapport 175
- Getting the Environment Right 177
- Goodwill towards All Learners 184
- Building Confidence 187
- Why We Get Nervous 191
- Breaking the Nervous Cycle 193
- Projecting Authority 195
- Dealing with Resistance 201
- The Who, Why, How Template 205

Priming Summary 208

Guiding 209
- From Lecturing to Storytelling 211
- The Ladder of Explanation 213
- Talk to Their Emotions 219
- Crafting Stories 221
- Show, Don't Tell 224
- Using Analogies 227
- From Showing to Asking 230
- How Not to Put People on the Spot 231

- Constructing Questions 234
- Experiential Learning Activities...241
- Choosing Experiential Learning Activities...242
- Designing Experiential Learning Activities..243
- Sample Experiential Learning Activities 245

Guiding Summary...248

Practicing 249
- Start with Objectives 250
- Defining the Behaviour 253
- Defining the Standards 257
- Defining the Conditions...260
- Training Objective Template 261
- The Stages of Mastery...263
- Planning Transfer Activities..267
- Design Practice by Testing Objectives...271
- Describe and Model Before Practice 273
- Practice in Context 276
- Focussed Practice...279
- Efficient Practice 283
- From Feedback to Feedforward 287

Practicing Summary..293

Reflecting..294
- Shallow Reflection—Recall and Apply 297
- Deep Reflection—Reviewing with the VACA Model.........................299
- V is for Vent...301
- A is for Analyse 303
- Conclude...305
- A is for Apply 306
- Designing Reflection Activities 307
- Energising Reflection Activities 311

- Increasing Reflection Throughout 316
- Reflection Activity Template 318

Reflecting Summary 321

Committing 322
- Compliance in the Process of Commitment 323
- The Elephant and The Rider 325
- The Habit Loop Theory 329
- Commitment Plans 333

Committing Summary 337

Part 5—Creating Materials 338

Designing for Visual Impact 339
- Choosing Your Tool 340
- Designing Templates 343
- Selecting Visuals 353
- Arranging Elements 357
- Using Slideshows 364
- Using Videos 369
- Using Flip Charts 371

Writing and Readability 374
- What is Readability? 375
- Layout 377
- Clear Writing Habits 379
- Eliminate Fluff 384
- Less Is More 386

Keeping Productive 387
- Brain Power 388
- Beating Procrastination 394
- Beating Blocks 395

Creating Materials Summary 398

Conclusion 399

Books that Inspired Me 402

About the Author 404

A Note from the Author (and Contact Information) 405

Why This Book?

There are many books out there on training, so why did I write another one?

In the early days of my career as a trainer, I looked through book after book after book for tips to help me become more proficient. I found a lot of great stuff, but I was also left with a lot of questions, such as:
- How can I make my training more valuable?
- How do I get people to use what they learnt at work?
- How can I minimise wasted time in the training room?
- Beyond engagement, what else is necessary for a good learning experience?
- How do I explain things effectively?
- How can I get people to answer my questions?
- How do I impact people on an emotional level?

And so on.

I discovered something quite interesting about a lot of trainers. Many trainers know how to engage people, how to help people remember things, how to tell stories and jokes, and how to play games. But, ironically, there are a lot of trainers that don't know and don't care about how to achieve behaviour change.

I actually had to go to other fields to understand more about behaviour change. In my opinion, the field of Learning and Development does not pay enough attention to actual behaviour change. And I think I know why.

Trainers and Training Managers are normally just responsible for organising and delivering learning activities, yet are not held accountable for the results these activities are supposed to deliver. In theory, the learners are responsible for enacting the results of the training (behaviour change) back at work. But, in reality, they are rarely held accountable. In fact, in reality, usually hardly anyone is held accountable. This means it's actually possible for us trainers to deliver a useless solution and still get paid!

This leads to frequent failure. Learners attend training, then go back to work and forget. Then people start asking questions, so Trainers and Training Managers seem to point fingers (out of habit) at the learners themselves or their managers for not being responsible enough. This finger-pointing, to me, seems ludicrous.

If you look at other fields of design, you see completely different attitudes. Take mobile phone apps, as an example. The designers design an app, but the people who decide to actually buy the app are the end users. Again, the result is out of the designers' hands. But if no one buys the app, then the person who designed the app doesn't get paid!

This means they approach their work with a completely different attitude. They don't just focus on delivering an app. They focus on delivering an app people will ACTUALLY USE. They take the latest lessons from neuroscience, they conduct tests, and they keep amending their app until they finally end up with something people *want* to use.

Whilst I'm not saying we can 100% definitely control our learners' behaviour post-training, I believe that we should approach training design with an attitude of wanting to ensure they behave back at work in the ways that we want them to behave.

So, how do we do that?

This book advocates designing usable tools and basing the entire training experience on that (whereas what a lot of trainers seem to advocate is just delivering an engaging and memorable experience).

Usable tools means tools people will ACTUALLY use. To get a tool people will actually use requires a lot of simplifying, a lot of understanding what goes on in the learners' worlds, and a lot of experimenting and amending, based on feedback. If we approach our training design with this goal in mind and couple it with the attitude of accountability for application, then we become capable of realising the full value of our training.

To me, this book is my guide. As I've researched and written each section, I have referred to it over and over again, to get ideas to improve various trainings I've been working on. It's been a big help to me, and the ideas I've shared with other trainers have been a big help to them. It's my hope that you find these ideas a big help to you, too.

How to Use this Book

I recommend using this as a dip-in-and-out book.

But if you want to read it from start to finish, you'll find it's been arranged in a logical structure, taking you from understanding the conditions for success (Part 1—Training Doesn't Work), to focussing on the right outcome (Part 2—Mapping the Gap), then to smoothly conducting the design process (Part 3—Designing for Lasting Impact), before looking at how to effectively and efficiently deliver an engaging training (Part 4—The Five Elements of Delivery), with one final look at how to create materials (Part 5—Creating Materials).

There's a lot of information in this book, so I've tried to simplify it into as many usable tools and reference aids as possible. Any time you see a visual in the book, it is there to serve as a summary or a tool.

I hope that, with these tools, you won't feel the need to remember things. Instead, you can enjoy reading through and see what ideas spark for you, and when you're ready to start using things, you can just flip to the tools and follow those. Or, if you find the tools don't work for you, then, at the very least, I hope they can give you some ideas for designing new tools that are better suited to you.

And just to emphasise, I recommend using this as a dip-in-and-out book. If you approach it as a read-from-start-to-finish book, you may find it a bit overwhelming. This book will be far more useful for you as a reference aid, in your times of need.

This book is split into 5 parts, and below is a summary of how each part can help you.

Part 1—Training Doesn't Work

Read this if you want to:
- Identify what conditions are necessary for training to be a success
- Determine if a training project is doomed to failure, and find what the missing ingredients are

Part 2—Mapping the Gap

Read this if you want to:
- Find the root cause of performance issues
- Determine if training is the right solution or not
- Conduct an effective needs analysis
- Ask stakeholders the right questions
- Get your training off to the right start

Part 3—Designing for Lasting Impact

Read this if you want to:
- Improve your research ability
- Design training that impacts learners at work
- Design practical tools that learners are more likely to use
- Design training that impacts learners on an emotional level

Part 4—The Five Elements of Delivery

Read this if you want to:
- Help learners get in the right mental state for learning
- Get yourself in the right mental state for delivering training
- Get the training off to a great start
- Give effective explanations to help learners understand
- Use storytelling techniques to generate more interest
- Use questioning techniques to increase engagement and help learners better understand
- Design and/or run experiential learning activities
- Design and/or run effective and efficient practice activities
- Plan learning transfer activities
- Achieve a deep learning impact
- Design and/or run reflection and debriefing activities
- Increase engagement in reflection and debriefing activities
- Help learners commit to following up on action plans after training

Part 5—Creating Materials

Read this if you want to:
- Design training materials with visual impact
- Improve the readability of training materials
- Improve your productivity as a training designer

Part 1—Training Doesn't Work?

You don't have to go far to find someone who believes this. Blog after article after research paper will tell you that billions of dollars are wasted every year on training. In every company, there is a Manager or Director who has lost faith in training. If you speak to enough people, you'll find plenty of reasons to believe that training doesn't work.

There is some truth to that. A lot of people (perhaps even you) have had bad experiences with training. You've probably sat in a classroom at some point and felt bored, or felt what was being taught was useless and quickly forgot everything afterwards.

But people still need to learn, and training is a way of helping people learn. We all know how fast the world is changing, and how much businesses need to adapt to that. If you're reading this book, it's probably because someone has asked you to deliver training for them.

On the one hand, there are many who believe training doesn't work. Yet on the other hand, there is still a demand for it. So does training work?

That's a lot like asking 'Does dieting work?' You're always going to find people with different opinions and experiences. The answer is never going to be 'Yes' or 'No'. Instead it will be 'It depends'.

With training, just like with dieting, it is possible to make it work. You can help people generate new insights for old problems. You can help people develop their skills to a higher level. You can help people achieve their goals.

Instead of asking 'Does training work?' we should be asking 'What **would** make training work?'

By asking this question, we start to realise that there **are** conditions under which training works. When we know these conditions, we can start designing and delivering training that switches on those conditions.

That's the purpose of this book. I want to make it easier for you to help people. I've identified these conditions, and arranged them into a framework for you. This framework is easy to use and will allow you to help your learners achieve more.

Later in this book, we're going to look at how to enable these conditions. First, let's have a look at what these conditions are.

- ## Outcome Focus

What would make training work? If you think about it, the first condition is quite obvious. It's being able to define what is meant by training working.

If your goal is to get 25 bums on seats for 2 days, and you achieve that, then frankly your training 'worked'. But if bums on seats is the only outcome you're after, then it's a bit of a sorry world we live in.

At the same time, if your goal is for 30 of your recent graduate recruits to come out of a 1-day training program and then go on to generate $100 million in revenue within the next 2 weeks, then your desired outcome may be a bit unrealistic.

This raises the question 'What is training capable of?' Again, this is another question for which the answer is 'It depends'. The possibilities of training and the boundaries of reasonable expectations are topics we will see pop up over and over again throughout this book.

The biggest benefit of being outcome-focussed is that we can then create a plan to achieve that outcome. We can then break the plan down into baby steps and focus on each step, one at a time, until we finally achieve our outcome.

Being outcome-focussed isn't just about what happens after the training. It's also a fundamental practice for pretty much every tiny step of designing and delivering your training.

For example, when we sit down to design a practice activity, we'll probably find it very difficult if we don't know what we are trying to achieve. Rather than design activities that help learners achieve a goal, we'll just end up searching the Internet for activities to fill the time.

When you conduct your Needs Analysis, you need to speak to your stakeholders. Imagine what would happen if you started speaking to them without knowing what you wanted to ask them or what information you wanted to get. The conversation would probably go around in circles, you'd probably get confused, and you'd leave feeling like you hadn't got what you needed.

When you are actually delivering your training, at different stages, you need to focus on achieving different outcomes. Sometimes you need to help your learners relax, whereas other times you need to push them. Sometimes you need to explain something, whereas other times you need to encourage them to reflect. And sometimes you need to show them whereas other times you need to let them try things on their own.

A further aim of this book is to give you an outcome focus for each step of the framework. When you know what you are trying to achieve, you'll be able to make better decisions and be more present throughout it all. You'll be able to design faster, and deliver with much more impact.

- **Direction**

By now you might be thinking, 'Okay, so what is training anyway?' That's a good question, so let's have a look.

Training is a formal, structured learning solution. Training is intentionally designed and/or delivered to help learners do specific things that they previously either couldn't do at all, or couldn't do to a certain standard.

There are lots of versions of training out there. Some are in-class, some are on the job, and others are online. This book has been written with classroom training in mind, but many of the principles still apply to other training contexts.

An important thing to remember is that training is not the only way of learning. There are also informal, non-structured, spontaneous, and natural ways of learning. There are lots of different terms for these but, for the sake of simplicity, I am going to refer to all of these in this book as learning by chance.

A lot of the things that you have learnt, you have probably learnt by chance, through a natural process of trial and error, reflection, and practice. Did you take formal lessons to learn how to type? Probably not. You probably picked it up by just trying. The same applies to learning how to use a phone or with learning how to live with your spouse (unless you needed marriage counselling!).

As training is purposefully designed and delivered with intention, it takes effort on the part of the designer and deliverer, as well as the learner. This means there is an investment of time and money. Whereas learning by chance, generally speaking, doesn't require an investment of money (unless learning by chance led to you making a mistake that cost a lot of money!). So if we are to justify the cost of training, then we need to make sure it does a much more efficient job than learning by chance. How do we do that? Direction.

Direction is what people go to training for. They have a problem and can't find a solution. They come to training to find a solution. They have reached a plateau in their skill development, and need help with finding a breakthrough. They come to training because they haven't found that breakthrough on their own. Direction is fundamental to effective training.

Direction shows learners what to do, how to do it, when to do it, and why they should do it. But remember, just because you told someone the direction doesn't mean they learnt it. We need to find ways of showing our learners the right direction, allowing them to reflect on it, and practice it. We need to spend less time teaching people, and more time helping people learn.

Direction reinforces the right way of doing things, and corrects the wrong way. Every so often, we need to step in with feedback to reinforce their direction. We need to raise awareness of areas that need more attention. We need to give them encouragement and nudge them in the right direction.

Direction is not just giving people some abstract ideas like 'Be in the moment'.

Direction is focussed on actions that our learners can take immediately when it counts.

If you were teaching someone meditation and the only direction you gave was to 'Be in the moment', then that doesn't help. What does 'Be in the moment' mean? How can I 'Be in the moment'? Direction is actionable; it doesn't require interpretation. 'Notice the sounds around you' is a much clearer direction because it's something you can do immediately.

Direction also needs to be relevant. It must both be something the learner can do, as well as something that gets the desired results. This is something self-defence classes get very wrong. Your partner throws a punch, and then freezes whilst you take your time to apply the technique you just learnt. But in real life, your attacker won't freeze when they punch you. You don't have that much time to react. For direction to be relevant, it must be applicable in the conditions under which it will be used in real life.

Finally, direction can either be provided or discovered. Either we design our training so that we show learners the direction they need to take, or we design activities that help learners discover the direction they need to take. Either way, training only works if, by the end of it, learners have a new direction to take, going forward.

Direction is something we need to take care to get right. We will see lots of ways of doing this throughout this book.

- ## Energy Budget

The purpose of training is to change behaviour. Change takes energy. If we want our learners to change, we need to make sure they have enough energy to change.

But this is not just about energy levels during the training. Far more important is making sure they have enough energy to sustain the change *after* the training. If they can't implement these changes back at work where they matter, then our training will be a failure.

This is actually where so much training fails. Learners walk out of the workshop with good intentions. But upon returning to work, reality hits. They get busy. They get tired. When they have an opportunity to use what they learnt, they struggle to remember it, or don't have enough energy to use it.

How do we make sure learners have enough energy to change?

We can't. But what we can do is make the change so energy efficient that our learners don't require more energy than they have available.

Consider just some of the different things that are required in order to sustain a change in someone's behaviour:

- **Cognitive Energy**—Remember when you first learnt to drive and how hard you had to concentrate? That's cognitive energy right there.
- **Physical Energy**—Writing is quite easy, isn't it? Well, try changing hands and seeing how easy it feels then. It might look easy, but you need to use a lot of energy to write with your other hand.
- **Time**—Doing something new means you can't do it fast. Have you ever tried to learn a new language? When having just learnt to speak a new language, most people take extra time to translate in their heads first before being able to say something in the new language. This all takes time.
- **Practice**—It takes practice to master a new skill. You don't learn to drive by taking just one lesson. You have to take lots of lessons, and practice over and over and over again.
- **Feedback**—People who enjoy long-distance running can injure themselves very easily if they don't have proper form. It's all well and good to practice, but if you end practicing the wrong thing, then you end up mastering the wrong thing. Feedback can help correct mistakes early on.

I think you get the point. Changing behaviour takes A LOT of energy as well as having the right conditions at the right time. The more complicated the behavioural change is, the less likely it is to happen.

But this doesn't mean we need to give up on our training. If we take the right approach, we can create valuable changes in behaviour. All we need to do is ensure that the energy requirements of the behavioural changes we want to make are within the energy budget of our learners.

What we do need to do is take a Zen razor to the design of our training. We must avoid overwhelming our learners, and instead spend as much time focussed on achieving realistic changes as possible.

We should focus on changes that create maximum value with the minimum investment of effort.

How do we do that? Again, this is something that will come up throughout this book.

- ## Intrinsic Motivation

A core and important assumption of adult learning is that adults learn for a reason. Adults don't just learn because their manager told them to. Adults invest time and energy into learning because they feel a need to do so.

For example, let's look at the scenario involving Jason. Jason is an engineer at a company that makes space ships. You are his boss. You have just told him that there is an important course in Geology that he must attend at the local University. He must attend and pass the course in order to keep his job. 'Oh, boy', Jason thinks. 'Geology…my favourite subject', he says to himself in a very sarcastic tone.

So Jason goes to the local University and takes the course. He turns up on time every day. He tries to focus on the class, but most of the time ends up wondering why he is there. He also daydreams a lot about getting back to making his spaceships. When the teacher sets homework, Jason does the homework. When the test comes up, Jason looks at the grading criteria and identifies what he must study in order to pass the test. He spends just enough time studying to pass the test, but not more than that.

In the end, Jason gets a C for this test. It's a satisfactory result because he passed, he can keep his job, and he never has to worry about Geology anymore.

But we could have helped Jason learn a lot more. So let's go back a bit and change how this course was presented to Jason.

This time, you sit down with Jason and show him a picture. The picture is of the surface of Mars. 'Our spaceship will be landing here', you say, pointing to a crater. 'It's a rocky surface, and we must ensure the spaceship lands safely on it.'

Jason nods his head.

'I need you to learn about these rocks so you can make a spaceship that can land on them.'

Jason nods his head and says, 'I see'.

'There is a course at the local University on Geology. I suggest you attend because it will help you understand what these rocks are like.'

'Good idea', Jason replies.

So Jason goes to the University course. This time, he turns up with a list of questions. He takes notes. At the end of each lecture, Jason goes up to the instructor to ask him his long list of questions. Jason also scours the textbooks for answers to his questions.

When it comes to the test, Jason doesn't need to remember so much. He's already studied a lot, and he already knows most of the answers. So, this time when he takes the test, he gets an A.

The difference between the first example and second example is extrinsic and intrinsic motivation.

Extrinsic motivators are factors outside of the training that will push learners to take the training. For example, their manager telling them they must go would be extrinsic. Taking a course in order to get a good grade would also be extrinsic. Intrinsic, on the other hand, is all the factors about the training itself that motivate learners to take the course. Two examples include the course that provides answers to their questions, and helping them develop skills that solve problems in their work.

Learning is not something that can be forced. Learners need a reason to learn. They need to care about the learning. Extrinsic motivators can only push our learners, they won't engage our learners. At the very most, extrinsic motivators will lead to learners who only perform when pushed. This result is not sustainable. But intrinsic motivation is.

If our learners are intrinsically motivated, they will be more active. They will pay attention, seek answers to questions, and actively apply new skills to their work. And we, as trainers, will see greater benefit coming from our training.

Your learners are not the only ones with an interest in the training. If your target audience is corporate, then you may have a lot of stakeholders such as HR, managers, senior leaders, etc. Each may have their own specific requests on what should be included in the training, but what is absolutely essential is that this training is designed with the learner in mind. If the learners have no intrinsic motivation, then, at the end of the day, no one is going to be happy.

We'll look at lots of ways of identifying and sustaining intrinsic motivation throughout the rest of this book.

- ## Involvement

Sitting in a classroom for two days can be quite demanding for some people, especially when the experience is not very engaging. People might switch off, get distracted, or lose interest. They might even sit there, staring at the ceiling, waiting for the time to pass.

Engagement is a lot like a door. If a door is shut, nothing gets in. Likewise, if learners are not engaged, nothing will get in, and no learning will happen. It doesn't matter what's happening in the world around them—if they are not engaged in it, they won't pay attention.

There are many reasons engagement might slip off.

For a start, learners may turn up to the training with other things on their mind. Maybe they have something urgent that they need to get done, so they sit there, constantly wondering when a good time to slip out would be. Maybe, during the training, they will receive emails or text messages with sudden demands. Maybe they will have a noisy classmate sitting next to them, constantly distracting their attention.

The room might be too warm. Maybe they will start to drift off. Maybe a lack of sunlight will create a dim atmosphere. Maybe they had a big lunch and in the afternoon they struggle to keep their head up. Perhaps they recently had a baby and didn't get much sleep last night.

Every facilitator has their own tricks for raising energy. It might involve telling a story, playing a game, doing some stretches, or using some subtle way of rearranging the room.

But the design of our training also has a big impact on engagement.

If one section goes on for too long, then our learners struggle to concentrate. They become overwhelmed and exhausted, and their minds can't keep up, so they switch off.

Or maybe that section was all theory and demanded that the facilitator lecture it. If a lecture goes on for too long, people will become overwhelmed and even bored. Again, their minds will switch off.

Perhaps the progression of content moves at the wrong pace. If it goes too slow, then learners will become bored. They might feel there is nothing challenging about it, they know it all already, and their minds will start to drift.

Maybe it progresses too quickly. Yet again, they will become overwhelmed. They also will become frustrated and might consciously decide to check out as they feel increasingly hopeless.

There are so many reasons engagement levels might drop. But what's important to remember is that **engagement is the foundation of a good learning experience.** If any section of the training doesn't engage them, then they won't learn anything from that section. They need to be engaged all the time.

Engagement is, essentially, very simple. Replace the word 'engage' with the word 'involve' and you can see how easy it is to engage people. All we need to do is to involve them as much as possible.

Lectures will suddenly become much more engaging if we involve the audience. Just ask a few questions. At the very least, you will get people to raise their hands. Maybe you will even get certain members of the audience to cover certain parts of the lecture.

Activities become much more engaging if everyone is involved. Sometimes we see a few individuals dominating discussions, whilst the quiet ones sit quietly in the corner. So instead, reduce group sizes so it's easier for every individual to be involved throughout. And even break it up into sections. Have an individual preparation stage, then a pair discussion stage before moving on to a group discussion stage. Ensure every individual is capable of being involved in every part of the activity.

Feedback also becomes much more engaging if you can involve everyone. Instead of just getting the instructor to provide feedback, ask other learners to give feedback to each other. Get them to pair up and share feedback with each other. Or break them into groups and give each group a certain area to focus on. Then allow them to share their feedback on that particular area.

When you think of engagement as involvement, it suddenly becomes really easy to design your training for maximum engagement. And when your learners are fully engaged, they are fully focussed on the learning experience and are ready to gain the most benefit from it.

- ## Flow

Flow is the state of being fully focussed on a task, so much so that you don't think about anything else. Time ceases to exist, and you, in a way, become the task. It's a higher level of engagement; it's more than simply being involved.

Flow is the state video game designers want players to enter. As players enter this state, everything in the real world seems to fade away. The calls from their parents or spouse (or maybe even their own children) go ignored.

Flow is also the state that many athletes and artists enter. Some call it 'being in the zone'. Others call it 'being in the moment'.

You may even find it through activities such as solving puzzles, reading books, or chatting with good friends.

There are certain conditions that bring on the flow state. These are:
- A challenging (yet achievable) and clear goal
- Timely feedback about progress towards that goal
- Confidence in the ability to achieve the goal

For example, say you are solving a 100-piece jigsaw puzzle and want to do so within 30 minutes.
- Is this a challenging (yet achievable) goal? For most people, yes. It's challenging yet entirely possible to complete it within that time limit.
- Is there feedback about progress towards that goal? Yes. When the pieces match, they click together. As you make further progress through the puzzle, more and more of the picture is revealed to you.
- Do you have confidence in your ability to achieve the goal? You most likely would have confidence. 100 pieces is not too daunting. And 30 minutes, although tricky, is also entirely possible.

Yet, if we change the conditions slightly, we get a slightly different state.

For example, say you have 2 hours to complete a 25-piece puzzle. Now you would feel bored because it's too simple.

What if you had only 15 minutes to complete a 1000-piece puzzle? Now you'd probably feel frustrated because that's too difficult.

Flow exists in the sweet spot between boredom and anxiety.
The conditions must be just right in order for it to exist.

Although flow is an internal state, there are three things we can do to increase the chances of a task creating a flow state:

1. **Define clear goals**
2. **Provide more feedback**
3. **Increase or decrease the level of difficulty**

This is why we sometimes hear of people changing jobs because they wanted a new challenge. They became so good at what they did that it became too easy. So the work went from inducing a flow state to inducing a state of boredom.

We also hear of people changing jobs because the job was too stressful. Maybe the goal was unachievable, or there just wasn't a goal. Maybe they weren't getting the right feedback. Maybe they didn't have the skills or support to confidently face the challenge. It's easy to see how someone would feel overwhelmed in such circumstances.

So, in training, we need to keep our learners in the flow zone. We need to be constantly challenging them, pushing them out of their comfort zone, and giving them puzzles to solve. But we need to make sure the challenge is just within their reach, and they are only just able to achieve it. It's only when they are in flow that they are focussed and driven enough to push themselves beyond their current boundaries and start improving.

- ## Reflection and Practice

Our brains are big bundles of neurons. Think of them as like little sparks of light that exist to transfer information to different places like nerves, muscles, and glands. Whenever you lift a cup of coffee, that's because neurons have transferred certain information to the relevant places to enable you to do that. The same thing happens when you drive a car, throw a ball, or read a book. Everything you are capable of doing is because of your neurons.

Our neurons transfer information through neural pathways. Think of them as like long streaks of light, like viewing a freeway from space at night time. When you lift a cup of coffee, a specific set of neurons travel through specific neural pathways. If you were to put your brain under an MRI scanner, you would see these pathways light up as electrical signals.

Learning is basically the process of developing new neural pathways. Any skill, thinking process, habit, knowledge, or memory, etc., that you have exists because you have neural pathways to enable them. When you can't do or remember something, you simply need to develop the right neural pathways required in order to do that.

You can also think of these neural pathways like treading paths in a grassy field. When we do something once, we tread a pathway through the grassy field. But after a short while, the grass grows back, and that pathway disappears. In order to keep our learning, just like to keep that pathway, we have to retrace it many, many times.

But we can't just give our learners these pathways. Our learners must burn the pathway themselves. It's no good us just telling them 'Do this'. Simply listening to instructions doesn't mean someone can do something. They actually have to take those instructions and convert them into actions.

Take experience, in particular, as an example. We all know that experience is an incredibly valuable learning tool. But the reality is that every day we experience lots of things, yet we don't learn from every experience. The only times we learn from experience are when we step back and figure things out, or, in other words, reflect.

Reflection is the process of actively forming new neural pathways. It's that time when we tilt our head to the side, look up, and scratch our chin. If I read a book and I see something interesting, I'll start to think of what that new idea brings to mind. I'll think of how something that previously made no sense to me now might make sense if I connect it to this new idea. I might even think about ways of testing that new idea, or other ways of using that new idea.

Reflection helps me see the connection I need to form. It helps me visualise that pathway. But it is practice that will help me tread that pathway. And practice isn't just about moving our arms and legs. Sometimes it is about developing a new thinking process.

If I am learning how to manage my time better, I still need to reflect and practice. As I reflect, I notice that I should be doing more scheduling, and I currently don't do that enough. I might think about when I should do that, and how I should do that. Then I go and practice scheduling my day to burn that new pathway.

A few years ago, I spent some time learning Tai Chi. When I was learning a Tai Chi form, it was both reflection and practice that helped me burn those new neural pathways. Reflection helped me see the path, whereas practice helped me tread the path. As I reflected, I would think about the difference between what I just did, and what I should do. I would realise that my elbow needs to come back further, and I would think about when I need to do that, and how to do that. I might think about the feeling I will feel in my back, or how my arm should look when I look in the mirror. As I start to practice next time, my attention is on bringing that new connection to life.

Training should show learners how they can solve their problems and achieve their goals. But it should do more than that. It should also provide the space for learners to reflect and practice, and ultimately make it their own.

Remember, learning is a cycle. It is not as simple as reflect once and practice once. The reality is we need to reflect and practice, reflect and practice, reflect and practice, and so on.

For training to be a successful learning experience, it needs to include as many opportunities for reflection and practice as possible. We'll look at different techniques we can use during training to encourage reflection, as well as ways of structuring our training design to include reflection activities throughout.

7 Training Success Factors Summary

There are 7 training success factors, which we have just looked at. They are:

Outcome Focus (1)
Direction (2)
Energy Budget (3)
Intrinsic Motivation (4)
Involvement (5)
Flow (6)
Reflection and Practice (7)

7 Training Success Factors

 Outcome Focus

 Direction

 Energy Budget

 Intrinsic Motivation

 Involvement

 Flow

 Reflection and Practice

Part 2—Mapping the Gap

When I was younger, I used to think that creative work just involved creating something. I'd sit down, decide what I wanted to create, and then create it. But shortly after I started designing training programs, I realised that is not how it works at all.

You've probably heard of writer's block. That's when your mind goes completely blank whenever you try to write something. The same blankness or lack of ideas can happen in any creative field (including designing training), but when you have the right conditions in place, creativity just flows. A big part of getting those conditions right involves doing enough planning beforehand. It involves brainstorming, setting objectives, finding inspiration, building a framework, and so on.

The purpose of Part 2 of this book is to look at how to set objectives for our training (we'll look at finding inspiration, building a framework, and other things in later parts).

As we saw earlier, one of the first conditions for training success is to be outcome-focussed. If we don't know what the outcome we want is, then we don't know what can be classified as success.

It's like going on a journey. To go on a journey, we first need a destination. We need to know where we are going, and we need to be able to tell if we got there or not.

We also need a map. We need to see where we are and where it is we want to go. We need to see the route between these two points. That is why this part is called 'Mapping the Gap'.

Training is all about improving performance, and the desired outcomes we want to define are all about improving and reaching the desired levels of performance. There is a gap between the current level of performance and the desired level of performance. Naturally, we can call this a 'Performance Gap'.

There are different types of performance gaps. For example, some people might not be performing because they don't have the motivation. We call that a 'motivation gap'. Others might not perform because they don't have the right skills. We call this a 'skill gap'.

Not every gap can be covered by training. Some gaps require different solutions. Training can be a bit of a knee-jerk reaction in some companies, and it can sometimes distract people from far more effective solutions as a result. It's a bit like trying to drive a car across the Atlantic Ocean from London to New York. It's not going to work and we'd be much better off taking a flight instead.

Before we get to defining outcomes, we're going to first look at the different types of performance gaps we are likely to encounter. This will help us make sure we are using training in the right way as well as setting realistic outcomes.

• Performance Gaps

If you've been asked to design or deliver training, it's because there is currently a gap. The gap is the difference between what the performance should be and what it currently is. We call this the performance gap.

For example, meet Sam. Sam is the team manager of a group of engineers who recently became sales people. Their company recognised them for their outstanding technical ability and product knowledge, and decided to put them in a more customer-facing role so that they could establish more credibility with customers. But there is a problem. Sam's team of new sales people have no sales skills. They've never done sales before. This is obvious to Sam whenever he takes them out on a client meeting. Sam's sales team have a performance gap. (Actually, they probably have a variety of performance gaps, which we'll see throughout this section.)

There are different performance gaps, each with their own special solution. Some performance gaps can be solved by training, whereas others require different solutions.

The gaps that training has most impact on include:
* knowledge gaps
* skill gaps
* mindset gaps

The gaps that training has minimal impact on include:
* motivation gaps
* communication gaps
* environment gaps

Sometimes performance gaps have much simpler solutions than training. Sometimes a simple tweak in working conditions can improve motivation. Or an organisational restructure can improve communication. Even something as simple as redecorating the office could have an impact on performance.

There are a lot of managers out there who believe that training is the solution for all performance problems. Our responsibility is to educate these managers, and let them know when a simpler, cheaper, and more effective solution exists.

In this section, we'll have a look at the different types of gaps, how to bridge them, and how to decide if training can help or not. We'll also look at some useful tools for helping us analyse our performance gaps.

- ## Knowledge Gaps

Knowledge is the information needed to complete a task. When you don't have this information, there is a knowledge gap. It's actually very simple to bridge this gap: get the information, and complete the task.

If I wanted to travel from one side of Shanghai to the other by subway, then I wouldn't need to learn the skill of taking the subway, I'd just need to know where my nearest subway station is, the one I need to go to, and which line I should change to on the way if a transfer of lines is necessary to get to where I'm going.

For a sales person, knowledge might be information about the product they are selling. For an IT technician, it might be information about the software they are using. For a pilot, it might be information about the functions of the different buttons in the cockpit of the new plane they are flying.

If you find that knowledge is the only gap, then training might not be the best solution. It's normally pretty easy to fill knowledge gaps. Things like books, videos, and wikis can solve the knowledge gap cheaply, simply, and effectively.

Another thing about knowledge gaps is that they can normally be bridged at the exact time of need. For example, the IT technician doesn't need to remember everything about the software he is using. When he encounters Error No. 2XY8HB3, all he needs to do is go to the company wiki and type it in. Straightaway, the wiki presents him with the procedure for dealing with this.

Frankly, it's good that a lot of knowledge gaps can be bridged at the exact time of need. The human memory isn't the most dependable of machines. When there is a lot of information to remember, some things can become blurry, inaccurate, and even forgotten.

With technology these days, bridging knowledge gaps at the exact time of need becomes even easier. Imagine trying to operate a piece of machinery that has a complicated start-up process. These days, you can paste a QR code to the machine. Then, when an operator comes to use it, they just scan the QR code using their mobile phone. Instantly, they are taken to an app and shown a video. The video then guides them, step by step, through the process. After completing each step, the app then gives them a checklist to make sure they have done everything correctly. (Of course, you could just stick those instructions on a piece of paper next to the operating panel to save a lot of time and money!)

Knowledge gaps can be bridged in ways that save a lot of money for organisations. For example, consider the cost of sending a team to attend one day of training delivered by a professional facilitator, in a professional venue. Compare this to the cost and effectiveness of setting up a company wiki to answer their questions instead.

For forward-thinking trainers, knowledge gaps also offer many opportunities. Because bridging them is so cost-effective, organisations will have a strong interest in any way of doing something that saves them money.

But this doesn't mean training is useless for knowledge gaps. Training can still sometimes help bridge knowledge gaps, especially when the knowledge is used in combination with skills and behaviour.

Going back to Sam's team of engineers who recently transitioned to sales people, let's think about what their knowledge gaps are. Obviously, they already know a lot about their products, so that's not it. Their knowledge gaps are more related to sales skills.

Sam's team needs to know what skills to use, how to use them, and when to use them. But knowing this information isn't enough to improve their performance. They will also need a lot of practice. Learning this knowledge will give them the direction they need to start practicing those skills.

Training Knowledge

This might be surprising to some people, but knowledge is HARD to train/teach. We can't just talk knowledge into our learners. Human brains have a very limited capacity for absorbing and embedding information. If we say too much, it's almost the same as saying nothing at all. And if we pass on knowledge just through one lecture, it will very quickly get forgotten or, more likely, not even remembered in the first place.

If we are training knowledge, we need to train it with care. We must ensure the amount of knowledge shared does not exceed their capacity for taking in new information. We need to make sure it is passed on in a meaningful way. We'll look at how we do this later in this book, especially during the Guiding section.

- **Skill Gaps**

If our learners need more practice, then this is a skill gap.

To be skilled at something means you can perform an action (or set of actions) at will, with the minimum of effort, in order to achieve a specific result, and you normally achieve that result.

We can say Lionel Messi, the Argentinian football mega-star who plays for Barcelona FC, is extremely skilled at football (or soccer if you are from the US). I don't think anyone on the planet would deny that. He can perform a number of different actions, many simultaneously, with the absolute minimum of effort, with the intention of achieving a result, and he normally achieves that result.

Sometimes he doesn't achieve that result. Sometimes other people or certain conditions prevent him from doing so. But we can say he is extremely skilled because the ratio of achieved results against intended results is much higher than most other players, and the consistency of those achievements is evidence of his ease in performing these actions. Lionel Messi is a truly great example of someone who is exceptionally skilled because of the consistency of his results.

Signs of High Skill

Consistency　　　　Creativity

Creativity is another sign of an extremely high skill level. Lionel Messi can perform some dazzling feats, all within a split second, without any pre-planning. Other players feel intimidated by him because they don't know what he is going to do next. Or they do know what he is going to do but, despite their best efforts at preventing him, he still finds a way past them.

The reason high skill leads to creativity is because the performer has enough cognitive resources to allocate some to creative thinking. For example, someone who has just learnt how to drive needs to expend a lot of cognitive resources on remembering which things to do at different times. They haven't naturalised all of the required actions, so need to spend a lot of time recalling and retrying the different actions until they finally get the result they are looking for.

A less-skilled opponent, put up against Lionel Messi, has to think a lot more. This means they must also invest much more effort and will react much more slowly.

The path from unskilled to skilled has 4 steps:

1. **Unconscious Incompetence**—Where someone doesn't know what they should be doing.
2. **Conscious Incompetence**—They know what they should be doing, but can't do it.
3. **Conscious Competence**—They know what they should be doing, and can finally do it. But they haven't mastered it, so need to use a lot of conscious effort to perform the actions effectively.
4. **Unconscious Competence**—They can finally perform the actions without the need for conscious effort. They can will the action into life and focus their conscious attention elsewhere.

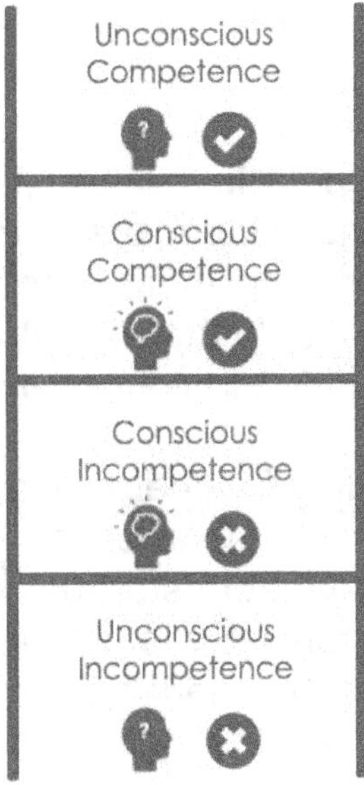

Did Lionel Messi become skilled at football from only going to one training session? No. He has been training his whole life to reach his current skill level. **A one-off training solution cannot bridge skill gaps. Instead, people need a continuous repetition of focussed reflection and practice.** They need numerous opportunities to finally reach the level of competence that is required to perform effectively.

It's Not Always about Mastery

Not every learner needs to reach the Unconscious Competence level of a skilled master like Lionel Messi. In some circumstances, simply being able to perform the action is enough. Sometimes, performance does not need to be to a high standard.

A bus driver may need to have some level of interpersonal skills for interacting with passengers, but they don't need the listening ability of a therapist. A manager responsible for managing a budget may occasionally need to use some advanced functions on Microsoft Excel, but not need to do it whilst under time pressure, nor need to do it frequently. That manager wouldn't struggle to perform their job effectively if they took their time to slowly work their way through those Excel functions on occasion.

Intention and Focus

To bridge skill gaps, we need to help learners practice (and we will look at this in more detail in the Practice section of this book). But learners can also practice by themselves. If they are learning by chance, then there is a good chance that they are still practicing, regardless of whether it's intentional or not. But intention is where training stands out from learning by chance.

For practice to be effective, it needs to be intentionally-focussed. **Learners need to be focussed on performing specific actions, to specific standards, under specific conditions.** We could help them practice individual actions or groups of actions simultaneously. We could help them practice in a relaxed environment or under real life conditions. We could help them practice deciding which actions to use, performing those actions, or a combination of deciding and performing.

Training also adds value by providing feedback, or as I prefer to call it, 'Feedforward'. Feedforward raises awareness on what learners must focus on, going forward. It tells them what to continue doing, and what to start doing next time. Learning by chance may provide feedback from the environment that lets our learners know if they performed well or not, but learning by chance does not give them direction on what they need to do going forward (or, at least, it does not do so as effectively as training does).

So, if our learners have skill gaps, then training is definitely something that can help them.

And coming back to Sam's sales team, they definitely have skill gaps. They will need a lot of guidance on how to sell, and then a lot of chances to practice selling. It will help them if they practice roleplaying with each other and receive 'feedforward' from other more experienced colleagues. It will also help them if they shadow more experienced colleagues to observe what they are doing, reflect on their insights from those observations, and then turn those insights into actions during their next practice.

- ## Mindset Gaps

When someone knows how to do something and is capable of doing it, yet still doesn't do it, then they probably have a mindset problem.

Take Simon, for example. Simon is very quiet in meetings, and we wish he'd contribute more. We know he has opinions, and we know he's capable of sharing these opinions because he's shared them many times before. But, for some reason, every time he's in a meeting, he just keeps silent.

Simon's behaviour suggests to us that there is something about his thinking that's holding him back. He's probably thinking too negatively, doubting the value of his contribution, and/or worrying of the consequences of sharing his opinions. If we wish to address his behaviour, then we probably need to address these thinking patterns.

Mindset is Invisible

The challenge with one's mindset is that we can't see it. Mindsets are interconnected webs of beliefs, values, thoughts, and feelings that are hidden away in the murky depths of our learners' brains. Thankfully, there is something we can see that reflects mindset, which is behaviour.

Mindset gaps generally address what are commonly known as interpersonal skills, or soft skills. So if they are still skills, then why are we calling these gaps mindset gaps and not categorising them as skills gaps?

Well, note how one of the terms for these is soft skills. *Soft* implies something that we can't see. Most skills involve simple actions that happen only on a physical level, and we call these technical or hard skills. They're pretty much all about what we can see. Soft skills are a bit more complex, though.

With hard skills, we only target the action. With soft skills, we target the mindset-behaviour connection. Because one's mindset is invisible, we can't offer directions for it so easily. Instead, we have to influence it.

Merriam-Webster defines 'mindset' as 'a mental attitude or inclination', and, in turn, defines 'attitude' as 'a feeling or way of thinking that affects a person's behaviour'. Roughly speaking, it leads to behaviour in 4 simple steps:
1. Perception—Sense something happening or about to happen
2. Thoughts—Think something about what's happening or about to happen
3. Feelings—Feel emotions as a result of those thoughts
4. Behaviour—React in accordance with those feelings

With Simon, he is perceiving the meeting. As he perceives the meeting, he thinks that it's an extremely important event, where what you say counts, and if you say the wrong thing, then negative consequences will result. Simon starts to feel worried and anxious about the possible consequences of saying the wrong thing, and so he decides to keep quiet because his feelings tell him that's probably the safest reaction.

From Mindset to Behaviour

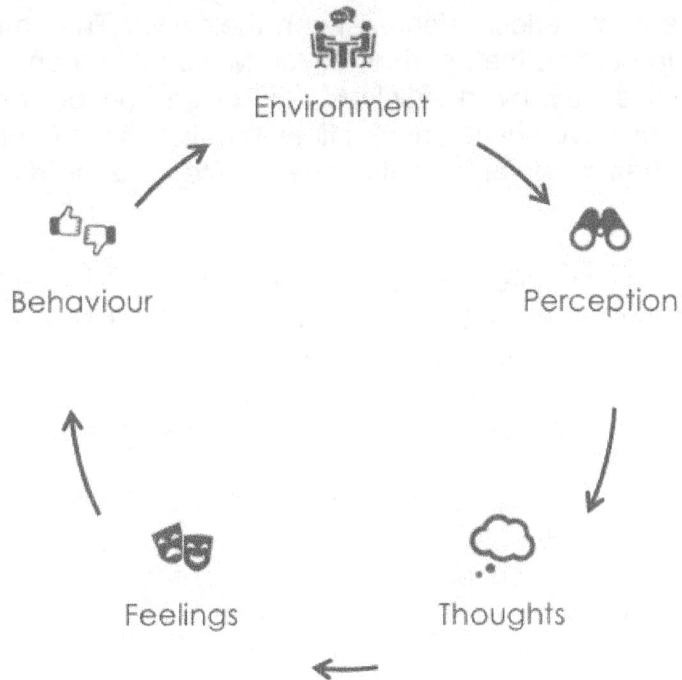

Training Mindsets

In order to address these mindset issues, we need to raise self-awareness of how people are perceiving things, what their thoughts and feelings are, and how those thoughts and feelings affect their behaviour. We can then offer new ways of thinking and behaving to change up the cycle. Through reflection and practice, they can start to change their thinking and behaviour.

Sometimes the mindset gap is easy to close. It might just involve informing the learners of what they currently do and what they are expected to do. Then, BAM! They change their behaviour!

But, other times, we might come up against resistance. They might not agree with our assessment of their behaviour, or even with the expected behaviour. They may not even agree that they are not currently meeting expectations. With this sort of resistance, we sometimes need to use more persuasive methods to inspire the will to change. Remember, without intrinsic motivation, or a belief that there is a need to change, learners will not push themselves to change.

When it comes to changing attitudes, it requires a lot more emphasis on reflection. Although reflection is the natural process of learning, it's interesting to note that, a lot of the time, people don't reflect adequately on their own. They may not perceive a problem, so they do not see the need to reflect. Maybe they don't reflect in the right way, or in an effective way, by themselves. And given how busy everyone is these days, maybe they don't even have enough time to reflect. **This is one of the biggest benefits training has to offer people—the space and guidance for effective reflection.**

We can use stories, case studies, and even experiential learning activities to stimulate that reflection. We can guide that reflection with well-structured debriefing activities. And we can encourage them to take the insights they gained from reflection and turn them into action plans they can apply in the real world. (We'll look at how to do all of this later on throughout The Five Elements of Delivery section.)

Coming back to Sam's sales team, they could also have mindset gaps. Less experienced sales people can have a lot of challenges with adapting their mindsets to their new roles. They may suddenly feel a lot of pressure to hit targets, which consequently makes them extremely anxious when talking to customers. They then will focus only on pushing the sale through, as opposed to taking the time to build long-term relationships and understand their clients' true needs. Sales people with these challenges will probably need a lot of coaching from their more experienced colleagues to gradually adapt or change their mindsets.

- ## Motivation Gaps

Motivation gaps, on the surface, may look like mindset gaps. People have the knowledge and skills to behave in certain ways, but for some mysterious reason, don't. When this mysterious reason is due to the fact that the organisation, or work, doesn't motivate the person, then this is a motivation gap.

For Sam's sales team, this could be a major issue. They used to be engineers, and suddenly they have been pushed into a sales role due to their in-depth knowledge of the products they helped make. But maybe some of them don't enjoy sales; they much prefer engineering. If they have no interest in the job in the first place, then, of course, they are not going to perform.

Motivation gaps, generally speaking, cannot be solved through training, as they are due to factors that training has little influence over. Remember, one of the fundamental conditions of success for training is intrinsic motivation, so if there is no motivation at all, then training won't work.

But it's useful to know what a motivation gap looks like so we can (1) avoid designing and delivering a training solution that inevitably won't work and (2) offer more effective solutions.

Traditional vs. Modern Motivation

The traditional approach to motivation has been carrots and sticks, otherwise known as rewards and punishments. This approach worked well in the old world, where many tasks were routine in nature.

For example, if I pay you £10 to spend 1 day cleaning windows, you are not going to be interested in cleaning more windows. You are probably going to find ways of passing the day so you get your money for the minimum amount of effort possible. But if I pay you £1 to clean 1 window, you will find a way of increasing the number of windows you can clean in 1 day so you will make more money.

The carrots-and-sticks approach is not very relevant to much of today's work. Because much of today's work is not routine in nature, it is creative. It requires more experimentation, more specialisation, and more mastery. It is less about doing the same thing the same way and more about improving the way we do things, or doing new things altogether.

That's not to say the carrots-and-sticks approach doesn't work. Offering monetary rewards for work does provide motivation, but only up to a certain level. Once the monetary reward moves beyond that threshold, it has minimal impact on motivation.

This is where other factors become more important.

According to Daniel Pink, author of the book *Drive: The Surprising Truth About What Motivates Us*, there are three ways of motivating people in the modern world:
1. Autonomy
2. Mastery
3. Purpose

Autonomy

Autonomy means people have freedom of choice over:
- The work they do
- The way the work is done
- When the work is done
- Who they do the work with

The more autonomy someone has, the more likely they are to be happy with their work and their working conditions.

This makes a lot of sense because, if intrinsic motivation comes from the inside, then the way the work is done should also come from the inside. When individuals works towards their own goals, in their own ways, at their own pace, in their own time, then they will be relatively free from any external pressures. That freedom opens up the chance for them to be fully engaged in their work.

If the goals, the way of working, the pace of working, and the time of working are all dictated by someone else, then this becomes demotivating, because there is a strong chance that these do not match the individual's criteria for satisfaction.

Furthermore, the individuals may feel they have little control over their work. And lack of control in itself is such a high cause of stress that, in some studies on rodents, it has even led to death. (*SCARF: A Brain-Based Model for Collaborating with and Influencing Others*, David Rock, Neuro Leadership Journal, Issue One, 2008.)

Mastery

Mastery is the desire to get better and better at something that matters. It's a big part of my own motivation for designing training.

Remember the concept of flow that I mentioned earlier? Well, flow is a pre-requisite for mastery. **In order to reach mastery, the nature of the work must help the individual enter a state of flow.**

Remember, with flow, there are certain conditions. Goals must be clear, with immediate feedback (for example, taking a penalty kick in football). And to achieve the goal requires stretching themselves just slightly more than they are currently capable of (add a goalkeeper to the penalty kick and you increase the challenge). It's not too difficult and it's not too easy; it's just right. It's in the sweet spot between boredom and anxiety.

But in order for flow to lead to mastery, Daniel Pink mentions that there are three other conditions.

Firstly, individuals must have a belief that they can improve. If they believe their abilities are fixed and they have limited room for improvement, then they won't seek mastery.

Secondly, mastery involves setbacks, which require grit to get through. If individuals give up at the first hurdle, then they're obviously not going to continue on the path to mastery.

Thirdly, mastery is never realised. It is a constant state of improvement. You may reach your goals, but that only makes you realise you have the potential to achieve even higher goals.

Consider Olympic athletes. They train incredibly hard, or *obsessively*. They break their sport down into fine details and perfect every single one of them. They keep themselves focussed on bettering their own personal record, beating their opponent's record, and even setting new world records. They endure struggles to push themselves beyond their limits. And the best only rise to the very top because they can push themselves further than others.

Does the push come from the dream of winning a medal? Perhaps, partially, but that's missing the point. Carl Lewis, Olympic gold medallist in 1988, 1992, and 1996, puts it perfectly: 'It's all about the journey, not the outcome.'

That is the essence of intrinsic motivation. It's not about the result. It's all about the activity.

Purpose

Why do you do what you do? **Purpose is all about *why* people do their work.** My purpose for working in training is to help people improve themselves. A fireman's purpose may be to help those in need. Anyone who works in entertainment may do so to make people happy, or to tell stories that inspire people.

The greater the purpose, the greater the motivation. If the purpose is simply to pay the bills, then only enough motivation is required to do that. But if the purpose is bigger than what an individual is capable of, then there is more drive to seek ways of expanding potential.

How can you increase someone's sense of purpose? Show them the bigger picture. Show them how their work helps grow the business. Show them how their work helps change society and/or the world. Show them what they work hard for and give them a reason to care.

What Motivates People

From Daniel Pink's *Drive: The Surprising Truth About What Motivates Us*

Training's Impact on Motivation

I have summarised 4 factors of motivation: the traditional carrots-and-sticks approach, autonomy, mastery, and purpose. Can training affect these?

Yes, but with a minimal effect. There are far better solutions out there for improving motivation.

For improving individual motivation, coaching is a solution that might be able to help them figure out how to feel more motivated in their current role. At the very least, coaching will help them find a new direction that they are more motivated by.

When the motivation issue is more widespread, then it could be a management issue, and the managers may need training on how to manage people better (which is something I talk about next, in Communication Gaps).

But it can also be due to organisational factors that are out of the control of the managers. In that case, training is definitely not the solution at all and a management or HR consultant may be able to offer better advice.

• Communication Gaps

Put simply, sometimes people aren't performing because they haven't been told to, or how to. Or maybe they have been told, just not in the right way.

A communication gap occurs when there is a breakdown in communication.

Communication is not a simple process of *I speak and then you understand*. There are numerous barriers that crop up at various steps of the communication process. Think of the communication process as having the following 6 steps:

1. Sender—The person sending the message
2. Encoding—Taking an idea, and putting it into a communicable format (such as the spoken or written word)
3. Channel—The channel through which the message is sent (e.g. email, telephone, face-to-face, etc.)
4. Receiver—The person receiving the message
5. Decoding—The receiver interpreting the message that has been sent
6. Feedback—The receiver responding to the message the sender sent

The Communication Process

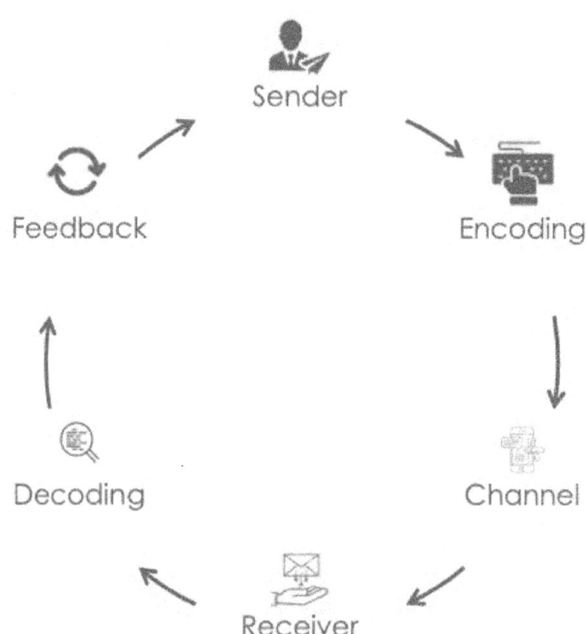

Communication issues can arise at every single step. The message may not be encoded clearly, or it was sent through the wrong channel, or the sender did not take the time to consider the impact the message will have. The channel itself may have technical issues, meaning the message is not fully communicated, or is not done so in a timely manner. The receiver may have their own biases which interfere during the decoding process. And so on.

For someone to perform effectively, they must know the following things:

- what they should do
- to what extent
- by when
- under what conditions
- why
- how

Wherever there is a communication gap, there is normally a management issue. Consider for a moment just why this is. Managers don't start their careers as managers, they start them as individual contributors in a specific function. They then get so good at that particular function that they get promoted to management. But managing uses a completely different skill set than their original function.

Managing involves a lot of communication, which, in my experience, most managers (especially the recently-promoted ones) are not fully capable of, particularly when it comes to giving feedback about performance.

Maybe the manager does not communicate performance expectations to their people because they haven't spotted a performance gap. (When performance discussion reviews only happen once or twice a year, then there's little wonder that performance gaps are not spotted or communicated in a timely manner.)

Or maybe they have spotted the performance gap, but struggle to communicate it. Maybe they tried giving feedback but they were too indirect. Or maybe they were too direct and ended up offending their people. Perhaps the feedback was simply not practical. Maybe the learners know they have a performance gap (they know what they should do but don't know how to do it) but they don't know how to correct it.

Maybe even the manager knows there is something wrong, but can't quite put a finger on it. If they don't know what specifically this problem is, why it exists, and/or how to solve it, then they naturally will struggle with communicating this.

This is possibly an issue with Sam's sales team. Sam really wants to give his staff effective feedback on how to improve their sales skills but, given that Sam's sales skills are at the level of unconscious competence, he has trouble putting a finger on what feedback they need and articulating that feedback in a way they can understand and implement.

Can Training Help?

When we spot communication gaps, there are several things we can do.

We could first look at coaching, or even training the managers (if they are open to the idea, of course). If their lack of communication skills are hindering performance improvement efforts, then directly coaching or training the managers in communication skills would be like killing two birds with one stone.

Or we could design and deliver training that bridges the communication gap. We would need to make sure it effectively communicates what is expected of our learners, explain why and how to do it, and when they should do it. It would involve lots of reflection and practice to ensure the message got through clearly.

We could even offer to bridge the communication gap directly ourselves, or help the managers do so more effectively.

Communication gaps normally point at deeper issues within the organisation that you, as a trainer, might be able to help resolve. You could also, at least, point the organisation in the direction of someone who can help. And if you do so, then you will be highly valued by that organisation, as opposed to being someone who wastes their time. It's a bit like the difference between a bad and good doctor. A bad doctor sees you have a headache and gives you painkillers to treat the symptom. But a good doctor sees you have a headache, and focusses on the cause of that headache to make sure you never get it again.

• Environment Gaps

Maybe optimal performance is just not possible because the environment does not allow it. If this is the case, there is an environment gap.

There are many ways the environment can have an impact on performance. For simplicity, we can split the environment into 3 different categories:
1. Business Environment
2. Organisational Environment
3. Physical Environment

Business Environment

Sales people are heavily dependent on their business environment for their performance. If the R&D department releases a faulty product, or the regulatory environment changes, or the economy hits a downturn, then obviously their performance is going to be poor. And there's going to be very little training can do to change it.

In such cases, a better solution may be for the business to reassess its strategy.

Organisational Environment

Perhaps organisational systems or processes are holding people back from achieving their optimal performance. Such systems and processes may mean employees are expected to follow certain rules (or steps) that are (or end up being) overly complex and time-consuming.

Maybe the technology doesn't enable them to perform optimally. For employees who need to work virtually, this raises all sorts of issues. Maybe they work with people in different time zones, and/or from different cultures, both of which create huge communication barriers. Maybe the quality of the technology they use for communicating with these people creates even bigger communication barriers.

There may even be a poor atmosphere. Large groups of people working together have a tendency to play the politics game, which can be enjoyable for some yet frustrating for others. Or there may be a high degree of tension amongst co-workers, leading to poor cooperation.

Or maybe there is a sense of uncertainty over what the future holds. Whenever an organisation undergoes a major change, one of the biggest causes of anxiety is the uncertainty the change brings. People worry if they'll still enjoy their jobs in the future, or if they'll even have a job.

Where the organisational environment is responsible for poor performance, training may be able to help, somewhat. However, rather than target the surface-level issues that arise as a result of the organisational environment, it would be far more effective to focus efforts on the underlying issues.

Sometimes facilitation or team-building may be more effective solutions for these issues than training. Sometimes it just involves helping people work through their issues together. It might also be as simple as just bringing co-workers together to form stronger bonds. These may even be combined with training to help them simultaneously learn new things and solve problems.

Physical Environment

The immediate physical environment can also impact performance. Given the physical environments of many of the offices I have visited, I would say the impact of this is greatly underestimated in many companies.

Noise and lighting have a big impact on performance. Low levels of natural light can lead to people feeling depressed, which naturally impacts their motivation. High noise levels are known to reduce productivity due to the distractions they cause. It can be very difficult to get into a deep state of focus with so much noise around.

The layout of the office can also impact people greatly. Open-layout office spaces may cause frequent distractions. Physical separations between people can hinder communication and cooperation. It is important that offices are, therefore, designed with optimal performance in mind.

Maybe the office has recently moved to a new location and is far away from where the employee lives. The long commutes exhaust them and also impacts their morale.

Coming back to Sam's sales team, their performance could be impacted by the environment. For example, the product may no longer fit customer needs, or might not compare to competing products. There may be internal competition between departments, or within the team, leading to less collaboration. They may even be impacted by the physical environment if their customers are based in different countries!

Whilst training might help improve their internal collaboration, and maybe offer them help with working with customers based in other countries, their overall performance will still be heavily impacted by these environmental factors.

The 3 Types of Environments

 Business

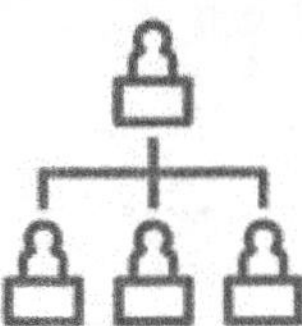 Organisational

 Physical

6 Performance Gaps Summary

There are 6 performance gaps, which we have just looked at. They are:

Knowledge Gaps (1)
Skill Gaps (2)
Mindset Gaps (3)
Motivation Gaps (4)
Communication Gaps (5)
Environment Gaps (6)

6 Performance Gaps

 Knowledge Gaps

 Skill Gaps

 Mindset Gaps

 Motivation Gaps

 Communication Gaps

 Environment Gaps

Defining Outcomes

Do you want your training to be successful?

If you answered yes to that question, then you need to set a measurable outcome. It's only once you can prove that the outcome has been achieved that you can consider your training a success.

The way to set this measurable outcome is by speaking to your stakeholders. Ultimately, it is their satisfaction that is your measure for success. If you want to measure the success of your training, then you need to know how to measure their satisfaction.

To define these outcomes, you will be asking your stakeholders the following questions:
1. Who decides if this training has been successful or not?
2. Why run this training?
3. What are the expectations?
4. How will this impact the business?
5. What will learners do differently?

I'll go into more detail of the things to look out for in each of these questions. There may be times when you ask just one or two of these questions and get all of the answers you need. Nonetheless, it is important to know what information will help you most with your design.

• Who Decides?

If we are asked to deliver training, it's because someone made a decision. Either a Senior Leader, an HR Manager, the learners themselves, or someone else decided that there was a need to run training. Whoever was involved in this decision is called a stakeholder.

Stakeholders are defined as anyone who has an interest in, or can influence a project. They are very important people. They determine if we get to run our training, and also if we get paid for our training. They don't necessarily have to be the person paying for the training, but they do have an impact on whether the training goes ahead or not.

You will probably have multiple stakeholders for any one training project. If you want your training to be successful, then you will need to please all of your stakeholders (or as many as possible), so it's a good idea to find out who they are.

Generally speaking, for training, that means we will encounter 4 types of stakeholders:

1. The Organiser
2. The Investor
3. The Learner
4. The Learner's Stakeholders

1. The Organiser

For corporate training, the organiser is normally HR, but it could be someone else. They will almost always be the person who comes to you and asks you to do the training.

Some organisers know exactly what they want, especially if they are the decision-maker. Some organisers won't be very clear, and that's normally because they are not the decision-maker.

A good way to start talking to them is to ask 'Why do you want to organise this training?' If their answer is 'My boss told me to', then ask to speak to their boss. If they can answer by themselves, then great! Either way, **you need to understand the reason for this training in order to be successful.**

So what are the sorts of reasons you should be looking for?

The normal reasons are:

A Vision

The boss or senior manager wants things to be done a certain way. They may have fallen in love with a certain methodology from a book they read. Or maybe they attended one of your classes before and loved it, so now they want the same thing for their staff. If this is the case, then ask to speak to the one who gave that command.

Problem/Solution

A problem has occurred and the natural solution is training. This line of thinking tends to be quite naive, so be sure that training would really be the best solution.

Trainees Requested It

Many companies will send out a survey to their staff, asking what training they want. When results come in, HR will go to vendors or internal trainers to supply the demand. Some companies even have a quota for the number of training days each year. Learners then choose which training to attend, in order to meet their quota. If the reason for training is just to meet the quota, then it's time to speak to the learners. They will tell you how to make this training worth their time.

Under Budget

A strange phenomenon occurs in a lot of companies. Towards the end of the year, training departments realise they are under budget. Terrified by the thought of having next year's budget slashed, they quickly try to spend it. Training companies suddenly receive lots of phone calls and become very busy. In this case, the most important stakeholder is likely to be the learner. So ask to speak to them.

The organiser is always a good person to start speaking to. Not only can they describe the reason for this training, they can also introduce you to other stakeholders, so be sure to ask them the following questions:
- Who approves the budget for this training?
- Who will attend the training?
- Who do the trainees normally interact with?

2. The Investor

This person has the power to invest money in the training. They will only do so for a very good reason. Speak to them and find out what that reason is. Once you know that reason, you will know how to get them to sign that cheque.

Normally, their expectations will match one of the following:

Seeing is believing—They want to see a change. They want to see their staff work with more confidence. They want to see smiles on their customers' faces. Whatever it is, they'll know the training has been a success when they see it.

Compliments—They want to hear their customers saying nice things about their staff. They want to hear less complaints about managers. They want to hear people talk about their brand in a positive way. As soon as they hear those things, they'll be happy.

Good Feelings—They can't quite put a finger on it. They'll just feel it's been successful. They'll walk into the office and feel something has changed. They'll feel less worried about sending their staff on sales meetings. They'll feel more confident things are going as planned. When they've got that feeling, you know you've done your job well.

3. The Learner

The learner will always be one of your stakeholders. After all, they'll be the one sitting through your training. If it's done badly, they'll be the ones writing nasty messages on your feedback forms. If it's done well, they'll be coming up to you and thanking you for changing their lives.

Do not forget these people, as they have expectations as well. Their expectations can be summed up as follows:

The Problem-Solver—They have an annoying customer that they just don't know how to communicate with. The first project they managed was a disaster and they never want to relive that experience. There is a big presentation coming up and the manager has high expectations of them. They have a very clear reason for attending your training.

The Curious Cat—They read a book about an amazing methodology, then they heard you're going to be training it. They just have to attend it! These trainees may start off with a bit of admiration for you, making your job easier. They will sit attentively and behave themselves. Be prepared for lots of questions from these guys. But don't worry, they tend to be patient. These guys are great to have in the classroom.

The 'I have nothing better to do' Person—These trainees might have a set number of training days to attend each year. Or they just really don't want to sit at their desks. Either way, they're not so interested in learning things; they're just interested in being there. These guys are probably going to be easily distracted, and will easily distract others. They also might not be honest with you if you ask them why they're attending. No one is going to say 'I have nothing better to do'. You'll most likely find out if they're this type by asking the organiser why they have arranged this training.

4. The Learner's Stakeholders

The work the learner does will affect other people. These people are the learner's stakeholders, and can include:

- Suppliers
- Customers
- Managers
- Colleagues

The training could be to help them sell with more confidence to their customers, or manage their suppliers better. Maybe it's to present better reports to their managers, or to communicate more efficiently with their colleagues. If you learn how they interact with these stakeholders, you will know more about their needs.

You won't always be able to speak directly to these stakeholders, but you should be able to hear what they have been saying about the learners. If customers have been complaining, then the managers will know about it.

4 Types of Stakeholders

• Why Run This Training?

The *why* question is always a great place to start.

It helps you understand all of the different reasons this training has come about. You may even get different reasons from each different stakeholder you speak to. And these different reasons give you lots of useful information about various things.

These reasons can give you valuable insight into how this training ties in with the business. If we can understand how this training will impact the business, then we will find it much easier to measure and justify its value.

For example, I was once asked to train a group of recent graduate recruits on communication skills and business etiquette for a consulting company. When I asked the *why* question, I found out that these new recruits spent a lot of time at the customer's site and weren't behaving as professionally as they should have been. They mentioned how this impacts their trust with the customer.

When the customer doesn't trust the consultants, it can impact the effectiveness of the projects they are working on, as the customer won't buy into their ideas as easily. All of this gave me great context and valuable information for measuring the immediate business impact as well as finding what would motivate this group to improve.

You may also get insights into what the learners will use the training for. We may learn about the problems they are trying to solve, the challenges they are facing, or the goals they are trying to achieve. If we can customise the training to help with these, then we make the training more practical for our learners.

Say you have been asked to design and deliver a course on using Photoshop to a group of internal trainers. You might initially assume that they need to learn super advanced functions. Upon further analysis, you learn that they are simply trimming photos down most of the time, changing colours, and combining pictures together (or with other elements). These specific needs eliminate a lot of what you were originally going to include, such as the super advanced functions, so you are able to design a solution that is more practical for these learners.

As you understand more about the business impact and the learner's problems, challenges, and goals, you may start to see if training is the right solution or not. The earlier you can determine this, the more time you will save everyone further down the line if it turns out that training is not the right solution.

Another thing that may come out from this question is information about what they have tried before. They may have tried training before and it didn't work. They may have tried something else as well and found that didn't work either. This is also useful information that gives you indicators as to challenges you might face later on.

- ## What Are the Expectations?

In business, when we make an investment, we expect a return on that investment. If I give you money to open an ice cream shop, it's not because I'm a nice person, it's because I want you to eventually give me more money back in return. I invest £10,000 now because I hope to get back £20,000 in the future. This extra money that we get back is known as Return On Investment, or ROI for short. And ROI is the language of business.

Businesses expect a good ROI when they make investments. Training is also an investment, so it would make sense for businesses to expect a Return On their training Investment. However, it actually doesn't.

Measuring the ROI of training is impossible. To do so requires that you link a monetary return (either an increase in revenue or a decrease in costs) back to training. For example, we run a sales training for our sales team. The most likely monetary return for a sales training would be an increase in sales figures. So 6 months after receiving sales training, Paul's sales figures have increased by 200%. Hooray, that means the sales training had a high ROI, right? Well, not necessarily.

How can we prove that the 200% increase was only because of the training? Maybe the economy improved in these 6 months after the training. Maybe the company ran a good marketing campaign. Maybe a competitor went out of business. There are lots of other factors that could have influenced that number. So we can't prove that training was the only factor because there are so many variables involved in performance improvement. But that's not the only problem.

There are many factors involved in performance improvement. Trying to put a number on the exact percentage of training's contribution to improvement is, in my very strong opinion, futile. It is literally impossible to do. Yes, there are ways of calculating a number, but any number you *do* get will be inaccurate. There are much better ways of using your time than measuring the ROI of training.

So measuring the ROI of training is futile. And in my experience, most companies agree. Most companies recognise that it's impossible to accurately calculate the true value of training. But that doesn't mean they don't expect any returns.

The types of returns that all companies look for on training are called ROE, which stands for Return On Expectations. If I invest in you training my staff, then, at the very least, I expect you to meet my expectations.

And so, as we speak to our stakeholders, we need to define their expectations.

What are the Expectations?

To get the most useful answers to this question, focus on what your stakeholders will see, hear, or (if they are the learners themselves) do after this training.

They may want to hear less complaints from customers, or see more professional behaviour. The learners may wish they can do things more smoothly and with more confidence.

The thing with this question is that our stakeholders aren't necessarily experts in the training's subject matter, which means they may struggle to define their expectations very specifically. So be prepared for some vague answers here. But as long as you get enough information to know what direction they want the training to go in, you may be able to fill in the blanks for them.

Scope

Another thing you should ask whilst on the subject of expectations is the scope of this training. For example, you'll want to know:

- Length—How much time they can allocate for this training (e.g. a few hours, 1 day, 2 days, etc.)
- Dates—When they can run the training, and if that matches your schedule
- Location—Where will the training be held, and if can you travel there easily
- Numbers—How many people will attend the training
- Venue—What kind of venue they have for the training, and if it has enough space to run the required activities
- Budget—How much money they can afford to spend on this training
- Specific Requests—If they want the training to include any specific concepts, techniques, case studies, etc.

Getting this information early can save you a lot of problems further down the line!

To make sure you've got absolutely everything you can about their expectations, one great final question to always ask is: 'Anything else?'

Keep asking this question until they really don't have anything else to offer. I find I generally ask this question 3 times before they finally feel they have clarified everything about their expectations.

- ## How Will This Impact the Business?

If a business is investing in our training, then our training should impact on that business in a positive way. If not, then why would they spend their money on training?

Speaking with your stakeholders about the business impact of training can give you (and even the stakeholders) extremely valuable information about the reasons for this training as well as the expected outcomes.

So how does training impact business?

Training impacts business by causing changes that either increase revenue or decrease costs. Some examples of these changes include:

- Increasing efficiency
- Increasing productivity
- Increasing sales
- Reducing waste
- Reducing turnover
- Saving time

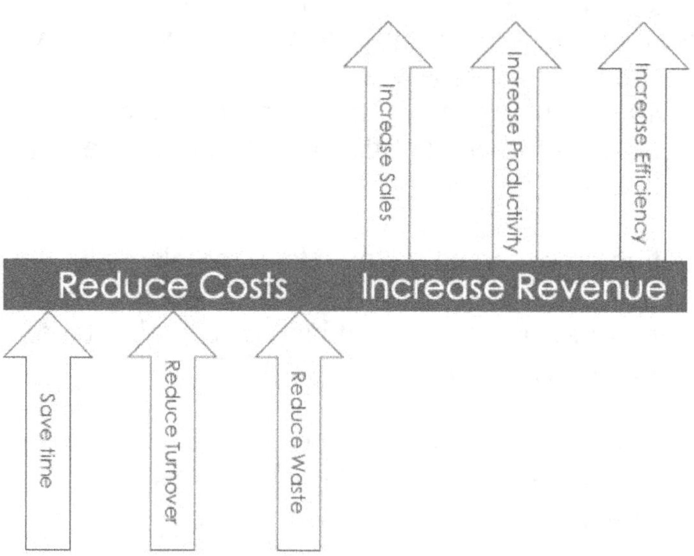

A great question to ask your stakeholders is: 'How will the changes you are looking to achieve help your business?'

Say you have been asked to deliver a course on consultative selling. This kind of course is probably going to help the business in the following ways:
- Increase selling price
- Increase sales conversion rates
- Increase customer retention

Maybe you've been asked to deliver something that has a less obvious link to business outcomes, such as a course on conflict management. If you think about it, you can start to see the links:
- Increased working efficiency
- Reduced staff turnover rates

If we can measure the impact of our training in terms of business results, and prove that it has been a success, then that's invaluable, because we can actually justify our value.

The link between training and business outcomes is not always going to be clear, but that's not always going to be a problem because it all depends on the stakeholder's expectations.

For example, I was once asked to design and deliver a half-day training on the topic of work-life balance for a group of engineers. I asked why they wanted this training and what their expectations were, and what I got was not much. They said they had a two day off-site meeting and wanted to spend a half-day of that time in training.

I pushed and pushed for a link to business outcomes, but there wasn't a very clear link. Eventually, one stakeholder was very upfront with me and said, 'We are having this two day off-site just to get out of the office and refocus our energy. It's something we do every year, and people are looking forward to it. Part of this off-site includes training because they don't want to be in meetings all the time. People have told me they have been very stressed out and would love to learn more about work-life balance. So if you can just give people some new ideas on this, then they'll be happy and I'll be happy.'

So was there a clear link to business outcomes? The closest link I could think of was how it would help staff feel supported and cared for, which would be one of many factors that can contribute to keeping their morale up. It's not a very clear link, nor a very significant one. Nonetheless, their expectations were reasonable. They just wanted people to spend time out of meetings, enjoy themselves, and get some new ideas on the topic of work-life balance. Knowing those expectations made it easy for me and in the end, it was a success.

- ## What Will Learners Do Differently?

Stakeholders who aren't familiar with how training works may have a tendency to tell you what they want the learners to *know*. But we care more about what they need to *do*.

Remember, the purpose of training is to change behaviour. That is why we are concerned with what learners need to do. **We want to change behaviour because changes in behaviour lead to changes in performance, and changes in performance lead to business outcomes.**

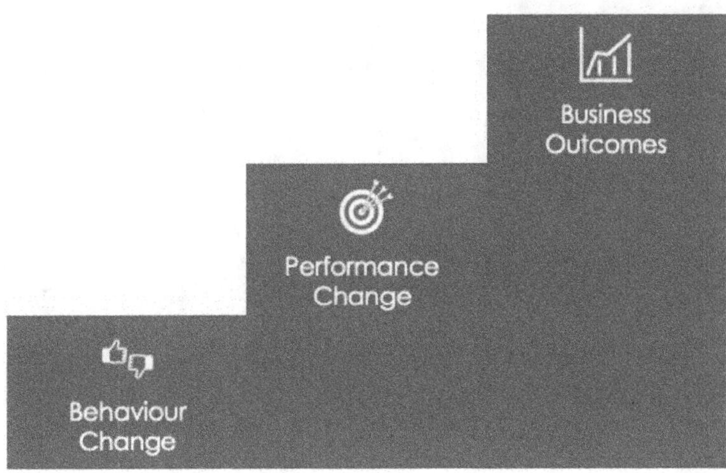

In the previous question, we clarified what the business outcomes are. With those in mind, we can work backwards to identify the changes in behaviour required. And this is a great opportunity to start exploring those performance gaps.

So here are some great questions to ask:

- **What do people need to do in order to achieve the desired outcomes?**
- **Why aren't they doing that right now?**

- **Do the business, organisational, and physical environments provide them with everything they need to do this?**
- **How clearly have these expectations been communicated to them?**
- **What would motivate them to do this?**
- **What attitude do they need to do this?**
- **When, how, and how often can they practice these actions at work?**
- **What information do they need to take those actions?**

What Will Learners Do Differently?

What do people need to do?
Why aren't they doing that right now?
Does the environment support this?
How clearly have these expectations been communicated?
What would motivate them?
What attitude do they need?
When, how, and how often can they practice at work?
What information do they need to take action?

Answers to these questions will help you clarify what exactly the performance gap is and what our training should be focussed on.

There is a chance that our stakeholders may not be able to answer all of these questions. Some of these questions (especially questions 6-8) require a certain level of expertise that our stakeholders may not have. If they don't, then we will need to speak to subject matter experts, or conduct some subject matter research. We'll look at how to do that in the following section.

5 Key Questions Summary

There are 5 key questions that we need to address. They are:

Who Decides? (1)
Why Run This Training? (2)
What are the Expectations? (3)
How Will This Impact the Business? (4)
What Will Learners Do Differently? (5)

5 Key Questions to Ask Stakeholders

Who decides?
Why run this training?
What are the expectations?
How will this impact the business?
What will learners do differently?

Part 3—Designing for Lasting Impact

Training gives us trainers plenty of room to hide. We turn up, deliver a fun and engaging workshop, and then go home and never come back again. Whether learners actually change or not is out of our control, and frequently we trainers are not even held accountable for that. Yes, that's right, we are not held accountable for our results!

The gap between input (the training) and output (learner's changing their behaviour on the job) is massive, and it is within this gap that waste thrives. It is so, so easy for us to not care, to not actually get results, to not even do a good job, and still survive.

Never has this been more obvious to me than on one particular occasion.

I turned up at the training room, eagerly anticipating catching up with the group I trained several months earlier. As they walked through the door, I was desperate to hear how they'd got on since. After the formalities, we got straight down to business, and I was shocked with what I heard:

'To be honest, we haven't really had that many opportunities to practice.'

All the effort I went to was down the drain. I'd designed an engaging session, and customised it to their needs. I'd sat down with the managers and emphasised the importance of follow-up. I'd set follow-up activities and even kept up with how the activities had been going. But there was one factor we'd all forgot to overlook: they didn't have enough opportunities to use what they had learnt for their work.

Despite the managers requesting their team go through a Presentation Skills course, they did not need to present enough in their jobs, so after a few weeks with no practice, they quickly forgot. Everything was done for no good reason and I left feeling quite disheartened.

Yet I was also quite shocked as well. I really should have spent more time enquiring about whether or not they would actually have chances to use this in their work, and when. I should have got the blame for that, and for wasting everyone's time. But the amazing thing was that I didn't! The managers were not bothered. They just saw it as a normal part of corporate life.

Let Us Learn from App Designers

The gap between our work and its impact is big, and we can easily avoid being held accountable for the impact. But that doesn't mean it has to be this way. In other industries, the gap between input and output is not so big. There is not much room to hide, so there is not much room for waste.

Smartphone apps are a great example of this. Successful apps integrate themselves into people's lives. People use them every day for joy or convenience. But it's not because the app developers are holding a gun to their user's heads that they use them every day. The users do it themselves, of their own free will, because the app has been painstakingly designed to fit into their life.

The best apps I've used are the ones that do their thing better than any other way I know, or that fit into my life better than any alternative. The worst ones are awkward, clunky, and just not relevant to my life. Make a bad app, and no one downloads it, and you don't make any money. Make a good app, and more and more people will download it, and recommend it to their friends, and it will make more and more money.

We should think like app designers when designing training. Whilst it is up to our 'users' to use it, we need to take great care to design it so that it fits into their life better than any alternative.

How?

How can we make training more relevant to our learners' lives? How can we increase the chances of them actually using what they learn back on the job?
The answer is to **be realistic, not idealistic**.

For example, one of biggest factors influencing training success is the learners' manager. The more managers follow up with learners about the training afterwards, the more likely our learners are to apply the training to their work.

But the reality is that this doesn't happen enough. Not every manager has the time (or frankly, the will) to follow up with the learners.

Should we blame the managers? I'm going to say *no*, because that doesn't change things. Instead, we should focus on what WE can do, not what other people SHOULD do.

Of course, it's up to the learners themselves to actively try applying what they've learnt back on the job. But again, reality does not always favour this. Learners don't always have the time, opportunity, or even the energy to start applying. So when it comes to designing training, we need to be realistic and not idealistic.

Going back to the smartphone app analogy, app designers set out to achieve what we are also seeking: behaviour change. And they do it extremely successfully. The best app designers know all about human nature. They can't afford to be idealistic because there are too many realistic app designers out there who will do a much better job of integrating into their user's lives.

We need think to think realistically as well. And that's what this part is all about—thinking realistically to design training solutions that will have a lasting impact.

So now we're going to learn about the following things:

- Researching a Solution
- Designing for Application
- Designing for Emotion

Researching a Solution

If you were to redesign your kitchen, you wouldn't just start by tearing it down and decorating it. You would first look through magazines and websites. You'd collect pictures of kitchens you liked. And then you would start planning your design based on those.

This is generally what happens in any design project. Design ideas don't just appear from thin air. They come from research. They come from analysing and combining existing ideas. They come from gathering inspiration.

That is what we also want to do when starting our design journey—collect ideas.

These ideas could include any of the following:
- Tools
- Models
- Concepts
- Theories
- Activities
- Stories
- Case Studies
- Examples
- Pictures
- Tips

At this stage, we are not looking for complete ideas, or even ideas that fit together. We're not even necessarily looking for relevant ideas. We're just looking for things we might work with.

Keep a Record

Before you begin your research, make sure you have somewhere to record all information you gather, either digitally or with pen and paper.

I find a good, old-fashioned notebook with lots of Post-it Notes a great way of collecting ideas. The act of writing down information helps our brains process it more.

But digital recording also has its advantages. It's much easier to search back through, later on. It's also easier to edit as you go through. My two favourite tools include Scapple and Scrivener, both by Literature and Latte (www.literatureandlatte.com).

Scapple is a brainstorming tool. You simply add notes onto a blank slate as you collect information. You can then move your notes around, link them together, and so on.

This is really helpful for just jotting down notes and ideas without having to worry about where to put them. Once you've finished collecting information, you can then start sorting it.

Scrivener is a tool primarily designed for authors, but is equally useful for instructional designers. I am actually using it to write this book right now. Think of it like a far more advanced word processor, the only difference being that you can store multiple documents in the same 'project' instead of only being able to write in one document at a time. So, instead of having to browse through various folders on your computer, it's all there in the same file.

Entire books have been written about using Scrivener. It is a fantastic tool and something I've been using for instructional design for years. You can create one file for your instructional design project. Any information you collect—even articles and website links—you can just drag into the file. You can then build entire booklets using it.

There are many more advantages to Scrivener that I won't go into detail about here. I strongly recommend you download the free trial from the website and just play around with it.

Don't Get Carried Away

It's easy to get lost in the research process. Subjects can seem like huge things, and sometimes you'll never quite feel like you've got everything you need.

It's important to allocate enough time for research at the beginning of the project. And it's equally important to resist the temptation to keep researching just because there might be one other thing you might be missing.

- ## The 4 Key Questions

Remember at the beginning of this book I talked about the importance of being outcome-focussed? Well, we want to do that here as well.

We want to know if our research is going in the right direction or not, and when to stop. It is very, very easy to get distracted by irrelevant information, run out of time, and finish our research with nothing useful!

But if we start our research with a clear goal of what information we need, then this helps us keep focussed.

Know vs. Do

The end result of our training is not for learners to know things, but instead for them to do things. It is only when they take action that they start to have an impact on their work and their business.

So we want to avoid making our training overly focussed on theory, concepts, and ideas. We want it to be focussed on strategies, actions, and things they can do. This is probably the most fundamental part of making training practical; prioritising DO over KNOW.

The 4 Key Questions are a great way of keeping focussed:

What
- What outcomes and learners should aim for
- What indicators of success will help learners measure their progress

Why
- Reasons for achieving those outcomes to help learners find motivation
- Relevant theories/concepts to help learners understand why those outcomes are worth seeking

How
- Action steps learners need to take to achieve those outcomes
- Step-by-step, detailed instructions

When
- The different contexts in which they can take those actions
- The cues and triggers they should use as reminders to take those actions

I find being able to answer all 4 of these questions in the training room helps create an instant buy-in for trainees.

In fact, as I write this, I am sitting on a train on the way back home after a successful day of training. Today, being able to answer these questions for one learner helped her take an action with immediate impact during the course itself.

She explained that she had problems communicating with her overseas colleagues. Being based in China, there is both a huge geographical and cultural distance between herself and her American colleague. This has led to communication problems, frequently evidenced by the fact that her email requests for help tend to go unanswered.

After learning more about her issue, I realised that there were several aspects to it. One part was the different communication styles. Chinese are generally quite indirect in what they say, whereas her American counterpart's couldn't decipher such indirect messages.

But another aspect of this issue was the fact that they didn't have any feeling of warmth in the relationship. Pretty much all communication was business-related, which meant they never took the time to learn about each other as human beings. When relationships lack this feeling of warmth, communication naturally becomes a struggle, especially across borders.

So I gave her a simple piece of advice.

'Aim to build a sense of liking with your colleague (WHAT). There is a lot of psychological research out there that shows how people are far more agreeable with people they like. In other words, people like people who are like them (WHY).

The key to building this sense of liking is to find things you have in common with each other, by gradually revealing things about yourself and encouraging them to reveal things about themselves. It might be telling them how frustrated you are today because of the bad traffic on your way to work in the morning, or maybe how your child is about to start primary school and you have been busy getting them ready for that. And when you reveal this information, they might just reveal something they have in common with you, like how the traffic is bad in their city, too, or how they have a child as well. And you can start all this by initiating every conversation with one simple question 'How are you today?" (HOW).

So the next time you send an email, ask them how they are. The next time they call you, ask them how they are. And the next time you have a teleconference with them, get on the line a few minutes earlier so you have time to talk about how you both are today (WHEN).'

She took my advice during the break. She emailed her overseas colleague, used one sentence to explain how she was today at the beginning before getting down to business, and asked how her colleague was today. A few hours later, she got a friendly reply and discovered something they had in common. And now they have a small foundation of liking upon which they can build on.

Use these 4 key questions to frame your research. When you can confidently answer all 4, you will give learners both the clarity and motivation to start taking practical actions.

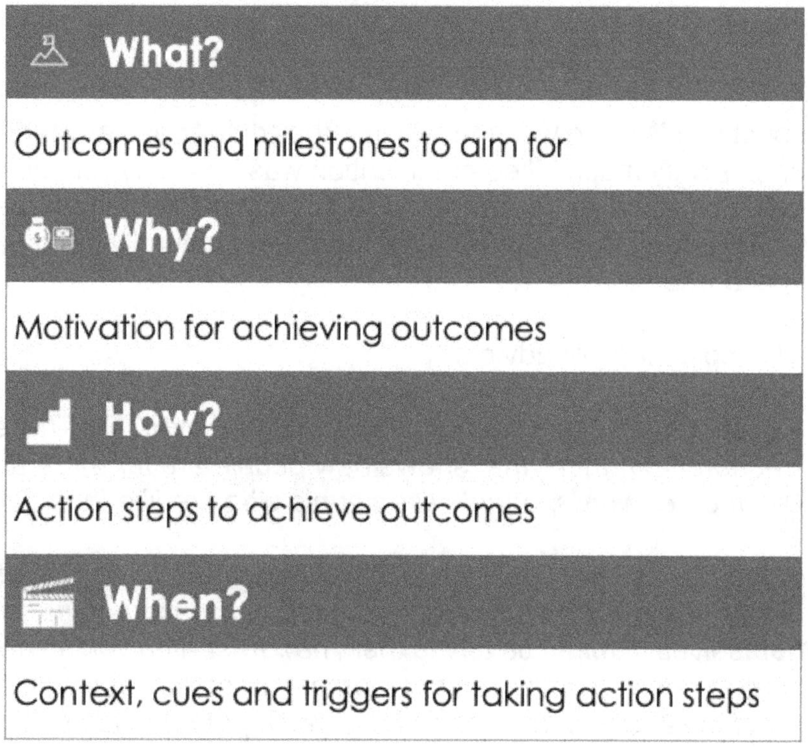

• Steal vs. Copy

Whether you like it or not, the iPhone is probably one of the most significant pieces of consumer technology to have been invented in modern history.

Since the rise of the iPhone, a wide range of things have arisen with it, from the app economy, to ride-sharing, mobile payments, fitness devices, the growth of social media, and a large amount of new anti-social habits such as staring at our phones whilst eating dinner with our families.

The iPhone may not be the only device that gave rise to all these changes in our culture, but it arguably had a significant impact.

What was truly unique about the first iPhone? Was it the first phone with a touchscreen? Was it the first phone that could access the Internet and check emails? Was it the first phone that could play music, download applications, or take photos?

The answer to all of those questions is NO. A lot of the things people loved about the first iPhone were not unique to the iPhone. Many of those features had come long, in many different products, before the iPhone.

What was unique about the iPhone was what it did with all of these features. It combined, presented, and used them in ways that had never been done before. The iPhone didn't copy these features; instead, it took all of these features and made them its own. The iPhone didn't copy, it stole.

Austin Kleon wrote a very inspirational book called *Steal Like an Artist*. If you are ever looking for ideas to inspire your creativity, I strongly recommend you dip in and out of his book. It is a joy to read. He has a great quote in there as well:

'What a good artist understands is that nothing comes from nowhere. All creative work builds on what came before. Nothing is completely original.' (Kleon, Austin. *Steal Like an Artist: 10 Things Nobody Told You About Being Creative.* 1st Edition, Page 7. Workman Publishing Company. Kindle Edition. 2012)

The very title of his book (*Steal Like an Artist*) even has a lineage of thievery. It comes from a famous quote 'Good Artists Copy, Great Artists Steal', which was made famous by Steve Jobs, who attributed it to Pablo Picasso. But did it come from Pablo Picasso, or someone else?

Maybe it came from T.S. Eliot.

In 1920, T.S. Eliot wrote:

'One of the surest of tests is the way in which a poet borrows. Immature poets imitate; mature poets steal; bad poets deface what they take, and good poets make it into something better, or at least something different. The good poet welds his theft into a whole of feeling which is unique, utterly different from that from which it was torn; the bad poet throws it into something which has no cohesion. A good poet will usually borrow from authors remote in time, or alien in language, or diverse in interest.'

Did he actually say that? And did he say that before Pablo Picasso said that?

I don't know. I don't care.

I just stole those words from http://quoteinvestigator.com/2013/03/06/artists-steal/.

But I think those words make a lot of sense. And if you think about all the significant products and technology that we use today, you'll notice that they are not original.

Was Facebook the first social media platform? Was Google the first search engine? Was the iPad the first tablet? No, no, and no.

So, should your training be original? Can you create a 100% unique idea? Is that even possible? No, no, and no.

In reality, when it comes to designing your training, you are probably going to be doing a combination of copying and stealing. Sometimes you will do more copying, and other times you will do more stealing. But there are advantages and disadvantages to each approach…

Stealing:

Advantages	Disadvantages
The end product is unique and belongs to you. You can then brand it and enjoy the advantages of that.	It can take a long time to create something unique, and sometimes even cost money.
It's fun to innovate and gives you a sense of achievement.	It might not work the way you want it to the first time. It may require a lot of attempts before you get it right.
Stealing means you have to go deeper into something, which helps you really understand it.	What you create may not reach the same level of quality as something created by someone with more expertise than you.

Copying:

Advantages	Disadvantages
Copying saves you a lot of time. It's ready to use immediately.	You might not have permission to use it.
It's probably been tried and tested and so more likely to work than something that has been created from scratch.	Because you didn't create it, you might not have a deep enough understanding of it.
If it's been created by a famous expert, then you can leverage that person's influence when delivering it.	It might not be suitable for your audience in the format it's in.

My philosophy is to copy for the short term, but steal for the long term. If I am in a rush to develop something, or want to try something I haven't tried before, then I'll take the copy approach, and be sure to attribute the sources I used. But if I use it again and again, I'll eventually find things I like and don't like about it, and gradually mould it into my own stolen version.

I have numerous courses that started off as a bunch of ideas taken from various books. I'd run them and get mixed results. Then I'd tweak them, run them again, tweak them again, and so on. After many iterations of this process, my courses end up being unique to me.

So if you find something that looks useful for your training, how do you decide if you should copy or steal it?

Well, here are some questions to consider when choosing which approach to take:
- **Do you need or have permission to use it?**
- **Is it relevant to your objectives?**
- **Is the content theoretically and practically valid?**
- **Do you understand it?**
- **Have you tried it?**
- **Is it easy for your learners to use?**
- **Is it easy for you to train?**
- **Do you have enough time to modify it to your needs?**

Steal or Copy?

Do you need or have permission to use it?
Is it relevant to your objectives?
Is the content theoretically and practically valid?
Do you understand it?
Have you tried it?
Is it easy for your learners to use?
Is it easy for you to train?
Do you have enough time to modify it to your needs?

• Working with Subject Matter Experts

These are more commonly known as SMEs. The title speaks for itself—people who are experts on the subject matter.

You might even be an SME yourself. This is normally the case for the training I do, as I work mostly with soft skills training. If a client asks me to design a course on communication skills, influencing, productivity, management, emotional intelligence, or any related topic, then I am good to go.

But whenever we get requests for training that we are not experts on, we might need to speak to an SME.

The Curse of Knowledge

The biggest challenge of working with SMEs is translating their expertise into information that can be easily absorbed by non-experts.

This concept is known as 'The Curse of Knowledge'.

The Curse of Knowledge was demonstrated in a famous experiment conducted at Stanford University. In this experiment, there were two roles, *tapper* and *listener*. The tapper's role was to tap out the rhythm of a song on a table, whereas the listener's role was to guess the song.

Throughout the whole experiment, only 2.5% of the listener's guesses were correct. But the tapper's predictions of accurate guesses were much higher, at 50%. What this essentially meant is that the tappers thought they'd get their message across one time in two, but in reality it was only one time in forty (source: https://hbr.org/2006/12/the-curse-of-knowledge).

If you were the tapper in that experiment, the song in your head would be very strong... so strong that you'd be unable to ignore it. As you tap that rhythm out on the table, it seems impossible for the listener to not guess correctly. But what our brains struggle to comprehend is the fact that the listener does not have that song going around in their head.

The Curse of Knowledge basically means that we are unable to ignore the knowledge that we already have. So when we start explaining things, we make assumptions that the listeners already have certain knowledge, when they actually don't.

We've all experienced working with IT professionals. Their expertise is notoriously difficult to communicate to non-experts. With so many technical words, complex processes, and functions, it can be difficult to remember what laymen know and don't know.

And as you work with SMEs, you may encounter this problem. But there are several ways around it.

Breaking The Curse of Knowledge

The best way is to find an SME who has only recently acquired a decent level of competence. These SMEs will be so fresh that they can remember what it was like to not be an expert. They can easily recall what things they struggled with, what they found helpful, and how they learnt in general.

But if we can't find that kind of SME, and can only find high-level SMEs, then we just need to find ways of breaking through The Curse of Knowledge.

The best way of breaking through is to take control of the conversation and focus it on action points, rather than knowledge points. Most people who are not an expert on training or instructional design tend to assume that people need knowledge in order to learn. As a result, these kinds of SMEs may talk a lot about what they think people need to know.

But we should divert their focus away from what they think learners need to know, and divert it towards what learners need to DO. So use the following questions to guide the conversation in that direction:
- **What do people need to do in order to achieve the desired business outcomes?**
- **Why aren't they taking those actions right now?**
- **How can we make them more likely to take those actions?**
- **How can they practice those actions?**
- **What mistakes do people commonly make?**
- **How can we help prevent them from making those mistakes?**
- **What information do they need to be successful?**

And if they do start to focus on knowledge, then test the necessity of that knowledge, but do so politely. These kinds of questions can help with that:
- **Can you give me an example of when the learner would use this?**
- **What is the consequence if the learner doesn't know/perform this?**
- **How often does that happen?**

And if your conversation with the SME does not get you the information you were hoping for, then don't worry. There are plenty of other sources we can use, as we will find out next.

From Know to Do

What do people need to do?
Why aren't they doing that now?
How can we make them more likely to do that?
How can they practice?
What mistakes do people commonly make?
How can we help them avoid those mistakes?
What information do they need?
Can you give me an example of when the learner would use this?
What is the consequence if the learner doesn't know/perform this?
How often does that happen?

- ## Using Other Sources

Books

As I work primarily with soft skills, and there are a lot of books on soft skills, books are my primary source of information.

You've read books before. You're reading one right now. So I'm not going to tell you how to read a book. But I do have **some tips to speed up your book-reading process:**
- Start with the most comprehensive book you can find
- Choose the book that is easiest to skim through (lots of headings, short paragraphs, detailed list of contents etc.)
- Jump straight to the most relevant sections

Some books invite you to read through in great detail. I advise staying away from these kinds of books when researching. Researching should not take forever, and you will be on a tight schedule a lot of the time.

Opt for books that allow you to find what you need *fast*. As a general reference point, I have always found the '…for Dummies' books to be the absolute best for research. They are short, snappy, and comprehensive. A lot of the courses I have developed have been based on things directly taken from these books. And when they don't answer my questions, they at least point me in the direction of areas for further research.

I would also advise against using paperback versions. Some of you may have a passion for paperbacks, but I have found they pale in comparison to e-books, when you're doing research. I can store hundreds of e-books on my computer. I can also take them with me wherever I go, as I can access them on my phone. I can even highlight and make notes for future reference. Most importantly, they have a search function, which makes skim-reading much, much faster.

Technical Manuals

The company you are designing for may have technical manuals with details of their standard operating procedures (SOPs) and so on. Be sure to get the latest editions because these are excellent resources.

Technical manuals have been written by technical writers whose job is somewhat similar to yours. So you may find a lot of the research work has already been prepared for you. So maybe all you need to do is find a way of training the manual.

A great way of using these is to take them to any SME and ask the SME what changes need to be made, and if anything is done differently in practice.

Industry Standards

These are also excellent reference points. These have been put together by industry experts, again saving you a lot of research time.

Look through these for best practices, competencies, frameworks, and so on. As these are the standards, you should be able to directly take them and design your training around them.

Existing Training Materials

These are also a great source of information, as they take technical manuals and industry standards one step further and put them into a trainable format. You may even find that the way they are right now is fine.

Maybe your client gives you these as previous versions of the training that you are working on. Or maybe you have similar training materials from another project you've worked on before. Maybe you've even purchased a stock of standard training materials.

The biggest thing to be careful of with these is any copyright issues.

To avoid these issues, seek permission when you can. At the very least, attribute the source in your work.

As well, I recommend rewriting, rewording, and reordering content in your own unique way. And absolutely avoid using any templates or stock graphics that are included in these.

As you browse through these materials, do so with a critical eye.

Think about how they could be improved, and use those improvements as a starting point for your training development.

Research Resources

 SMEs

 Books

 Technical Manuals

 Industry Standards

 Existing Training Materials

- ## Finding the Vital Few

With all of the content that we collect through research, it's likely that we'll end up with more than we need.

Even if you are reluctant to let go of anything, it's important to remember that **less is more**. Over the years, if there is one thing that has been and is consistent about my improvement as a trainer and instructional designer, it is simplicity. The more content I let go of, the better my training becomes.

Furthermore, the more content you include, the more challenging it is for the learners (and even the person delivering the training). It ends up becoming a cramming session where you desperately try to get to the next point before time runs out.

For the trainer, this feels stressful. For the learner, this feels overwhelming. And once it's over, the learners leave feeling exhausted and remember nothing.

So we need to let go of things. We need to look at all the content we have collected, discard as much as we can, and only keep the vital few.

The vital few is the least amount of content that delivers the highest value.

This is also known as Pareto's Principle, or the 80/20 rule. For example, 80% of your business might come from 20% of your customers. As you sift through the content you have collected, you will eventually discover that 20% of it has an 80% impact on the learners.

So let's have a look at how we decide what to let go of, and how to identify the vital few.

Mix and Match

The first step to finding the vital few is to clarify what is unique and what is the same.

Some of the stories you will have collected may talk about exactly the same point. Some of the techniques may achieve exactly the same goal. And some of the theories may talk about exactly the same thing, just from a slightly different angle.

Start by going through everything and mixing and matching.

If two things look the slightest bit similar, then group them together.

At this step, you are not removing anything, just identifying what is unique and what is the same.

Connecting all of the relationships between different pieces of content helps me a lot when I come to actually finding the vital few. It removes any doubt in my mind that something might be useful, as I can clearly see that another piece of content does the job just as well. You'll be surprised by the amount of similarities you identify when going through this process.

Take the Garbage Out

Some of what you will have collected might not be valid. It might be flawed theories, models that only work in some situations, or even someone's personal opinion. I call this garbage.

Taking out the garbage is a great and easy place to start filtering out unnecessary content.

So as you look at your collection of content, think about the following questions:
- **Is there any way this might not work?**
- **Would this work for the learner's situation?**
- **Does anyone disagree with this?**
- **Do I have proof that this works?**
- **Does something else achieve the same goals more efficiently?**

Aim to be left with only content that will work for your learners. There is nothing worse than training something that gets challenged. There have been a few times in the past when I fell in love with a piece of content, but eventually got challenged in the training room on it.

When you are designing training, you ideally want to identify anything that is irrelevant, impractical or theoretically flawed before your learners do.

Taking the Garbage Out

Is there any way this might not work?

Would this work for the learner's situation?

Does anyone disagree with this?

Do I have proof that this works?

Does something else achieve the same goals more efficiently?

Keep Within Their Grasp

Remember, not everyone comes to the training with the goal of becoming a master. For most learners, their goal will simply be to reduce the inconvenience of not being a master.

A lot of learners are looking for quick fixes, and quite frankly, need quick fixes. They have far too many other priorities in their work. Perhaps the most common need I observe amongst the people I train is to reduce complexity.

So what we train them on should not be complex. It should be as simple as possible.

It should be something they can take away and use immediately without much effort. The more effort it takes, the more barriers they have to using it.

With that in mind, we should only keep things that are within their grasp. Anything that requires a significant amount of time to master, or a significant amount of further reading to understand, or significant amount of energy to even use should not be included in our training. If it is beyond the reach of the normal person, then it should be removed.

Finding the Vital Few

 Mix and Match

 Take the Garbage Out

 Keep Within Their Grasp

And Now Begin

You should be left with only relevant content. And now it is time to being designing!

Researching a Solution Summary

The following flowchart is a summary of everything we have looked at in this section:

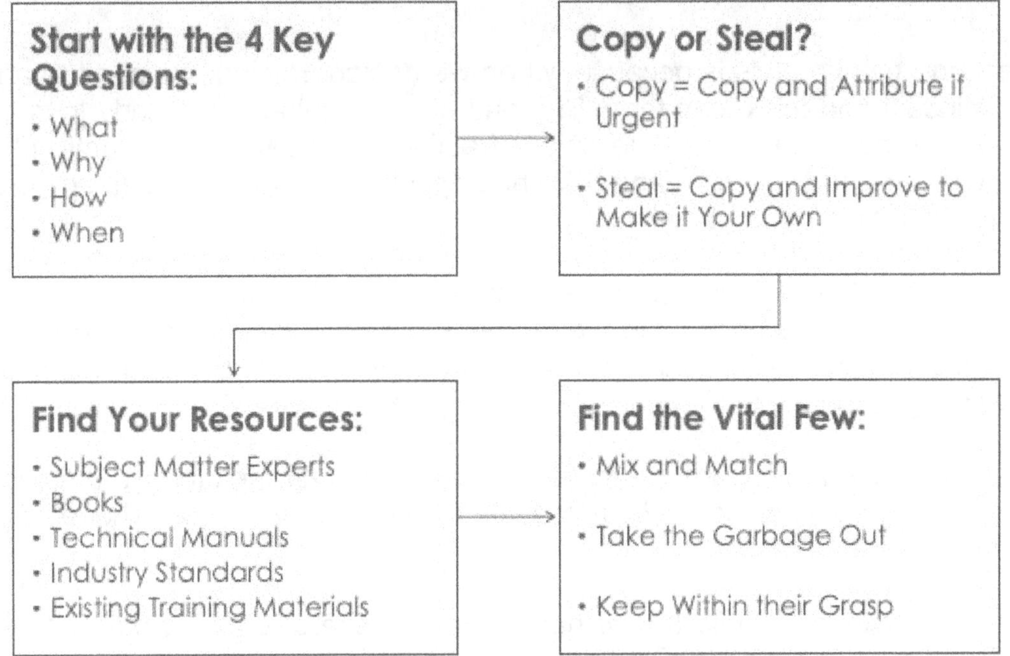

Designing for Application

In 1972, during Richard Nixon's visit to China, Zhou Enlai, Premier of the People's Republic of China, was asked what he thought the impact of the French Revolution was. Despite the French Revolution taking place two centuries earlier, Zhou famously responded that it was 'too early to say'.

That saying has gone down in history as an example of the Chinese tendency to think long-term, in contrast with Western impatience and short-sightedness.

And just to be factually correct, it was later revealed that the question was misunderstood by Zhou Enlai. Zhou thought it referred to the 1968 students' riots in Paris!

The reason I mention this is because, when we design training, we need to adopt a similar mindset and think long-term. The end of the training is too early to say what impact it has had. The real value of our training won't reveal itself until after our learners have returned to work and have had opportunities to implement and practice what they learnt during the training.

This presents a huge challenge to us because the justification of the value of our training is out of our hands. It's in the learner's hands. Even worse, it's only in their hands once they get back into the real world. And the real world is a dangerous place for any changes to take place in.

Have you ever tried to change a bad habit? Have you ever tried to give up smoking? Or stop drinking so much coffee? Or stop surfing the Internet on your phone as you're about to go to bed?

Have you ever tried to build a new habit, such as exercise more, eat healthier, or spend less time on your phone?

Unless you are superhuman, you have probably realised from experience that changing your habits is not an easy thing. We tend to fail more times than we succeed. And it becomes even more difficult when we're trying to change someone else's habits.

Have you ever tried desperately to bring something to mind when you needed to, but really struggled? For example, in an exam, when you try to recall some fact that you know but, for some reason, can't seem to remember right now? Or when you are looking for your car keys in the morning because you can't remember where you put them last night?

As we'll see shortly, the human memory sucks. It sucks so much that to believe our learners will remember anything from our training is simply foolish.

As you might be able to see, getting learners to apply what they have learnt is far from simple. There are numerous barriers to application, and it is our responsibility to overcome those barriers. That is the focus of this section.

• 3 Conditions for Habit Change

Changing our own habits is hard enough. But changing other people's habits is a whole other challenge.

Under certain conditions, habits can change. There are even certain conditions for changing other people's habits.

In order to help people change their habits, the habits we train them in must:
- be within their reach
- require no decision-making in the moment of action
- be rewarding

Within Their Reach

Doing something new requires willpower.

If you're a regular smoker, and you want to stop smoking, you need willpower. If you're a very nice person, but suddenly have to start giving very direct negative feedback to your team members, you will need willpower to do so.

You will also need willpower if you are used to giving presentations using PPT (PowerPoint) and then very suddenly have to start giving presentations without PPT.

The problem with willpower is that it runs out very quickly.

Think of it like a muscle. The more it gets used, the more tired it becomes. When it becomes tired, it doesn't work well. But if you let it rest, it recovers. You can also train your willpower muscle to become stronger.

But our job isn't to train our learners' willpower muscles. Instead, our job is to limit how much our training depends on their willpower muscles... much like what I mentioned earlier, in the section on Energy Budget.

Throughout their working day, learners have numerous drains on their willpower energy store. Their commute to work through the morning rush hour traffic, scanning their email inbox, and even a simple phone call all require some amount of willpower. By the time they have a chance to apply what they've learnt from our training, they will probably have very little willpower left over.

And even if they do have enough willpower left over, in my extremely strong opinion, it is far more reliable to just assume they will have hardly any willpower left over.

So, first of all, we need to make sure that the behaviour we train our learners to do requires as little willpower as possible. The easier it is, the more likely they are to do it.

Require No Decision-Making in the Moment of Action

The biggest barrier to taking action is decision-making in the moment of action.

Imagine you set the goal of eating healthy. 'Eat healthy' is the only thing you told yourself. Then you enter a convenience store. You're hungry and in a rush, so you need to choose something fast. You notice dried mango, a sports drink, a delicious-looking sandwich, and lots more. You remember 'Eat healthy' and then your mind starts analysing your choices.

Dried mango. Is that healthy? How about the sports drink? How about the sandwich? Arrghhh, I don't know!

This causes your brain to enter **analysis paralysis**.

You stand, frozen, in the snacks section, unable to make a decision. Your watch is counting down the time and you feel an increasing sense of urgency to buy something to eat before it's too late. Under the stress, your higher cognitive functions start to shut down. And without being aware of it, your hand reaches for a chocolate bar and you suddenly find yourself paying for it, walking out, and stuffing the chocolate bar into your mouth.

Analysis paralysis, according to Wikipedia, **occurs 'when the fear for potential error exceeds the potential for success, and prevents a decision from being made. An overload of options can overwhelm the situation and cause this "paralysis", rendering one unable to come to a conclusion'.**

Now, let's change the scenario a bit. Instead of 'Eat healthy', your goal is 'Eat natural foods'.

Is dried mango natural? No. It's been processed and is probably coated in sugar. How about the sports drink? No. What about the sandwich? No. But then you see a banana, which is. Because it is the only natural food you see, you choose the banana!

The less decision-making a person has to do in the moment of application, the easier it is to take action.

And we need to make sure that any decision-making there is to be done is done in the training room and not out in the real world.

Rewarding

About 5 or 6 times a week, I do a variety of exercises, including bodyweight workouts, yoga, and running. I have found that exercising gives me great benefits. It increases my energy levels, makes me happier, and even encourages me to eat healthier.

There is some struggle involved in the exercise, though. At times, it can be demanding, and even painful. But if that were all I got from it, then I wouldn't keep up exercising for very long. I know that I am much healthier, overall, for exercising, and that is why I continue to exercise.

Like me with exercising, when it comes to giving our learners new habits, there has to be something in it for them. Otherwise, it becomes a huge struggle. (It is important to note that I don't mean there has to be something in it for the business, or for their managers. I mean there has to be something in it FOR THEM.)

We talked earlier about intrinsic motivation. Whatever behaviour we are training our learners in, we should ensure that it is something they have an interest in. It must solve a problem, help them overcome a challenge, or achieve a goal.

We also talked about flow.

The behaviour we want our learners to embrace must not be so challenging that it becomes frustrating, and it must not be so easy that it becomes boring.

It should be just challenging enough to give them a sense of progression and achievement.

It's All about Application

Whatever we train our learners in, we want to do the most we can to ensure that they apply it back in the real world.

When we are designing our training, we can control which behaviours, habits, techniques, strategies, and so on get included. We can also control how these are customised and presented to our learners. And we have a lot of control over simplifying them to ensure they adhere to these 3 rules.

Now we are going to look at how to apply these 3 rules to our training design to make it easier for learners to apply what they learn back in the real world.

3 Conditions for Habit Change

 Within Reach

 Require no Decision-making in moment of action

 Rewarding

- ## They Will Forget

Apple is a company most of us know very well. You are probably quite familiar with their logo. Walking down the street, you'd probably recognise that logo from very far away. But if you were asked to draw that logo entirely from memory, you might struggle a little.

At least, according to one study, you would. In this study, 85 university students were asked to reproduce the Apple logo from memory. Before they drew it, they were asked how confident they felt at being able to draw it correctly. Most of the participants were extremely confident of their ability. But in the end, only 1 participant out of 85 could accurately draw the logo. (Source: _https://hbr.org/2015/06/we-cant-recall-logos-we-see-every-day_)

Most of them made little mistakes. Some drew the leaf in the wrong direction. Others forgot to remove a chunk. And so on.

What this shows is that our memories are limited in what they can accurately recall. Perhaps of more concern is that we tend to be overconfident in the strength of our memories.

The implication of this for training is that our learners are probably not going to remember everything they learnt. Normally, that's not a problem. After all, if you attend a training on using Photoshop, for example, then you don't really need to recall how to use Photoshop when you're taking the subway to work. But this becomes a problem when our learners cannot recall what they need to (e.g. how to use Photoshop) at exactly the time they need to (e.g. when they are using Photoshop).

• The Barriers to Recall

At the exact time of need, there are many barriers to accurately recalling and using necessary information.

This exhaustive list of the different types of barriers includes:
- Lack of Encoding
- Wrong Encoding
- No Contextual Encoding
- Overconfidence
- Lack of Reinforcement
- No Unconscious Competence
- Lack of Cognitive Capacity
- Too Much Unconscious Competence
- Lack of Attention
- Overriding Habits
- Too Much Similarity
- Distraction Whilst in Process

We will look at each of these in a bit more detail now.

Lack of Encoding

Perhaps the knowledge wasn't even stored into the memory in the first place. Maybe, during the training, our learners got called out for a meeting and so they missed a part. Maybe they had too much on their mind so they couldn't pay attention. Maybe our training didn't engage them. Maybe information was presented in an overly complicated way preventing them from taking any of it in.

Wrong Encoding

Maybe that training you went through on using Photoshop was delivered as a lecture, and you were given a whole load of facts on what Photoshop can do. You actually found it quite interesting. It finished with a multiple choice test and you aced it. But there was actually no practice in using Photoshop. So when you go to use Photoshop after the class, you can remember all these facts about its various features and functions, but you can't actually apply them. **Instead of encoding facts, that training should have encoded procedures and habits.**

No Contextual Encoding

Maybe the training did not take into account the context of application. For example, self-defence classes make self-defence look easy. The attacker punches, then the attacker freezes whilst holding their fist in the air, giving you a chance to apply that complicated manoeuvre you just learnt… all whilst laughing and giggling with your partner. After practicing several times, you master it. But when you get attacked in real life, the attacker doesn't hold their fist in the air, nor do they freeze. In fact, they have a knife, and they punched you from behind, and now you're curled up in a ball on the floor, crying!

Overconfidence

Maybe the training has given learners so much confidence that they actively seek out challenging opportunities to apply their new skill. This is a common mistake of self-defence classes as well—giving people so much confidence that they actually put themselves in danger. Whereas it would be wise to not walk down that dark pathway at night, they are excited about applying what they've learnt. Overconfidence means learners put themselves in situations that they can't handle, and overestimate the usefulness of the knowledge available for recall.

Lack of Reinforcement

Maybe the knowledge was encoded well, but as soon as our learners got back to work, they became busy. They didn't have enough time to look over their notes or practice what they learnt. Only after a significant period of time did they get a chance to practice what they had learnt, but by that time the memory had already faded.

No Unconscious Competence

If you are good at riding a bike, then you probably don't need to think about riding a bike. You don't need to think about pushing the pedals and balancing yourself; it all comes naturally.

When we become that good at something, we reach a state of unconscious competence, where we don't need to think about doing it, we just do it. But when we don't have unconscious competence, we need to actually think about it and concentrate on it. This requires a lot more brain capacity, which there might not be enough of at that time.

If we are too busy focussing on avoiding the traffic coming our way, we might lose balance and fall off of our wobbly bike.

Lack of Cognitive Capacity

When in the midst of a task or situation, our brains may be so overwhelmed that we don't actually have enough mental capacity to even think about doing what we need to do. To make this point easier to understand, try a simple experiment. Move your right arm in a circle in a clockwise direction. Then move your left arm in a square in an anti-clockwise direction. Now move your right ankle in a figure of eight shape. Do these all at the same time. Easy? No!

Too Much Unconscious Competence

When we become good at things, we no longer need to pay much attention to them. As a result, we can miss subtle mistakes that would be very obvious to beginners.

For example, have a look at the following phrase:

'Paris in the the summer.'

Native English speakers are far more likely to miss the second 'the' than non-native English speakers. (Didn't notice it? Then look again!)

People with limited English language abilities are very likely going to spot that second 'the' because they pay more attention to each individual word, whereas native-speakers only pay attention to the entire sentence, or even just the meaning of the sentence.

Lack of Attention

You're very angry about what your boss said to you this morning. As you start your drive to a customer meeting, thoughts are racing around and around in your head. When you reach your destination, you get out of your car and look up. But instead of arriving at your customer's office, you've actually driven back home. As your mind was racing with thoughts, your brain switched into auto-pilot and you drove your most familiar route because you were not paying attention to your driving.

Overriding Habits

Anyone who has ever made the switch from Windows to Mac will have experienced this. As you start up your Mac, you find yourself dragging the mouse to the bottom left, to find the Start button. Oops! Your old habits from your Windows days have somehow found their way into your Mac days. Overriding old habits takes time and a lot of reinforcement.

Too Much Similarity

Ever go to throw your dirty clothes in the laundry basket, but accidentally throw them in the rubbish bin instead? This sort of mistake can happen when the target of our actions is similar to another object. If the laundry basket and rubbish bin look exactly the same, you are quite likely to mix the two up. This sort of error happens quite a lot, such as when our spouses have a similar name to someone we've been working quite closely with recently and we address our spouse by the other person's name accidentally!

Distraction Whilst in Process

For many day-to-day actions, we tend to follow a procedure. For example, withdrawing cash from an ATM involves these steps: Put card in. Enter PIN number. Select amount to withdraw. Take card. Take cash. Walk away.

But if a distraction occurs in the midst of that process, then we may forget to take subsequent steps. For example, after you take your card, you might suddenly get a phone call. As you walk away to answer the phone, you completely forget that the cash is there waiting for you!

The barriers to recall:
- Lack of Encoding
- Wrong Encoding
- No Contextual Encoding
- Overconfidence
- Lack of Reinforcement
- No Unconscious Competence
- Lack of Cognitive Capacity
- Too Much Unconscious Competence
- Lack of Attention
- Overriding Habits
- Too Much Similarity
- Distraction Whilst in Process

As you can see, it's pretty risky to depend entirely on our learners' memories. Even if we have encoded things well, lots of different things can happen at the time of need that render memory useless. So we should definitely not rely only on knowledge in the head. Instead, we can also rely on knowledge that we can put into the environment.

- ## Knowledge in the Head and Environment

A group of University students in the US were given a set of drawings depicting a US one-cent coin. The different drawings all looked very similar, but with subtle differences. They were asked to select the correct image. Despite using these coins every day, less than half of the students were able to select the correct image. (Source: Norman, Don. *The Design of Everyday Things: Revised and Expanded Edition*, Page 75. Basic Books. Kindle Edition.)

The above example demonstrates how limited our memories are. But in reality, the above results aren't a problem. In reality, when we use coins, we don't need to just remember what they look like. We can actually see them, and compare them to other coins. **Despite the limitations of our memory, we are able to use coins successfully because we combine knowledge in the head (memory) with knowledge in the environment (the coins).**

In our training, if we can put more knowledge in the environment, then we can spend less time on helping learners memorise that knowledge. The time that we save through doing this can instead be spent on helping learners apply that knowledge, which raises all sorts of new possibilities.

Tools in the Environment

Tools are a fantastic way of putting knowledge into the environment. A tool is something that makes a skill easier to perform, or even performs the skill for you. When designed well, tools also help our learners apply that knowledge at the EXACT time of need.

In ancient times, navigating by the stars was a skill. Nowadays, we just use a compass or GPS. Arithmetic was a skill. Now, we use calculators. Driving is a skill. Soon, robots might do that for us.

It's easy to forget this but, in skill development, not everyone wants to become a master. Sometimes they're just looking to minimise the inconvenience of not being a master.

An engineer doesn't require training in presentation skills so that they can run for president or deliver a TED talk. They just want to be able to get their ideas across to the people that matter.

A sales director isn't looking to take a course on stress management so that they can become a Zen Master. They just want to feel less stressed.

And a project manager isn't looking to take Microsoft Office training so that they can mesmerise you with the amazing functions they can perform in Excel. They just want to manage their project better.

And that's OK. We shouldn't expect people to become masters in everything. An engineer should master engineering, just like a sales director should master directing a sales team, or a project manager should master managing a project. But other things beyond the scope of their expertise, they only need to perform well enough to work effectively.

To help them with those other things, we can provide them with tools such as:
- templates
- checklists
- forms
- models
- processes
- instructions
- reference aids

Types of Tools

 Templates

Checklists

Forms

 Models

Processes

Instructions

Reference Aids

And we mustn't forget that we can still use knowledge in the head, at times. Whilst we, ideally, want to put as much knowledge in the environment as possible, there are times when our learners must still rely on knowledge in the head.

For knowledge in the head, we have a special tool called mnemonics. We'll look at this and other tools in more detail momentarily, but let's first look at how to design tools that help us put knowledge into the environment.

• How Tools Aid Application

Tools provide people with a reference. They guide people on what to do, why, how, and when. They minimise the thinking required to perform effectively.

Checklists are a fantastic example of highly effective tools. Pilots use them when performing safety checks on planes. Without checklists, they'd be dependent on their memories alone, and more likely to forget important information.

Things like checklists minimise the conscious effort required to perform a behaviour, which is vital for overcoming the barriers to developing new skills.

Let's look at an example. Mark is an engineer and he needs to prepare a presentation to introduce his new product to his customers. Mark is also a busy guy. Despite his best intentions, events in his day conspired against his plans and he's only left with 30 minutes to prepare his presentation.

In Mark's situation, which of the following is more likely to happen?

1. He tries hard to remember what he learnt in the training. He digs around his drawers for the handouts and notes he took. He looks through them and thinks of how best to use this to prepare his presentation.
2. He panics and reverts to his old habits of just writing everything that comes to mind on two dozen PPT slides.

I'm going with 2 because people tend to revert to their old habits when they are under pressure. Pressure depletes precious energy, our capacity for conscious effort, and our stores of willpower. And when those are low, the only thing we can do is revert back to behaviours that require the least amount of energy, which are our old habits.

But if we change Mark's situation slightly, we might get a different result.

Maybe we taught Mark a structure that he can use to prepare his presentations. This structure is logical, it's easy to use, and it helps his customers understand his ideas more easily.

We could put this structure on a sheet of paper as a simple template that shows the structure and what information to include at each part of it. It might even include some good examples. Then Mark hangs this on his office wall, right next to where his computer is.

When Mark needs to prepare a presentation in a rush, he sees that template hanging on his wall next to his computer and instantly refers to it. He no longer has to think about what that structure was, or dig through his drawers to find it. It's just there, and it does all his thinking for him.

Tools Help Learners Find Their Way

Learning is about discovery. It requires reflection and finding one's own way. So if we design a tool for our learners, are we taking away their opportunity for self-discovery? Are we being too prescriptive and forcing a methodology down their throats?

To answer this question, consider (if you are old enough) your experience of using a VCR. Remember those things? They were all different. They all had different functions and they were all goddamn complicated.

What did you do when you first got your VCR?

You whipped out the instruction manual and looked up how to set the timer so that you could record that cheesy soap opera that's on at 7pm.

After doing that one time, you just about got it, but couldn't fully remember it. So the next 3 or 4 times you have to keep on getting out the instruction manual. But by the 5th time, you can suddenly do it without the instruction manual. You've learnt that new function by heart.

That's how tools work. They give learners a reference to use whilst they haven't fully learnt it yet. Eventually, after using the tool often, they internalise their knowledge. Then they never need to use the tool again.

When you're fiddling with your VCR, maybe you accidentally discover a secret hack that allows you to set the timer faster and easier. That then becomes your way, and you forget what you learnt from the instructions.

If that happens with tools, then that's fine. In fact, that's great. The learner finds their way. And that's the goal!

Tools simply support learners. They don't have to use them. But whilst they have no way, the tools provide a way. And by following that way, they either internalise it, or find their own better way. At the very least, they achieve the results they are looking for with the minimum amount of effort. Ultimately, the tools help them find their way faster.

But, as we'll see in the following sections, we need to design our tools with care.

- ## Follow the Path of Desire

Just because we have created a tool does not mean our learners will use it. Human nature (in other words, laziness) can get in the way of our learners using these tools.

When our learners don't use the tools the way they are supposed to, it's very easy to point fingers at our learners and say they're just too lazy. But the reality is that humans ARE lazy. If something is difficult to do, then our learners probably won't do it.

Human nature ALWAYS WINS.

So don't treat human nature as your enemy, because you will lose. Treat it as your friend, and **design your tools for lazy people.**

Training that uses practical tools is better than training that doesn't use tools. And training that uses tools that are not practical is exactly the same as training that doesn't use tools.

I have seen all sorts of attempts at tools. Where these tools tend to fail is that they focus too much on 'best practices'. When a best practice is complicated and takes more time and effort than learners have available at the time of need, then it's not a best practice, is it?

As an analogy, consider the path to my building in the compound I live in.

If I follow that path from the main entrance to my building, it takes a total of 4 minutes. That's 4 minutes of walking time. And for people who sometimes just want to get home, crash out on their sofa, and watch Netflix, 4 minutes is a long time.

So something interesting happened…

People created a new path. If you take a left turn straight after the main entrance, you will walk through a series of bushes and trees directly to my building.

Walking this shortcut takes a grand total of 30 seconds. And that's what I started to do. So did a whole bunch of other people. We took the shortcut through the bushes and trees, and we took it so often that eventually we created a new path.

In the field of design, this phenomenon is known as the path of desire. If we are going to design a product, a service, or even a tool, it had better follow the user's path of desire, because otherwise they won't use it.

Put yourself in the position of a web or app designer. These people know all about practicality. If the users don't like their website or app, the users just won't use it. It's that simple. How are you going to make money from websites and apps if no one wants to use them?

This requires thinking of the tool from the perspective of the learner. It requires asking the following types of questions;

- **How will they use it?**
- **Why will they use it?**
- **What will they use it for?**
- **When will they use it?**
- **What might distract them from using it?**
- **What would be easier than using this tool?**
- **How can I increase the chances of them using it?**

Follow the Path of Desire

How will they use it?
Why will they use it?
What will they use it for?
When will they use it?
What might distract them from using it?
What would be easier than using this tool?
How can I increase the chances of them using it?

To design the right tool requires an obsession with getting it right. Your first attempt at that tool won't work. Maybe it doesn't fit into their world. Maybe it doesn't do what it's supposed to do. But you can get it to work.

With enough trial and error, you can design a tool that compensates for a learner's lack of mastery. Learners will use it and they will start performing better at work as a result of it.

- ## Design for Context

To follow their path of desire, start by thinking of the context learners will use the tool in.

Where are they going to be?
What will they be doing?
What is the environment like?
What will they see? Will they be in a hurry?
Will they be under pressure?

Design for Context

Where are they going to be?
What will they be doing?
What is the environment like?
What will they see? Will they be in a hurry?
Will they be under pressure?

If they are operating a machine, then they'll be in the factory, standing by the control panel. It'll probably be quite noisy. They probably won't be in a hurry. There is probably a culture of safety in that environment, so it's important they take the time to use the machine right.

All of the above reveals lot of useful information about how a tool can be of help to the learner.

Let's change the example. Say we've been asked to design a course on how to prepare a presentation. What will the learner's context be like in this situation?

After speaking to some learners, you discover that they don't have much time for preparing presentations. They're pretty busy. Most likely they'll go straight to PPT, as that's their habit. So naturally they'll be at their computer, which is likely a laptop, which also means they could be anywhere at the time they prepare it.

Now we know that the tool should appear on their computer. We also know that PPT is a place they'll go from habit. Why not work with their habits? How about build a template into PPT that they can follow to prepare their presentation according to the way you teach them?

Maybe we get called back to teach the next part of the course: How to deliver a presentation. We teach them about body language, voice control, eye contact, etc. What's the context going to be like now?

We know they're going to be in a small meeting room. They're going to be talking to a small audience. They're going to be under a lot of pressure. They won't have time to look at reference aids in their environment. And even if they did, it wouldn't be appropriate for that situation. So what can we do here?

In this context, putting knowledge in the environment won't help. Ideally, our learners would develop good habits so that they naturally show good body language, voice control, and eye contact. Whilst developing those habits is the ultimate goal, development is still a process that can be greatly aided by a tool. So we still need to give them a tool, but we can't put it in the environment.

So where do we put it? In their heads.

This is where mnemonics come in handy. Mnemonics organise overwhelming amounts of knowledge into digestible mental models. Learners can easily encode mnemonics into memory. They can then, just as easily, retrieve them at the time of need.

So when our learner stumbles in the midst of their presentation and they need a moment to get back on track, they can access that mnemonic in exactly that moment.

It's even better if your mnemonic can take cues from the context to make it even easier to recall. Every time the audience drops their heads and lose interest, that could cue our learner to change their speaking speed. Every time our learner turns (out of habit) to face the PPT screen, that could be a cue for them to make more eye contact. And so on.

Context Analysis

Analysing the context of application gives us a great deal of insight. It tells us what format the tool should be in, where we should place the tool, how to present the tool, and what knowledge should be in the tool.

If we turn our insight into action, we can reduce the gap between access and application.

- ## Reduce the Gap

Our training tools are a way of putting vital knowledge into the environment. If our learners can refer to these tools at their exact time of need, they don't require much thinking capacity and are more likely to turn that vital knowledge into vital actions.

The challenge is reducing the gap between accessing and applying that knowledge.

For example, if our tool is a set of instructions on how to operate a piece of machinery, where should we put it? Should we put it in a big booklet together with instructions for all the other machinery, and then store it away in a drawer? Should we put it on the company's Wiki or Intranet? Or stick it on a notice board in the office upstairs?

None of those will reduce the gap. In fact, they will all increase the gap.

To reduce the gap, we need to put it in a place the learner will see at the exact time they use that machinery and need that knowledge. So, to reduce the gap, we should actually stick it on the machine itself, right above the control panel.

Relevant Format

What is the most relevant format for this tool? Is it a sheet of paper? Is it a word/text document? An email template? A PPT template? Or a poster that hangs on the wall in their meeting room?

I will assume that you will make your tools into documents (e.g. Word, PDF, PPT, etc.) as opposed to making your own computer software. There are many great tools out there, in various app stores, and you will probably find that your training tools could be used to create fantastic new apps, but that is time-consuming and costly. It takes far less time and money to make a document.

Think of what your learners will be looking at and using at the time they use the tool.

If they are writing an email and you want them to follow a certain structure, then save the structure in an email template. If they are coaching or mentoring one of their team members, then stick a poster with the GROW model on the wall behind where their mentee is sitting. If they are trying to operate a piece of machinery, then stick the instructions by the relevant controls so they get this information whilst they are operating it.

Whatever you do, aim to reduce the gap.

- ## **Mnemonics Aid Recall**

The way we store knowledge in the head is through mnemonics.

Any attempt to make something easier to remember is basically a mnemonic. There are many (and I mean MANY!) different types of mnemonics. For the sake of simplicity, I have identified 4 key ideas that are at the core of most of them:

- **Association**
- **Chunking**
- **Logical Sequencing**
- **Visualisation**

Types of Mnemonics

We will have a look at each one of these in-depth, but **make sure you use a combination of the above 4 ideas to create your mnemonics.** This is another thing that you can have a lot of fun creating, and you can come up with some really good ideas.

- ## Memory through Association

The simplest way to create a long-term memory is to associate new knowledge with existing knowledge.

Think of it a bit like a subway system in a city. In most subway systems, there are multiple subway lines, and some of the lines intersect at the same station. The stations with more connecting lines have more people travelling through them. Just like these stations, the more connections a memory has to other memories, the stronger it will be.

For example, look at the two lists below and see which one is easier to remember:
List 1:
- NASA
- NBA
- FBI

List 2:
- QHEV
- RYKL
- DRCI

Most likely, List 1 is easier to remember because those abbreviations meant something to you.

To use association to create mnemonics, **think first about the things your learners already know.** Some common things most people know include:

- **Words**
- **Names**
- **Places**
- **Dates**
- **Pictures**
- **Symbols**
- **Shapes**
- **Famous people**
- **Body parts**
- **Furniture**

And many, many more.

Then think about how those things can be associated with what you want them to remember.

Things Everyone Knows

- 💬 Words
- 🪪 Names
- 🚏 Places
- 📅 Dates
- 🖼 Pictures
- 🌐 Symbols
- 🔲 Shapes
- ♟ Famous People
- 🧍 Body Parts
- 🛋 Furniture

Metaphors and Analogies

Metaphors and analogies are powerful ways of using association.

One of my favourite metaphors is the 'elephant and rider' metaphor. It describes how our behaviour is driven by two forces: the rational force (the rider of the elephant), and the automated force (the elephant). For example, our rider (the rational force) might tell us that we should go for a run every morning to stay fit. Our rider will tell us that is a great idea. But when we wake up in the morning, our elephant tells us to stay in bed.

Another thing I love about the elephant and rider metaphor is that it not only describes the challenges we face when trying to change behaviour, but it can also be used to create solutions. The elephant and rider metaphor tells us that, when trying to change behaviour, we need to set a direction (the rider's job), then provide incentives and shape the path to motivate the elephant towards that direction. (I'll talk more about this particular analogy later on.)

Stories are another way of helping people remember. I have noticed an interesting phenomenon. Whenever I follow up on my training several months later, what people remember most vividly are the stories that I told. Stories are great memory aids. But how do they relate to association?

Because each story tends to follow a similar structure, we have had that structure burned into our brains. This means that we tend to only need to remember one part of the story, and then the rest of the structure that exists in our minds will help us unravel the rest of it. (We'll look at storytelling in more detail later on as well.)

Association is a powerful memory aid. Find as many ways as possible of connecting your learning points to your learners' existing memories and you will have greatly increased the chances of them remembering.

- ## Memory through Chunking

Chunking is the act of breaking down a big piece information into smaller chunks of similar information. The idea is to break it into small enough chunks so as to fit within the limits of the short-term memory. Chunking also uses association because any item of information used as a chunk needs to be meaningful.

For example, say we have to remember a long list of numbers such as 114997450712.

With 12 digits, this is a long list and it is longer than our short-term memory can handle. So we can use chunking to present it (and remember it) in a digestible quantity.

There are 2 things we need to do to effectively use chunking:

1. **Break the information down into smaller chunks (no more than 5)**
2. **Ensure each chunk is a meaningful item of information (in other words, associated to existing memories)**

So here is how I would 'chunk' the list of those 12 digits:

11:49 – Is it time to get ready for lunch?
97 - The year Hong Kong was handed back to China
45 - The end of WWII
07 - The year the first iPhone was released
12 - The year of the London Olympics

To me, these numbers mean something. I have broken the list of digits down into enough items of meaningful information to fit into my short-term memory. It's already become much easier for me to remember. You might create a slightly different list because the numbers might mean something different to you.

To use chunking in training, we obviously don't want to think about what is meaningful for us. **We want to think about what is meaningful to our learners, and find a chunking technique that helps them.**

Acronyms

A great way to do this is to use acronyms, where we use the first letter of each word in a list to form a word. An example of this is the famous coaching model, GROW:
- Goal
- Reality
- Options
- Will

One of the things I love about acronyms is that you can actually find a word that is closely related to the concept you are talking about. The GROW model is a great example, because GROWing is exactly what coaching is all about.

Acrostics

Another way of using chunking is to use what is called an acrostic, where we make a meaningful sentence out of the first letter of each word. A famous example of an acrostic to remember each line of the treble clef is to use the phrase 'Every Good Boy Does Fine' (E, G, B, D, F). Some of you might know these lines by using 'Every Good Boy Deserves Fudge'. Whichever acrostic you use, you end up remembering the same 5 lines, which is the whole point!

Techniques like acronyms and acrostics are a bit like the nesting Russian Dolls. With Russian Dolls, you find many dolls all within one single doll. You don't need to make space for all of the dolls to store them. You only need to make space for **one** of them. Similarly, with acronyms and acrostics, all you need to do is remember one piece of information (a word or a sentence), and once you recall it, you will be able to unpack all of the other pieces of information that are linked to it.

Principles

If you think about it, principles are also examples of chunking. Principles are rules that can be applied across a number of different situations.

For example, Robert Cialdini wrote a fantastic book called *Influence: The Psychology of Persuasion* in which he describes 6 key principles of influence. His book is filled with numerous examples of how these principles have been applied in real life. But if you were to remember all the examples and different applications, you would really struggle, because there are hundreds! So instead he chunks them all into 6 different principles which are much easier to remember (Reciprocity, Commitment and Consistency, Social Proof, Liking, Authority, and Scarcity).

One of my favourite of those principles is that of 'Liking' (I actually shared an example earlier on of how this principle helped someone I trained). It means that when people like us, they treat us more favourably and become more agreeable with us. And the best way to get people to like us is to find ways of being like them.

This means that, when I'm chatting with friends, I can try to emphasise points of views that I have that are like theirs. Or when I meet a new customer, I can emphasise parts of our professional backgrounds that we have in common. Or if I'm listening to a friend in need, I'll try to emphasise things about their viewpoint that I agree with.

All coming from one principle are these many different applications. All I need to do is remember that one word, 'Liking', and I can start to find ways of applying that in the moment.

You can easily find ways of enhancing your training by actively involving your learners in chunking exercises that will make what you are teaching meaningful and memorable to them.

- ## Memory through Logical Sequence

The idea with logical sequencing is to remember things in a logical order.

For example, when you walk into a room, you wouldn't first sit on the sofa, then hit the light switch, and then walk through the door. That's just not logical. A logical sequence would be to first walk through the door, then hit the light switch, and sit on the sofa.

The great thing about logical sequences is that you don't actually have to remember that much. You just need to remember one or two items in the sequence. As you apply logic to them, the memories start to come back.

I know I've referred to this model a lot, but it's a really fantastic example of packaging for knowledge in the head, and that's the example of the **GROW** model for coaching. Not only does this use association and chunking, but it uses logical sequencing as well. It's logical to start by setting **G**OALS, and then examining the **REALITY** before moving on to brainstorming **OPTIONS** and finally identifying what actions they have the **WILL** to take.

I created an acronym that uses logical sequencing for remembering how to effectively facilitate a meeting. The acronym is **EASE** and it stands for:
- **E**ngage—Get participants in the right mental state for discussing
- **A**lign—Get participants to focus on the same questions in the same order
- **S**upervise—As the discussion begins, step back and only come in to get things back on track
- **E**nact—Only finish the discussion when they have agreed on an action plan

This is especially useful for when the order of information is important, and it combines well with chunking methods such as acronyms and acrostics.

- ## Memory through Visualisation

One famous method for memory enhancement that athletes use (even used by ancient Romans) is called The Method of Loci. This uses visualization in conjunction with spatial memory and familiar information about your environment to enable you to recall information quickly and efficiently.

The idea is that you bring to mind a place that you are very familiar with. It might be your bedroom, or a library, maybe even a garden, but it must be somewhere you are very familiar with. Then, with that place firmly in mind, start to place the information you have just learnt into different parts of that place.

There are a few tips to make this technique work better. Firstly, as you place the information you want to learn in different places, make sure it is placed with something that really exists in that place (e.g. a bookshelf or a bedside table in a bedroom). Again, you are using the power of association here, and these things act as triggers that help bring back the new information to mind.

When you have prepared your Method of Loci, all you need to do is imagine that place (e.g. your bedroom) and then, as you notice the things in that place (e.g. the bookshelf, the bedside table), you then start to trigger the memory of the information you have just learnt.

Another tip to make this method more effective is to place the items in a meaningful way. Maybe you want to remember that you have to do the cleaning tomorrow, and you also need to prepare a shopping list. So you could place the task of cleaning with the bedside table (because it needs dusting), and place writing the shopping list with the bookshelf (because that's where you're more likely to find paper). Here, we're using both association and logical sequencing to strengthen this technique.

The core idea behind the Method of Loci is to use your imagination. This is what visualisation is all about—engaging your senses whilst creating the memory.

When we think about the senses, we tend to think about sights, sounds, smells, etc. But we should also think about emotion.

For example, think about September 11th, 2001, and (if you're old enough) the assassination of JFK. People say that everyone remembers what they were doing at those times. I can remember I was walking in Churchill Square in Brighton when the September 11th terrorist attacks happened, and my mum remembers that she was working in a pharmacy when she first heard about the assassination of JFK.

There are probably significant events that have happened in your life as well that you remember clearly, such as the phone call that informed you a loved one had passed away, the birth of your first child, your first kiss, and so on.

These kinds of memories are called flashbulb memories, and the reason they are so strong is because of the emotion associated with them.

Emotion is like an industrial strength superglue for forming memories. This is also a survival mechanism learned through evolution. It was important to remember moments of sheer terror, extreme joy, or any other extreme emotional reaction because it's a lesson in survival. The terror we felt when we were being chased by a lion means that every time we see a lion now, our heart starts to race.

Using Visualisation in Training

How can we use visualisation to help our learners remember more? Obviously, we don't want to scare them half to death, or wait for some terrible tragedy to happen. Instead, there are two things we can do:
1. **Create emotional experiences.**
2. **Use their imagination.**

If you have ever watched a video clip of a Tony Robbins seminar, you likely have noticed that it is quite emotional. There are a lot of tears, but also a lot of cheers. People really open up and dig deep down inside themselves. All of that must create extreme emotional experiences that they will remember forever.

The imagination is also very easy to use. One way I have done this is when I created a model for remembering all of the techniques I taught for presenting with confidence. I associated all of the different techniques with a different part of the body (eye contact with eyes, voice control with mouth, gestures with arms, etc.).

Then I arranged the body parts in order, from top to bottom (from mind to eyes to mouth to arms to legs). So I was actually combining this technique with both association and logical sequencing. To make it engage their senses even more, I got people to stand up and repeat the different body parts after me whilst touching them. After we'd reviewed each new technique, we'd then stand up and repeat the whole model again.

The core idea with visualisation is to involve as many senses as possible. The more vivid the experience, the stronger the memory will be.

Designing for Application Summary

The following flowchart is a summary of everything we have looked at in this section:

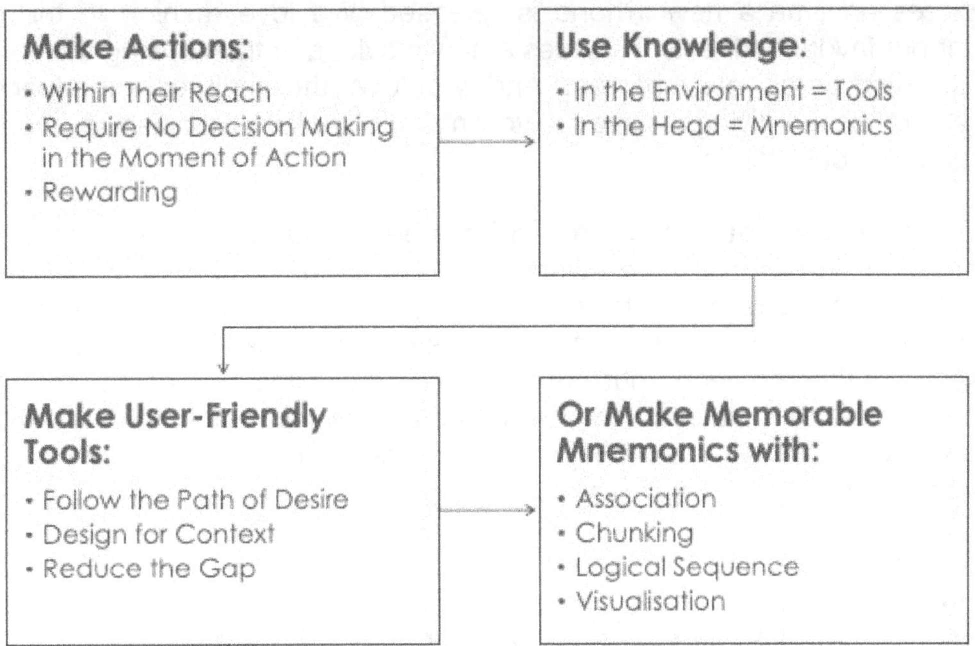

Designing for Emotion

I bet that somewhere in your home, you have proudly on display something that you adore. It might be a family photograph, your grandad's war medals, or maybe even your latest gadget. Whatever it is, you absolutely adore it. You might even say you love it.

You probably love quite a lot of things in your life. Not just objects, but brands as well, perhaps some famous movie directors or actors and actresses, or even certain experiences.

We love to show our devotion to brands, as can be evidenced by the line-ups outside Apple stores anytime a new iPhone is released. We love rushing to the cinema whenever our favourite director releases a new movie, and then buying the collector's edition to display on our shelves. And we love the thrill of experiences like rollercoasters, scuba diving, or even skydiving, and we love reminiscing about these good times with our friends.

Emotion affects both our decisions and our behaviour. A famous example is that of a team of designers in Sweden who wanted to get more people to use the stairs instead of the escalators in a metro station. They used sensors and speakers to make the stairs look like a piano and made each step sound like a different piano key. Because every time someone put their foot on a step, flocks of commuters hopped their way up and down the stairs to play out tunes they loved or just have a bit of fun. The end result was that 66% more people took the stairs! (Source: https://www.youtube.com/watch?v=2lXh2n0aPyw).

There is so much potential for emotion to greatly enhance the impact of our training. **By using emotion, our training can become:**
- **an experience to be cherished and reminisced upon**
- **a symbol of status and achievement**
- **an extremely satisfactory solution to a problem**
- **a methodology with a fan base**
- **a club to be associated with**

And much, much more.

Positive and Negative Affect

It's a fine day and you're in a great mood as you leisurely walk through a shopping mall. You walk past a furniture store with an attractive window display that catches your attention. You look at the bright white sofa and start to picture how it might look in your lounge. Then you go into a clothes shop and see a scarf that you like. It's quite affordable, and you think you deserve a treat, so you buy it.

The next day, you are walking through the shopping mall again, but this time you are in a hurry. You missed your alarm clock and are running late for a meeting at your office just around the corner. You walk past both the furniture store and clothes store again, but this time you barely notice them. All you can notice is the time on your watch and the exit door way ahead in the distance.

These two examples demonstrate the two basic modes our brain can be in. In his book, *Emotional Design*, Donald Norman describes these as Positive Affect and Negative Affect.

Positive affect is the state of being relaxed, when our brains are more receptive to interruptions and can pay more attention to novel ideas, which is what was happening in the first example. We are far more curious and creative when in a state of positive affect. As a result, we are better equipped to learn.

In the second example, we were in a state of negative affect. In such a state, our brains become super focussed. We focus in on the details of one particular thing at the expense of all other stimuli in our environment. It's not such a great state for learning, but it's essential for survival and taking action. When faced with a lion charging at you, you don't want to stop and take a moment to admire the pretty flowers around you. Instead, you want to focus on getting as far away as possible.

Positive Affect   Negative Affect

In training, we generally want to keep our learners in a state of positive affect for as long as possible. We want them to be curious and creative so they can imagine new possibilities and form new connections in their minds.

But, at times, we also want to push them into negative affect. When we need them to make decisions, take action, or make a commitment, they need to be focussed, and a little push can help them with that. Of course, we don't want to threaten to feed them to the lions! But we want to do enough to give them the push they need.

In the next section, we will look at priming to see what we can do in the training room to move our learners between positive and negative affect. For now, we are going to look at how we can create these changes through the design of our training in order to achieve optimum emotional impact.

• Three Levels of Emotional Design

A great place to learn more about emotional design is Donald Norman's book, *Emotional Design: Why We Love (Or Hate) Everyday Things.*

In this book, he talks about how we process the emotional aspect of design on three different levels, which correspond with different parts of our brain.

The better we understand these 3 different levels, the better we will be able to use them to enhance the emotional impact of our training.

3 Layers of the Brain

Over millions of years, our brains have evolved 3 different layers, one on the top of the other. These different layers control different functions, with the most basic and essential at the core of the brain, and increase in complexity as we go to the outermost layer.

At the very heart of the brain is our brainstem, or what we call the 'reticular brain' or 'lizard brain' (so called because it has been passed down to us from our earliest lizard ancestors). We share this part of the brain with all animals. It controls the body's most basic functions such as breathing, heart-rate, sleeping, balance, body temperature, etc. It's responsible for things like pulling our hands away when we touch a hot stove.

On top of the brainstem is what we call the 'limbic Brain' or 'mammalian brain' (so called because we share it with many mammals). This part is concerned with our survival, and controls some core functions such as fighting, feeding, and fleeing. (It also controls one other F word that describes reproductive behaviour!)

The mammalian brain is also responsible for learned behaviour and memory. It can remember what behaviours led to agreeable and disagreeable results, which is quite handy for when we make decisions about how to behave in the present moment.

It's also sometimes known as the 'emotional brain', because this is where emotions and emotional memories are housed. Emotional memories of the past are what we use to judge our present environment and make appropriate decisions. If I have a memory of a lion eating a family member, when I see another lion in this moment, my emotional brain uses emotions of that experience to tell me what this lion means to me. The fear generated from my emotional brain then links back to the lizard brain, and before I know it, I am running away. What's quite incredible is that my act of running away can be completely unconscious.

At the outermost layer is the most advanced part of the brain known as the 'cerebral cortex'. This is what makes us human. It's responsible for the development of human language, abstract thought, imagination, and consciousness. It visualises the future and makes plans. It can even imagine alternate universes.

3 Levels of Processing

Don Norman's 3 levels of processing relates how we process the design of objects and experiences to the 3 different layers of the brain. The 3 levels of processing are:
- the visceral level
- the behavioural level
- the reflective level

The visceral level is the most basic level, and is about how we make fast judgements about something that tell us essentially if it's good or bad. This is mostly controlled by our lizard brain, but also somewhat by our mammalian brain. The visceral level explains why people are afraid of spiders, heights and the dark. It also explains why we love sweet things, flowers, and bright colours. All of these things have had an impact on our survival throughout our evolutionary development. They are not just memories from our own life experiences, but also memories from the evolutionary development of our species and ancestors.

In design, the visceral level relates to appearance and aesthetics. It is all about what the senses can perceive and how we instinctively interpret our sensory experiences. For example, if you stand on a glass walkway on top of a skyscraper, your heart will beat faster as you notice the great height.

The behavioural level is slightly more advanced and is mostly concerned with the mammalian brain. Whereas the visceral level is concerned with instinctive reactions (e.g. 'Spider. RUN!'), the behavioural level is concerned with learned behaviour. For example, if you pick up something with one hand, and then try to pick up more things with that hand, you will be able to do so, but you won't know how you did it. You just willed your hand to pick things up, and your fingers moved accordingly. **The behavioural level happens unconsciously.**

But the behavioural level is also driven by expectation. Your mouth waters at the thought of eating that chocolate cake sitting in front of you. So you will your hands to grab it and put it in your mouth. If you then get to enjoy the taste of that chocolate cake, you feel a sense of satisfaction as your expectations are met, so you probably continue to eat it. If, however, the chocolate cake tastes awful, then you feel a sense of disappointment, and throw the plate on the ground out of frustration.

At the highest level is the reflective level, which is closely linked to the cerebral

cortex but also somewhat the mammalian brain as well. This is the home of conscious thought, rational thinking, and decision-making. It is where we reflect on our experiences and create conceptualisations about the world that help us change our future. Because of many generations of reflective thought, we are now able to build skyscrapers, circumnavigate the planet, and send people to the moon.

It is also because of conscious thought that we have developed the ability to override visceral and behavioural levels. Riding a rollercoaster is a good example of this. At a visceral level, it is quite terrifying, and therefore likely to put off people who are afraid of heights. But, for some, there is the appeal of being able to reflect on doing something that others were afraid to do, and brag to their friends about it.

It's All Theory

The above is simply theory and a framework for considering design from an emotional perspective. Nonetheless, it is a very useful theory if we focus on applying it.

To apply that theory, we have to look at our training and ask 3 key questions:
1. **Is it attractive?**
2. **Is it satisfactory?**
3. **Is it meaningful?**

Over the next few sections, we'll look closely at how to apply this in more detail.

• Making a Strong First Impression

Your life is in danger and you need to go in for life-saving surgery, but the operation has a 50-50 chance of survival. Whoever performs this surgery must be good, really good. So you go to visit two different doctors to decide which one to use.

You walk into the first doctor's office. It's a mess. On the floor are empty pizza boxes and bottles of beer. Papers are strewn all over the desk. There's a strange stain on the floor in the corner. The doctor looks like he hasn't washed his hair in months. He's sitting there wearing a T-shirt with a picture of a heavy metal band on it. He's wearing shorts and flip flops. He's smoking and his hand doesn't look too steady.

Then you walk into the second doctor's office. Straight away, you notice pictures on his wall of him shaking hands with famous people. You see a certificate from a prestigious university hanging on the wall and various awards standing on his shelves. The doctor has grey hair, he's wearing glasses, and he looks fit and healthy for a man of his age. He greets you with a smile.

Which doctor would you trust more? Personally, I'd go with the second one.

First impressions count for a lot. They determine our initial emotional reactions to people and things. And those emotional reactions, in turn, determine how we perceive those people and things.

For example, in 2002, when BMW released its new version of the Mini Cooper, Tony Swan of *The New York Times* had this to say about it:

'Whatever one may think of the Mini Cooper's dynamic attributes, which range from very good to marginal, it is fair to say that almost no new vehicle in recent memory has provoked more smiles.'

(Source: http://www.nytimes.com/2002/06/02/automobiles/behind-the-wheel-mini-cooper-animated-short-dubbed-in-german.html?mcubz=3).

He is suggesting that, even though it's not an especially outstanding car, the very look of it is enough to invite a positive emotional reaction, where you even overlook its flaws.

This is all about the power of the visceral level of design. First impressions count. It's why birds attract mates through their bright plumage, it's why flowers attract insects to spread their pollen, and it's why fruits attract mammals to spread their seeds.

One study on gamification also identified the power of the visceral level. In this study,

90 psychology undergraduate students from Aarhus University were given a task to discuss student satisfaction issues. The researchers wanted to investigate how the appearance of the task would affect the students' motivation. So the students were split into 3 different groups:
1. The Control Group, who conducted the task with simple worksheets.
2. The Gaming Group, who were placed around a colourful game board and given questions on glossy playing cards. As they answered questions, they got to move pieces a certain distance around the board in accordance with ratings given during the discussion.
3. The Framing Group, who were seated around the same game board as the Gaming Group. But instead of moving pieces based on the ratings given during discussion, they just moved one square after finishing each turn.

How did each group's levels of motivation vary? Well, the experiment reached an interesting conclusion. It found that there was no significant difference between the two groups who had been seated around the game materials. What this experiment showed was that simply presenting a task as a game, even if it didn't have the rules and mechanisms of a game, turned on the game switch in the participants.

(Source: http://gamification-research.org/2015/02/aarhus-gamification-experiment/.)

From this study, you can clearly see that first impressions count!

So how do we apply this to training? It all comes down to what we want our training to remind learners of, and what it actually reminds learners of, which we'll look at next.

- ## What Do You Remind Me Of?

The visceral level essentially comes down to one simple question: What do you remind me of?

Through your own life experiences, you have accumulated an incredible amount of memories. These memories tie sensory experiences (things we have seen, heard, tasted, etc.) to emotions. Now, whenever you encounter something new, your brain processes it by associating it with your memories to tell you how you should feel about it.

For example, Jeremy was asked to resign from his last job due to his poor performance. On his last day, he had to fill out a form confirming his resignation. He felt terrible filling it in. Now, whenever he lays his eyes on a form, especially forms that look exactly like that form, he feels terrible again.

Whilst every individual has their own unique life experiences, there are still a lot of common experiences we've all had.

These common experiences serve as a database for us to base our design decisions on.

How Do We Apply This to Training?

First, clarify what expectation your learners have, then describe these expectations via a series of key adjectives. For example: professional, innovative, inspirational, enjoyable, impressive, etc.

Second, use Google or another search engine to conduct an image search using those keywords. Collect a sample of images that you feel match those key words.

Third, analyse those images and consider what aspects of those you can apply to the design of the materials, the training experience, and the impression of the trainer.

In summary, we can apply this to training if we:

1. Summarise key adjectives
2. Find relevant images
3. Take inspiration

Designing for Visceral Impact

Design of Materials

If you can, hire a professional graphic designer to help you with these. Show them the impression you want to achieve and they will be able to translate that into a set of professionally designed materials.

If you want to do it yourself (which I don't recommend, unless you happen to be a graphic designer), then I recommend seeking inspiration from brands that already match the impression you want to achieve by visiting their websites, looking at their videos on YouTube, browsing their stores or product catalogues, etc.

As you do so, pay attention to the following:
- **Fonts**
- **Sizes**
- **Shapes**
- **Colours**
- **Language**
- **Layout**
- **Visuals**

Take Inspiration from Brands

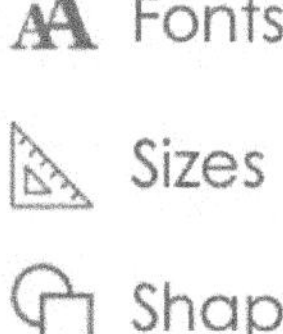

Fonts

Sizes

Shapes

Colours

Language

Layout

Visuals

These are all things you can replicate in the design of your own materials that will have a direct impact on the impression they give learners.

First Impressions of the Trainer

If you're attending a training on health and wellness, then you'd expect the trainer to be someone who is healthy. If they were in poor shape, then this person would instantly lose credibility for training on this topic.

Likewise, if you were attending a training on sales skills, then you'd probably expect the trainer to be confident, persuasive, and professional. A trainer delivering presentation skills should be a good presenter. And a trainer delivering a training on communication skills for introverts should be an introvert with good communication skills.

Also consider what your learners expect of the person delivering the training. Consider the trainer's:
* **age**
* **professional background**
* **appearance**
* **passions**
* **experience**
* **expertise**
* **personality**

Expectations of Trainer

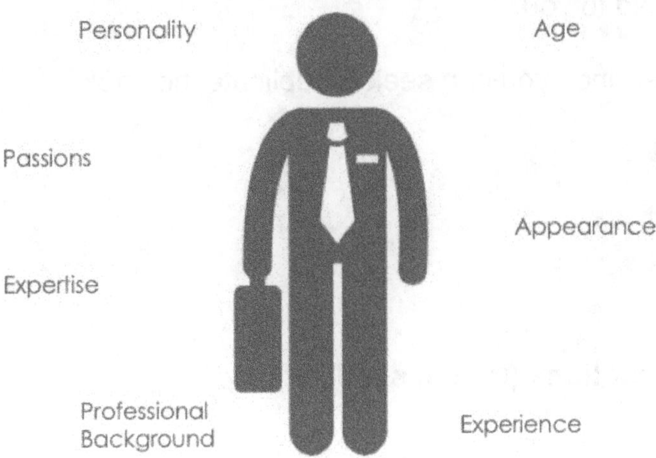

Search for famous people who already match that impression and see what inspiration you can take from them, but don't try to be something you are not. Authenticity is important in the training room. Without it, people see right through you and will think of you as a fake. Even worse, you'll probably find it exhausting trying to 'stay in character' for a whole day. So, instead of trying to be someone you are not, seek inspiration from your idols to show aspects of yourself that you may not be showing enough of at the moment.

First Impressions of the Training Experience

If you were paying a lot of money to attend a training, then you would expect it to be held in a venue that looked like it cost a lot of money. If you spent all that money only to attend a training in some run-down basement somewhere, then you'd be left with the impression that it wasn't worth it.

Similarly, if you signed up for an event that was advertised as 'Life-Changing!' then you would expect it to be life-changing. You'd expect the trainer to have high energy, and be powerful and impacting. You might even expect people to be crying as they make powerful revelations. Anything less and you'd demand your money back.

Think of life experiences you've had that made you feel the way you want your learners to feel. Think of museums, concerts, or even watching movies in cinemas. Think of the things you've done during your holidays, things you did when you were growing up, or even just normal, everyday experiences that impacted you. You can also think of things you signed up for, things you were forced to do, and things you couldn't predict that happened to you.

Aspects of the experience you can seek to replicate include:
- **mood**
- **energy**
- **pace**
- **lighting**
- **sound**
- **challenges**
- **visuals**
- **physical sensations (touch, smell, etc.)**

Expectations of Training Experience

The key to making a good first impression on your learners is to make a positive impact on them.

• Expectations and Satisfaction

Expectations drives behaviour. It is all about what you believe will happen. If you believe you'll have a good future if you pass your exams, or a bad future if you fail your exams, then that will drive you to study. If you believe that buying that new gadget will give you hours of entertainment, then you'll probably buy it. And if you believe that motivational speaker will change your life, then you'll probably sign up for their seminar at the very first opportunity.

At the heart of the behavioural level of design is this simple question: Is it satisfactory?

The simplest way to deliver here is to find out what your learners expect and make sure your training meets those expectations.

Here are some things they probably expect:
- Answers to their questions
- Solutions to their problems
- An enjoyable experience
- An experienced trainer

Think as well about agreements you make with learners. If you say lunchtime will be at 12:00, then make sure you break for lunch at 12:00. If you say you'll be sure to finish 15 minutes earlier so they can beat the rush hour traffic, then finish 15 minutes earlier. And if you say you'll deliver a section on something, then make sure you deliver it. Agreeing to do something, and then doing it, is the easiest way of setting yourself up for success.

Meeting Expectations

Your experience of delivering your training is a great opportunity to spot expectations that are not currently being met. They could be simple things such as wanting to have coffee and snacks available at all times. They could be amusing things like wanting some time to draw their name on their name tents because there are coloured pens on the table.

Previously, I talked about condensing your content into practical tools. From my experience, I have found that when my tools align with learner expectations, I then get comments in my feedback forms saying things like 'very practical' and 'relevant to my work'. It pays to pay attention to what they want to use these tools for and how they want to use them. Notice when they do something differently to what you intended and when they suggest an alteration you can make. Over time, you can evolve a tool that meets more and more expectations, helping you to deliver a more satisfactory experience.

It also comes down to how you communicate during the delivery. Frequently, when running activities, you will give them instructions to do one thing, but then discover they go off and do something completely different. So the next time you run that activity, adjust your instructions. Or even better, redesign the activity to run the way they want it to run.

Likewise with the training materials they receive. Do they work the way they expect them to? Or do they have to spend time figuring out how to reference them? Do they follow a logical order, or are they a random mess?

Plan vs. Reality

In summary, keep adapting your training to match their expectations. Make a plan, run it, and see what works and what doesn't.

Don't change the experience to match the plan, change the plan to match the experience.

- ## Using Rewards

Rewards create satisfactory experiences. Rewards could be anything from praise to money to a free holiday, etc. Look at what is at your disposal. At the very least, you'll have praise and recognition.

Do you have the budget for any other rewards? Or any other resources at your disposal that you can offer to your learners? Should you offer rewards before, during, or after the training?

For example, say you've just delivered a training for your team members on how to write reports. In the past, their reports have never given you the information you needed, so you decided to create a template for them to follow and train them on it. But it's a bit challenging for them to use this template because it means a bit more work than they were previously used to.

So you have decided to offer them a reward. Every time they submit a report that follows the template perfectly, you will give them coupons to use at the employee store. It's not much, but it should hopefully be enough to motivate them to get into the habit of following the template.

When we use rewards, keep in mind that we can offer rewards at different schedules. For example, I can reward you every time you do the right thing, or every 10 times you do the right thing, or even at random intervals. Depending on which schedule we use, we'll get different results.

There are 3 main reward schedules, and each consistently produces specific results. Here they are:

1. Continuous Schedule

This is where we give a reward every time someone does something. For example, every time a team member successfully submits a completed report according to the template, you give them a coupon.

This is great for establishing a new behaviour. People get a slight kick out of getting the reward, so will start to look forward to it. However, over time, the results will wear off. The coupons become a bit routine, or they've saved enough to buy what they want, and they stop submitting their completed reports as frequently.

Continuous reinforcement is great for getting people to learn a new behaviour. But once that behaviour has been learned, we need to switch to another reward interval.

2. Fixed Schedule

This is where we give people a reward after a certain time period, or certain number of successful completions.

We see fixed intervals used in coffee shops quite a lot. After buying a coffee, they will give you a card that can get stamped. Each time you get a new coffee, you get a stamp on the card. After 10 stamps, you get a free coffee.

We can use this with our team members submitting reports. Once they've successfully submitted 10 reports, we give them their coupon. We can even keep a tally on our notice board to get them excited about it.

This creates a sudden burst in behaviour. The coffee shop customer will quickly buy up their 10 coffees with any opportunity they get. But once they've gotten their free coffee, they are less likely to keep up the behaviour. And likewise with our team members—once they get the coupon, they may no longer feel interested in a second coupon as submitting another 10 reports seems so far away.

This is the schedule that annual bonuses use. You get your annual bonus once a year. But this seems to backfire in some companies. People might only work harder during the period of time when they are getting evaluated for their annual bonus. And then once they've got the bonus, they quit.

3. Variable Schedule

This is where the interval between each reward varies each time. When a gambler plays a slot machine, they might get a reward after 3 tries. But then the next time, they get a reward after 10 tries. And then the next time, after 26 tries.

This can create continuous behaviour, as the person doesn't know when they are going to get the next reward. They have a constant sense of anticipation. In the case of a gambler, this can even create an addiction.

With our team members, take them by surprise. After submitting a few successful reports, thank them and give them a coupon. Then explain to them that if they keep this behaviour up, then sometime within the next month, you'll give them another coupon worth even more money.

This is how surprise inspections work. Although not a reward, surprise inspections create a sense of anticipation because the workers don't know when they are going to get evaluated. So, a shopkeeper expecting a surprise shop floor inspection would keep their shop in top shape at all times. Whereas if we told them exactly when the inspection is going to happen, they are only likely to have the shop in top shape at that specific time.

The 3 Reward Schedules

If you are thinking of using rewards to enhance your training, consider which of the reward schedules would be best for you:

Continuous Schedule
- Reward every time they do something
- Great for establishing a new behaviour
- Effect wears off after a while

Fixed Schedule:
- Reward after a certain time period, or successful number of completions
- Good for creating a sudden burst in behaviour
- But effect can wear off after the reward comes

Variable Schedule:
- Frequency of the reward varies each time
- Good for creating continuous behaviour
- Can create addiction!

The 3 Reward Schedules

Continuous Schedule:
- Reward every time they do something
- Great for establishing a new behaviour
- Effect wears off after a while

Fixed Schedule:
- Reward after a certain time period, or successful number of completions
- Good for creating a sudden burst in behaviour
- But effect can wear off after the reward comes

Variable Schedule:
- Frequency of the reward varies each time
- Good for creating continuous behaviour
- Can create addiction!

- **Make it Meaningful**

Think about that family photo that you took when you went on holiday as a child, or that necklace that has been passed down through several generations, or that shirt you wore on your first date with your spouse. All of these things have value to you but not to other people, because of the subjective value your experience has assigned to it. They mean something only to you.

This is what Donald Norman's third and highest level of emotional design, the Reflective Level, is all about: making things meaningful.

To make something meaningful to someone, we have to attach it to an emotional experience. It could be something as simple as listening to a moving story from a grandparent or hero, or a reward for accomplishing a great feat.

Recently, I completed my very first Spartan Sprint. It's a 7-km obstacle course where you have to climb over walls, wade through muddy water, climb ropes, and so on. And whenever you fail an obstacle, you have to do 30 burpees as a penalty.

I noticed most people around me decided not to do the burpees, and just charged through, having fun at each station. That was their choice. But to me, I knew I would get a medal at the end for completing it, and I wanted the medal to mean something. I didn't want it to remind me that I cheated my way through the race—I wanted it to remind me that I worked hard for it. Now, that medal hangs proudly in my living room, and makes me feel proud every time I look at it. It means something to me.

There are 6 things we can implement in our training to make it more meaningful:
1. **Joy**
2. **Surprise**
3. **Mystery**
4. **Gamification**
5. **Status**
6. **Belonging**

Make it Meaningful

 Joy

 Surprise

 Mystery

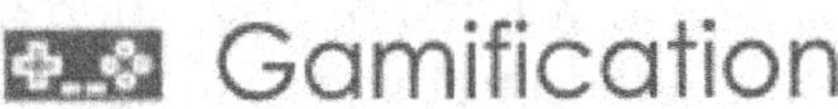 Gamification

 Status

 Belonging

- ## Adding Joy

What makes you smile, giggle, or just shout out, 'That's so cool!'?

Just last week, my wife and I took a trip to the Shanghai Tower, one of the tallest buildings in the world. We went to the observatory, over 500 meters up in the air, and it was incredible seeing Shanghai like we'd never seen before, with the cars beneath us looking so small. But one thing, in particular, really made me smile. As we walked around, without realising it, we stepped on one area of the floor that was actually a computer screen that had been carefully disguised as a typical part of the floor. As we stepped on it, suddenly cracks started to appear, and then chunks of the floor started to fall, and then, all of a sudden, directly beneath us was the ground, 500 meters below. We knew it was due to a computer because of the cheesy animations and sound effects, but it was a fun little touch that really made us smile.

A joyful experience is a positive memory to reflect fondly back upon. We love recalling positive memories, because memories can help us feel right now what we felt back then. Try it for yourself. Recall a time you felt happy, such as your wedding day, a nice holiday or even a time you achieved something significant.

Why not make our training experience a positive memory to make our learners feel happy every time they recall it?

- ## **Surprise!**

Our brains are actually stimulated by the element of surprise. Whenever something new and unexpected appears within something routine, our brains release dopamine. For a very brief moment, we experience a high.

This is part of the appeal of fortune cookies. You are never quite sure what they are going to say. A lot of board games use the element of surprise as well. Take a card at random from the deck and see what you get. Sometimes it's disappointment but sometimes it's something great. This also applies to birthday or Christmas presents, as half the fun is in the unwrapping to see the surprise you get.

For surprises to work, they must be both unpredictable and pleasant.

One of the most fun uses of a slideshow I have ever seen is when a facilitator friend of mine (Jimbo Clark) displayed random words on the screen, and then, as he walked up to the screen, he blew on the projector screen and suddenly the words reorganised themselves into the shape of a cube. We all knew he had secretly pressed the animation button on his remote control (hidden in his pocket), but that didn't stop us from smiling!

Another thing I've seen frequently done in trainings is giving gifts by surprise. I once attended a training by the legendary facilitation expert, Thiagi. At the end of the training day, he gave each of us two gifts: one was a whistle used to grab people's attention, and the other was one of his books. He could have very easily given these at the beginning of the training, but it wouldn't have created as much joy as surprising us with these gifts at the very end of the day. It was a very nice touch.

- **Mystery**

Something that drives our brains crazy is curiosity. Curiosity is where we have a gap in our information. We only know half of the story, and have to find out the rest. This curiosity gap is the essence of a mystery.

These gaps in information sometimes drive us to do incredible things. It's what set Christopher Columbus around the world, took man to the moon, and why I stapled my finger when I was 4 years old (I wanted to find out what would happen!).

In Stephen P. Anderson's book, *Seductive Interactive Design*, a great example of how a restaurant uses curiosity is given: At the end of his dinner, he was given a Thank You envelope with the words 'Don't Open It!' written in bold letters on the front.

The idea with this envelope is that inside is a coupon that you bring with you on your next visit to the restaurant. But the coupon is only valid so long as the envelope remains unopened. Only the restaurant manager can open it.

This sort of thing would drive a lot of people crazy. The desire to know what's inside would either drive people to open it up, or go to the restaurant again at the next opportunity.

So, how could you use curiosity in your training?

The key is to give them a gap of information. Give them one half of the puzzle, but leave the rest up to the learners to figure out themselves.

For example, say you are training people on how to use advanced functions in Microsoft Excel. You could give them a worksheet that suggests some experiments. 'What happens if you press _____?' would be a great thing for getting people to try out new functions in a piece of software you are training people to use.

- ## Gamification

People, obviously, love games. We love video games, we love board games, and we even love social games like playing pranks on people. Games are fun, addictive, and make us smile. As we learnt earlier, sometimes simply making something look like a game, even though it doesn't have the full mechanisms of a game, can be enough to improve motivation.

Therefore, gamification is something we can use to spice up our training. We can do so with a few simple components:
1. **Challenge**
2. **Context**
3. **Symbols**

Challenge

The most fundamental element of a game is the challenge. Games present the players with a challenge, and the players must then use their skills and put in effort to overcome the challenge. Ideally, the challenge should be just within their abilities so that it requires a bit of effort to achieve, but isn't too difficult or too easy (so that they can easily reach a state of flow). Sometimes, all it takes to gamify parts of our training is to add in the element of a challenge.

For example, when I do training on email writing, there is one exercise where I show the learners a sample email that has been poorly written. Then I show them a proofreading technique where, before sending, we first think from the perspective of the reader as we review our email, and imagine what questions the reader will have.

Many years ago, when I first got them to practice this technique, I would ask them to read through the email and think of how many questions the reader might have. It was an OK activity, but I always felt it could be a bit more engaging.

So, one day, I decided to up the challenge by adding in a simple element of competition: I divided the learners into groups and then made the activity into a contest by asking, 'Which group can find the most questions within the time limit?'

This simple change noticeably increased engagement. There was more laughter and giggles—and a lot more focus from each participant—as they tried to think of as many questions as they could in the time available. Such a simple thing had a big impact.

Let's look at another example. Say you've been asked to deliver training on some advanced functions in Microsoft Excel, and now it's time for the learners to practice. How can we make the practice more challenging?

One way could be to give them a case study about a shop that's looking for investors so it can start opening new branches. Give them all the data from past sales and ask them to use the Excel functions you've just taught them to create a projection of future sales.

You can make it even more challenging by explaining that they'll have to present their projections to a potential investor (yourself). Then, as they do, ask them difficult questions that test whether or not they actually used the functions to get the right kind of data.

Challenge + Context

In the last example, not only did we have a challenge, but we also had a context for the challenge. In other words, the challenge took place within a story.

The formula of **Context + Challenge** really gets the imagination going. And frankly, it makes the challenge more relevant as well.

Let's look at another example. Say you've just trained a group of stressed-out engineers on the subject of assertiveness. You've just spent an afternoon looking at a range of principles and techniques for saying 'No'. Now, it's time to practice.

You *could* give them a template for using those techniques and get them to practice preparing a few examples of how they might use them with certain people when they get back to work. But that seems a little dull.

Instead, try a role-play. Their partner role-plays their stressed-out and disappointed supervisor who desperately needs their help with something extremely important over the weekend. But they've booked a holiday for the weekend with their family. Do they say 'No' to their stressed-out supervisor? Or do they cancel the holiday?

Up the challenge of this a bit more by giving their partner a few details about their role. Tell them why this supervisor is stressed-out and disappointed, and why it's so important they work overtime this weekend. The stronger the reasons they have, the harder it is for this person to say 'No'. Then add in a time limit as well and see how they do.

In fact, I have a similar role-play activity to the above, and it's always very interesting when I run it. Each partner gets very involved and the one trying to say 'No' really feels the pressure. And a lot of them feel so much pressure that they cave in and cancel their family holiday. This then makes for some great follow-up discussions, and keeps their imaginations going for many hours afterwards.

When providing the context, keep in mind that it must be both digestible and relatable.

By digestible, I mean that it needs to be something they can understand very quickly. If they spend more time trying to learn and understand their roles than actually doing the role-play, then it's not a very effective activity. **We want more time spent practicing than preparing.**

And by relatable, I mean it should be something they have first- or second-hand experience of. With the above example, most people have an experience of trying to balance family life with working life, and so can start to imagine how they'd feel in such a situation.

Symbols

When you think of gamification, you probably think of symbols. Once you achieve something, you get a virtual reward. It might be something as simple as a picture of a trophy, or maybe having your name written in gold as opposed to silver, but it represents something you have achieved and therefore means something important to you.

This is what we see in a lot of video games. Upon successful completion of a certain task in a game, you could get one of the following rewards:
- Level up
- New abilities
- More currency to spend on new tools and abilities
- Extra points to move you up higher in a leader board
- A special badge, title, or award to show off

We now see these concepts, originally from games, in all sorts of places. I have a number of apps that use similar mechanisms to motivate me.

For example, Forest is a focus timer app available on iOS. It allows you to set a timer for how long you will focus on a task, and encourages you to stop procrastinating on your phone. As you start the timer, a virtual tree gradually grows on the screen. If you manage to go through the whole timed session without leaving the app, then your tree gets added to a field. But if you leave the app before the session is up, then a dead tree gets added to the field!

The Forest app works really well for me because I care about completing the task, and the thought of having a dead tree in my field brings out the Obsessive Compulsive Disorder in me and makes me want to keep that tree alive!
There are lots of other apps that I use with similar mechanisms. But this is not to say

that these mechanisms work with everyone. There are some services I use that give me points and other similar things for completing tasks, and I couldn't care less about them. For the ones that work for me, I do care about the rewards I get, but only because the task is important to me (e.g. finishing my work, meditating, working out) and so the points help me track how well I am doing at these tasks.

Symbols are easy to use in training. At the very least, give people a tick on the whiteboard every time they do something favourable. At a more advanced level, use an online Learning Management System to track every time a learner completes a follow-up assignment after the training. Every time they complete one, give them a virtual trophy. And then, with enough virtual trophies, give them a real-life prize like a Smartphone or vouchers to their favourite restaurant.

Gamification

Challenge

Context

Symbols

- ## Elevating Status

When I was a child and wanted to play football with my friends at school, we'd always go through this horrible ritual of selecting teammates. The best players in the class would be captains and, one by one, they'd select players to be on their team. If you got called up sooner than later, it meant you were a good player and they liked you! And if you got called up last, then it meant you were a bad player and they didn't like you!

The above experience was always pretty nerve-wracking because it was all about status. The better players had higher status and the poorer players had much lower status. Naturally, I was happier if I had a higher status!

In fact, it's not just me who would be happy with a higher sense of status. Studies have shown that, even in primate communities, higher-status monkeys have lower baseline cortisol levels and live longer! (*SCARF: A Brain-Based Model for Collaborating with and Influencing Others*, David Rock, NeuroLeadership Journal, Issue One, 2008.)

And if there is one industry that knows this all too well, then it's the luxury industry!

The luxury industry creates value by elevating the status of their customers. Wearing a Rolex watch or driving a Rolls Royce are status symbols. Universities, as well, make fortunes from the feeling of status they give their graduates. Harvard, Oxford, and MIT are all world famous universities, and simply having a degree from such a prestigious institution is sometimes enough to land a well-paying job. **Why not do the same with training?**

In fact, many companies already do. They offer certification in certain assessment tools or methodologies like MBTI or SCRUM.

They offer courses with big brand names such as **The 7 Habits of Highly Effective People** (http://www.franklincovey.com/leadership/7-habits).

There is a lot of value that can be created by simply elevating the status of customers, users, and learners. Experts on branding and marketing are better placed to talk about how meaning creates value and elevates status, so one such book I would strongly recommend is the appropriately titled *Meaningful* by Bernadette Jiwa. **But, for the sake of training, let me offer some suggestions.**

Firstly, by elevating your own status, you can, in turn, elevate the status of your learners. Think about martial arts communities and the sense of status some martial artists get by claiming they trained with certain Grandmasters. By enhancing your own status through experience, credentials, publicity, and perhaps even fame, you therefore offer an opportunity to enhance the status of your learners when they are trained by you.

Secondly, offer your learners opportunities for accomplishment. For example, some cultures offer rite-of-passage rituals to elevate the status of certain people, such as the Aboriginal 'Walkabout', where Aboriginal males would make the transition into manhood. Why not offer a similar experience in training?

Well, many trainers actually do. Anthony Robbins, for example, offers his infamous Firewalk Experience, where participants walk on burning coals. One of my good friends, Andy Clark, uses board breaking in a similar way in his trainings. These sorts of activities are daunting at first but, once successfully completed, give a huge sense of accomplishment that naturally elevates status.

Thirdly, offer symbols of the elevated status your learners have achieved. Certificates are a common example, and where that certificate is more than just a piece of paper and is actually a qualification that can lead to formal recognition by an authorising body, that certificate offers a huge increase in status. Some training companies even offer their learners 'badges' they can put on their email signature or business cards, or actual badges they can pin on their shirt when attending certain events. It doesn't have to be much, and the object itself doesn't have to cost much, but so long as it means something, it can significantly elevate a learner's feeling of status.

• A Sense of Belonging

I am a member of a small and close-knit community of trainers and facilitators spread throughout Asia. We keep in touch on a daily basis through WeChat. Every few months, we hold short retreats in different parts of Asia.

Over time, we have come to form extremely strong bonds with each other, and have started to reveal more and more personal details about ourselves to each other. We support each other both professionally and personally.

But the best thing about being part of this group is that, whenever I go on business trips to some distant city, I have friends there waiting for me. And we'll turn up wearing the T-shirts from previous retreats. We'll crack running jokes that have been part of our conversations for the last few months, and we have special greetings for each other as well. We frequently joke that we're part of a cult, and we probably are!

It's great to be a member of such a community and feel this sense of belonging. I'm sure you can relate to this feeling, because we are all part of many communities in our lives, be it a family, a neighbourhood, a community that is hobby-based, or a professional community. Wanting to feel this sense of belonging is part of being human, and we can achieve this in our learners through our training.

By making our training become a group to belong to, we can make our training more meaningful.

For example, some trainings are about a certain methodology, such as the Getting Things Done (also known as GTD) methodology by David Allen (https://gettingthingsdone.com/). I actually use this methodology. As a result, it gives me things in common with other people who use it. We can say things like 'I use GTD as well!' and then compare our GTD systems.

One powerful thing we can do to add this sense of belonging is, again, allow the learners to overcome a great challenge, such as board breaking or Anthony Robbins' Firewalk experience. It doesn't necessarily have to be as extreme as the Firewalk experience, but it does need to be a challenge in order to create a sense of accomplishment. For example, imagine if you climbed Mount Everest and met a complete stranger in a cafe who had also climbed Everest. The memory of the experience—and, more importantly, the sense of achievement you both shared— would create very strong rapport between the two of you.

On a simpler level, it can be things such as running jokes. Running jokes are a great way of strengthening rapport throughout the day. For example, maybe several people have been late to class due to roadworks on a certain street on their route to work.

Then, every time someone is a bit slow in coming back to class during breaks, you can crack a joke about how they must be taking that road back to the classroom from the bathroom.

All of this helps strengthen the learning effect long after the training. Every time these people are together, there is a chance of them reflecting on that shared accomplishment during the conversation. Every time they look at that photo on their desk of them and their classmates smiling happily during training, fond memories of the experience will come straight to their minds. And maybe every time they meet someone who has been trained or even certified in the same methodology as them, they will feel like they are part of the same tribe. All of these help to strengthen the memory of the learning experience.

Designing for Emotion Summary

The following flowchart is a summary of everything we have looked at in this section:

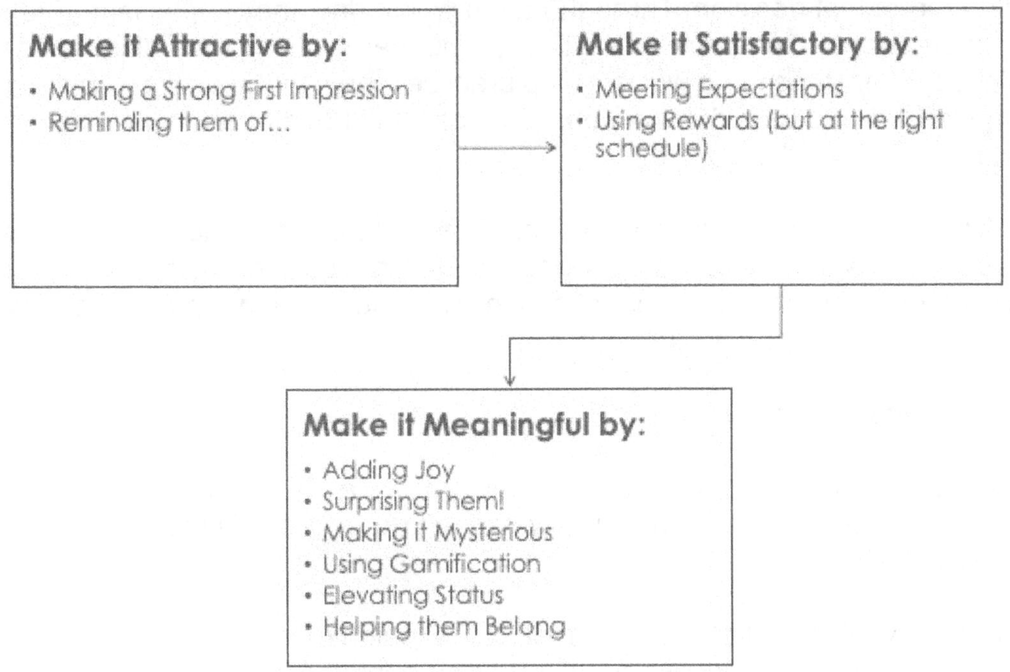

Part 4—The Five Elements of Delivery

Let me begin this section by telling you a true story. I turned up to the training room 15 minutes late, thanks to bad traffic. The learners were sitting there, waiting for me, and had been for some time. I felt rushed and flustered. I thought, *'Do I just go straight into the training? Or should I still go through with the icebreaker I had originally planned?'*

This was the second time I'd run this course for this company. The first time went smoothly (probably because I turned up on time!). And this time was quite like last time in that it was for the same company on the same topic, with trainees coming from different departments throughout the company. Therefore, they were not familiar with each other. *I thought, 'There's not enough time. No need for an icebreaker today. Let's just get straight down to training.'*

Boy, did I regret that decision. Throughout the whole day, they kept silent. Every time I asked a question, no one answered. Every time there was a group discussion, there was silence. Every time there was a group practice, some of the group would play with their phones whilst others did the work. This couldn't have been more different from the last time I trained this company.

The difference a little thing like an icebreaker made to that training was massive. The first time I ran it with an icebreaker, I encountered none of the problems I described above. But, this time, thanks to that one little difference, it didn't work out as I wanted it to.

The Five Elements Matter

There are some things that we absolutely must do as a trainer to make training work. Of course, there are things we absolutely mustn't do, as well. That's what this part of this book is all about.

For example, you've probably heard that you shouldn't lecture for too long. Why is that, and what should you do instead? You also shouldn't single out individuals, put them on the spot, or speak too negatively towards them. Why is that, and what should you do instead?

You probably know that we should give our learners plenty of time to practice and think things through. Again, why is that? And how can we do that in the right way?

The above questions (and many more) will be answered in this part as we go through each of the 5 elements of delivery. Once you can master each of the 5 elements, you can rest assured that you are doing everything you can to deliver a successful training experience.

The Five Elements of Delivery

1. **Priming**—Where we get learners into the right mental state for learning. The success of every other element depends on how well we prime our learners, and it's something we must pay attention to throughout the entire training experience.
2. **Guiding**—Where we give learners direction. We help them understand what to do, how to do it, when to do it, and why.
3. **Practice**—Where we provide learners with the opportunity and space to apply what they have learnt. Through application and reinforcement, learners improve their skill level.
4. **Reflection**—Where we give learners the space to process what they have learnt and form new mental connections. This is where the real learning takes place.
5. **Commitment**—Where we help learners plan how to apply what they've learnt in the workplace. Proper planning greatly increases their chances of achieving successful change.

The 5 Elements of Delivery

Priming

Earlier, I described the concept of positive affect, where our brains are in a relaxed state and far better primed to learn, and negative affect, where our brains are narrowly focussed on taking action. Let's see how this plays out in the training room.

For Michelle, today's training couldn't have come at a worse time. This afternoon, she has a conference call with the senior management team in the US. She needs to prepare a report for them, describing the market situation in her region. She's pretty well prepared, but still feels nervous because she knows it's important. At some point, she's going to have to explain to you that she needs to escape for part of the afternoon to attend the call, and she's not quite figured out how to explain this to you yet.

Then there's Mark. Mark's lucky. He doesn't have any important meetings today and he was able to catch up on his emails the night before. His manager knows he's going to be in training for the next 2 days and has offered to cover any work that needs doing during the training.

How will the training experience be different for Mark and Michelle?

Mark's will be considerably better. He will be relaxed. His mind will be empty of any concerns, allowing him to enjoy the experience and take inspiration from anything new he learns.

Michelle, on the other hand, will be very distracted. She'll try her hardest to focus on the training, but the fact that she has to try is far from ideal. Every few minutes, she'll probably have flashes of concern rushing through her mind about the afternoon meeting. She may even feel bad that she has to leave for some of the afternoon, and so might even think of ways to make it up to you.

Mark is in a state of positive affect, whereas Michelle is in a state of negative affect. Another way of thinking of these two states is relaxed and focussed.
Mark is relaxed. He can enjoy the training experience and be highly receptive to any stimulus from the training, much like a person walking through a shopping mall and imagining how the sofa in that window display would look in their lounge.

Michelle is focussed, just not focussed on the training. She's focussed on the undesirable situations that she needs to resolve. Her brain focusses in like a laser, filtering out anything that is unrelated to her concerns, and prepares both her mind and body to take action. Thoughts rush around in her agitated mind, her heart is probably beating faster than Mark's, and she probably has more blood being diverted to her arms and legs, prepping her to take action. With all this extra blood spread throughout her body, she probably gets fidgety, and shuffles about in her seat a lot.

You might even notice her fingers constantly tapping on each other. Due to this extra blood in her extremities, her brain probably has less blood available, making it harder for her to concentrate.

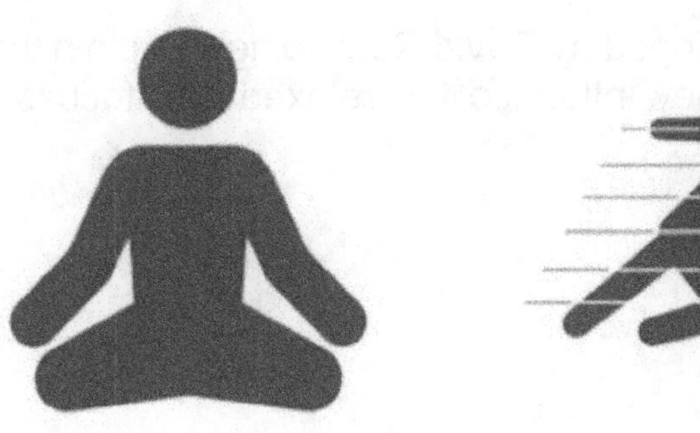

Looking at how Mark and Michelle behave in our training, we may naturally start to like Mark more because, from the outside, he looks like he's trying harder. But we should also sympathise with Michelle. It's not her fault that she's distracted. It's just bad timing. If we start to pick on her and tell her off for how distracted she is, then she's just going to feel worse. And to be fair to her, she is actually the one trying the hardest.

Our goal in training is to keep as many people as possible, for as long as possible, in a relaxed state (like the one Mark is in). Another goal is to help people in a focussed (and therefore, ironically, distracted) state deal with their distractions, rather than add to those distractions.

But that doesn't mean the focussed state is bad. It can actually be useful for training, especially when they are focussed on the training as opposed to anything else. At times, when we need learners to act, such as when they are practicing, or even committing to future actions they'll take at work, a (relevant) focussed state can actually be more useful than a relaxed state.

That's the goal of this section: how to effectively manage relaxed and focussed states.

- ## The Drivers of Social Behaviour—SCARF

Training is a social experience and social factors have a significant impact on whether learners are in a state of positive affect (relaxed) or negative affect (focussed).

The SCARF model was developed by David Rock to help explain the factors that drive social behaviour and how they influence the relaxed and focussed states. SCARF stands for:
- **Status**
- **Certainty**
- **Autonomy**
- **Relatedness**
- **Fairness**

The Drivers of Social Behaviour

Status

Certainty

Autonomy

Relatedness

Fairness

Let's have a look at how this plays out in the training room.

Status

Research has shown that, in primate communities, higher-status monkeys are healthier and live longer. (I mentioned this before.) Conversely, the stress associated with a perceived low status is detrimental to health. (*SCARF: A Brain-Based Model for Collaborating with and Influencing Others*, David Rock, Neuro Leadership Journal, Issue One, 2008.)

Recall how children sometimes select sports teams. Two captains get to select who joins their team. They both start off by choosing the better players. The poorest players are left until last. Think about how it feels to be selected first and, conversely, how it feels to be selected last.

Within a training room, status is a very sensitive issue. If you are the trainer, you automatically have a higher status than the learners who are sitting down in front of you. You, therefore, have the power to influence their feeling of status.

Typically, this comes with any feedback you give them. Praise an individual and they'll feel good, whilst others may feel bad in comparison. If you publicly criticise an individual, they will feel very bad. Even the question 'Can I give you some feedback?' can create the same sense of dread as hearing fast footsteps behind you at night.

But it's not just feedback where trainers can affect status. Even something as small as giving someone instructions can minimise someone's sense of status. If you deliver your training as a dictator (telling people what they should do and why they should listen to you), then you risk lowering their sense of status.

Sometimes, you will want to lower someone's status to bring them back down to earth, or to create a focussed state to drive them to action. Other times, you will want to raise their sense of status to give them more confidence. But most of the time you will want to maintain neutral status.

Here are some tips for doing this:

- Frame feedback as recommendations. Rather than saying 'You should…' say 'If you tried this instead, then…'
- Standardise your feedback. Give everyone the same amount of praise and recommendations. Be careful of giving some people too much praise and others too many recommendations. For example, each time you give feedback to any person you could give 2 recommendations and 1 instance of praise.
- Avoid comparing learners to each other. Instead, focus on comparing their

performance to their own previous performance. Focus on individual accomplishment as opposed to peer comparison.

- Avoid any form of SERIOUS competition or reward, and use these elements only when the competition is just a bit of light-hearted fun. When someone doesn't win something, their status decreases.

Certainty

Any sense of uncertainty during the training experience can be incredibly distracting. This sense creates tension, forcing the brain to focus on resolving the uncertainty. If it can't be resolved, then the brain will continue to focus on it anyway.

Imagine you have arrived at the training knowing that, sometime before lunch time, you need to make an important phone call to a client. Ideally, you'd like to do it during the morning break. But then the trainer doesn't tell you when the morning break is. So you start thinking if you should call them now, or wait a little while. Then you start looking for opportune moments to slip out. Whilst you are focussed on this, you are completely distracted from the training.

There are many issues that can create a sense of uncertainty. For example:
- hunger making people wonder when they can eat
- needing to go to the toilet and not knowing where the toilet is
- having to leave the training early to catch a flight
- wanting to learn something particular and not knowing if (or when) it will be included in the training
- whether or not they will need to do something embarrassing in an activity like public speaking or acting in a role-play

Ideally, you want to eliminate any sense of uncertainty as early as possible. The simplest way of doing this is to start the training by managing expectations.

To manage expectations, the following three areas should be made clear:
1. **Training outcomes—what they can expect to learn from this training**
2. **Timing—when the breaks are, what time the training will finish, what time different sections will be presented.**
3. **Content—what content will be covered, how it will be covered, etc.**

But try not to go into too much detail. Only go into as much detail as necessary to eliminate uncertainty. Taking some time to understand your learners and what they are concerned about before the training starts will help you here.

Another way of giving learners more certainty is to give them some time to manage their distractions. The way I do this at the beginning of the training is by asking them to spend some time sharing with a partner the things that might distract them during the training and brainstorming some strategies for dealing with those distractions. Just spending a few minutes at the beginning of the day can help minimise the impact of distractions throughout the whole training.

Managing Expectations

Training outcomes

- What they can expect to learn from this training

Timing

- When the breaks are, what time the training will finish, what time different sections will be presented.

Content

- What content will be covered, how it will be covered, etc.

Autonomy

Being micromanaged is stressful. You feel you have less influence over what you do and how you do it, and therefore less power to do the things you want to do in the way you want to do them.

In the training room, there are subtle ways we can increase people's sense of autonomy.

For a start, we can involve them in simple decisions about timing. When to have breaks and when to go for lunch can be left open for discussion and agreement.

Participation is another area. Sometimes we, as trainers, ask the audience questions. Instead of selecting certain individuals to respond, leave it open and wait for volunteers to answer. Choosing a particular individual to respond can give them a lot of pressure, especially when they are not prepared to respond.

We can also give them options about how they carry out activities. If it involves doing something that some people might be embarrassed about, then we could give them the option of leaving something out.

Of course, remember that we sometimes want to give them pressure. And taking away autonomy is a great way of doing this.

For example, sometimes we should let learners volunteer to participate, and sometimes we should push them to participate. When we want them to create new ideas, allow them to volunteer. But when we want to push them to action, force them to participate by choosing certain people to share their action plans or to demonstrate something in particular.

Action-planning towards the end of the training is another area where we want to increase pressure. Action plans need to be practical and need to have a level of commitment. So, challenge learners to share their plans, justify the practicality of their actions, and make public commitments.

Relatedness

The more we perceive people as being like us, the more relaxed we feel. But the less familiar we are with other people, the less comfortable we feel around them. For some people, meeting strangers brings about a sense of social anxiety.

Consider what would go through your mind if you sat in a training room with a feeling of social anxiety. You'd be incredibly self-conscious, worrying about how you look, how you behave, and even the way you say things. All of this would distract you from the learning experience.

Furthermore, the less familiar we are with people, the less we trust them. And when we don't trust people, we hide things from them. Yet, training sometimes requires people to be open and vulnerable. It sometimes requires people to share the challenges they face, the weaknesses they have, and their dreams and aspirations. How can people do that when they don't trust each other?

The key to building a sense of relatedness amongst participants is to create connections between each other. This is the value of using ice-breaking activities at the beginning of training. People get to know each other quickly and feel more comfortable as a result.

There are several things to remember in order to effectively break the ice:

- **Each individual should interact with as many individuals as possible**
- **Individuals should share personal details, working backgrounds, and their reasons for attending the training**
- **Through sharing, they should be able to quickly identify things they have in common with each other**

Ice-Breaking Rules

Optimum Interaction

Share Personal Details

Discover Things in Common

One simple activity I use with smaller groups is to put people in pairs and show a list of questions via PPT. Their task is then to use those questions to introduce themselves to each other within ten minutes. After ten minutes, they then need to introduce their partner to the group. The questions I typically use are:

- Who are they and where do they come from?
- What are their hobbies and interests?
- What is their job and how long have they been at the company?
- What things might distract them during the training and how will they manage this?
- Why did they come to this training?

I find there are many benefits to doing this.

Firstly, by sharing where they are from, their hobbies and interests, and their working backgrounds, they start to identify things they have in common. Some people might come from the same hometown, have the same hobby, or used to work for the same boss. When they realise they have something in common with each other, this creates an instant rapport.

Secondly, having people introduce each other strengthens their rapport. For a start, they focus more intently on each other's sharing because they know they need to remember the details. Although sharing those details about the person they've just met is a challenge, but because everyone is doing that challenge, they then have a subtle sense of togetherness for having all gone through it. Finally, as they each take turns introducing one another, everyone gets to listen to each introduction. So even people who haven't spoken with each other yet already know what they have in common with that person, which also creates and strengthens that rapport.

The third advantage is that all of this doesn't have to take long. When managed well and with smaller numbers (e.g. less than ten participants), it doesn't have to take more than twenty minutes. Given the great benefits that come from having an enhanced sense of relatedness amongst the group, I'd say that's a good twenty minutes well spent.

Fairness

We don't like being treated unfairly. If we perceive that someone else is getting preferential treatment, or that we are getting unfair treatment, then this creates a 'threat response' in the mind.

Consider what the sense of fairness has led some people to do throughout history. It has led to wars, people sacrificing their freedom and even purposefully sacrificing their lives. Political revolutions have been sparked, dictators have been overthrown, and powerful institutions have been brought to their knees.

Obviously, in training, we are not going to be sparking political revolutions or starting wars. But when an individual perceives that they are being treated unfairly, it can create big problems.

For a start, they will feel threatened. They will demand explanations or apologies for their unfair treatment. Or, even worse, they will seek to get revenge and treat you in the same way. They start to become disruptive, they challenge everything you say, and maybe they will even encourage others to do the same.

Maybe their grievance is not with you, but with another participant in the room. So they start mini-battles. Group discussions turn into arguments. Any open question you throw to the group becomes an opportunity for stabbing their opponent in the back.

Obviously we don't want any of this.

A great way to build a sense of fairness is to use ground rules… rules about what you expect of the group (e.g. no phones, computers off, etc.). When you make clear your expectations at the beginning of the day, they are more likely to live up to them. Furthermore, when you tell someone off for breaking the rules, they are more likely to feel it's reasonable because you explained the rules at the beginning of the day.

But at the same time, we don't want to take away our learners' sense of autonomy. Some groups know they shouldn't use their phones and should keep their computers switched off, so explaining those rules to them can seem patronising.

If you set rules that they can't live up to (e.g. don't leave the room until break time) then they are going to feel their sense of autonomy is taken away, their sense of status will be lowered ('I'm a rule breaker!'), and they will feel that it's unfair, as they can't live up to that. So another solution is to collaboratively set rules. Ask people what they expect of each other. But don't forget that you, as the trainer, can still have expectations of them, and that it is perfectly reasonable to explain those expectations. Just make sure they are reasonable expectations after all.

SCARF All Day

These SCARF factors are mostly within our control as trainers. Whilst it is important to get the training off to a good start with them, it is equally important to maintain the right conditions throughout the whole training.

And don't forget that, whilst we generally want our learners to be in a relaxed state, sometimes we also want them to be in a focussed state. So we can use SCARF both to relax our learners but also to put pressure on them when necessary.

- ## Generating Interest

It is better for learners to be interested in the training rather than not interested at all. This interest will incite their curiosity, excite them and drive their motivation for learning. Learners with interest will be better primed for learning.

So how do we generate interest?

Think WIIFM

What's In It For Me? This is a radio station that marketers and sales people have been tuning into for a long time. They know that, when selling their products, there is a difference between features and benefits. Features are what the product does, but benefits are what those features mean to the customer. Let's look at an example.

In our house, we have a really cool vacuum cleaner. These are some of its features:
- wireless
- changeable heads
- a clip to hang it on the wall

Now, let's translate these features into benefits:
- Wireless—Carry it ANYWHERE without getting tangled up in a wiry mess!
- Changeable heads—Reach those hard-to-get areas with ease
- A clip to hang it on the wall—It saves you valuable cupboard space, and means you'll never lose it

So instead of just telling your learners the topics they will learn, focus more on the benefits of those topics. Here are some examples:

Topic	Benefit
Assertiveness	Ensure your opinion gets heard.
Effective Meeting Skills	Spend less time in meetings.
Email Writing	Write faster and get the response you want.

I was once asked by a client to train some of its soon-to-be graduate recruits on how to be more proactive. If I only considered the manager's side of things, I would have turned up lecturing all of these students on how much it would help managers if they could just be more proactive. But I didn't do that.

Instead, I considered the benefits to these students of being more proactive. I shared stories from my career experience of how not being proactive made others trust me less, and the problems it caused me later on. I gave them some team games to play, where the more proactive they were, the better they performed. I gave them some scenarios to analyse and discuss what proactive and passive responses would be, and then asked them to reflect on how being proactive would help them in those scenarios.

My entire course focussed on the benefits to them, not just the managers. As a result, they were very engaged and made serious commitments to behaving more proactively.

Sell It

Maybe your training has already been approved by senior management and successfully booked. But that doesn't mean that the learners are interested yet. Maybe they have just received an email informing them they have a training, and they know nothing more about it. They might then turn up to the training just thinking 'Let's get this over with'.

If you can sell the training to your learners beforehand, they are more likely to turn up already primed for learning.

So put your salesman's hat on, and start selling your training to them.

Here are some suggestions of what you can do:

- Phone each learner, ask them why they are interested in this training, tell them what to expect, and how it can help them.
- Send a welcome pack either via email or straight to their desks. It should include information about what the course will cover (ideally including pictures of previous sessions). It might even include little puzzles to get them curious.
- Greet each participant as they walk in. Take the opportunity to learn about their expectations and then tell them the benefits.
- Start the class by sharing some of the benefits, and even sharing some of the feedback from previous sessions.

- ## Making a Strong First Impression

We have talked about this topic already. I'm including it in this section because there are certain things I have not yet mentioned and this topic also relates to the 5 Elements of Delivery.

The learners' training experience is also about you because you will have an impact on them, whether you intend to or not. So it's best to make sure you make a good impact and a good first impression.

Whether we like it or not, we judge people on a superficial level within seconds of meeting them. The way they dress, talk, behave, and so on will all leave an impression on us that will affect how we interact with them.

One of my friends told me about his experience of attending a B2B (Business to Business) sales training course. At the very beginning of the course, one of the participants mentioned how her business was focused on B2C (Business to Customer/Consumer) and realised this training might not be for her.

My friend shared with me how that instantly lowered the trainer's and training company's credibility in his eyes. If you're going to train others on how to sell to businesses, then, surely, you should be selling your course to the right people from the very beginning!

I have also witnessed another trainer delivering a public demonstration to potential clients on the topic of communication skills.

I later met with one of those clients for lunch and she told me that she would never invite that trainer to her company because "If you're going to train others on communication skills, then you need good communication skills to start with!" This trainer was not very good at making his points clear, and just criticised his learners whenever someone said that they didn't understand.

The first impression we give to learners lets them judge if we are credible or not. When they judge us as not being credible, our words will be met with skepticism, no matter what we say or how we say it, from that point on. But if we get off to the right start, then they will deem us as credible, more easily accept what we say, and the whole training is likely to go a lot more smoothly.

So, think about your learners. They are taking time out from their jobs. Some of them may have even paid money to come and attend your training. What do they expect of you?

They probably expect you to be the following:
- Professional
- Confident
- Knowledgeable
- Authoritative
- Experienced
- Caring

So think about what aspects of your appearance would they associate the above expectations with? For example:

Expectation	Associated Appearance
Professional	Suit and tie, well groomed, politically correct
Confident	Good posture, eye contact, strong voice
Knowledgeable	Can share relevant theories, answer questions
Authoritative	Can answer any question, strong voice, able to command the room
Experience	Lots of relevant examples, personal anecdotes, effective training, and facilitation skills
Caring	Listens, responds positively to everyone, offers honest and practical feedback

Some of these expectations will vary in different companies. For example, I once went to train a high-tech company, and I turned up in a suit and tie. Because they were all software engineers in a very modern high-tech company with a very casual working environment, my suit and tie stood out quite a bit. In the end, the HR manager recommended I turn up in jeans and T-shirt the next day to make them feel more comfortable.

Spend some time familiarising yourself with their expectations of you. These kinds of expectations are not normally things people will share openly through a phone call, as they may not even be consciously aware of them themselves. Sometimes a quick visit to their office, or even their website, can give you an impression of what they expect of your appearance.

Matching Expectations

Expectation	Associated Appearance

- ## Building Rapport

Rapport is the feeling of warmth between two people. If you are good friends with someone then you have rapport with them. When you meet someone for the first time and instantly get along, that's because you have rapport. When a whole group of learners like you as a person, that's because you have rapport with them. And rapport with a whole group of learners you're about to train is a pretty handy thing to have!

So how do we build rapport? The answer lies in this fact: **We like people who are like us.**

Imagine you are in a foreign country where no one speaks the same language as you. Then, one day, as you are walking down the street, you suddenly hear someone behind you speaking your native language. Furthermore, they're speaking with exactly the same accent as you. They're even the same gender as you, and sound around the same age as you. How would you feel about that person?

Normally, when I ask this question in my training, the answer I get is 'I'd feel a close connection with them'. Without having even seen them, you already feel close to them. And the reason is because, in that foreign country, that one person is the person most like you.

It's interesting that the word 'like' has two meanings. One meaning is to be similar to, and another meaning is to find agreeable, enjoyable or satisfactory. And if we want people to like us, then a simple way is to be more like them.

There are lots of ways we can be like other people. For example:
- personality
- background
- hometown
- favourite food, drink, movie, etc.
- hobbies
- dress
- behaviour

And so on.

We should start finding things we have in common with our learners as soon as possible. Use any informal interaction you have with them as an opportunity to find out more about them. Once you find what you have in common with them, you will find that rapport comes naturally.

There are lots of opportunities to find out what you have in common with your learners,

such as:
- pre-training phone calls
- greeting them as they walk in
- self-introductions at the beginning of the session
- break and lunch times

One particularly easy way of building rapport is by giving your own self-introduction at the beginning of the session. Be sure to share details about where you're from, your working background, and especially personal details such as your hobbies and interests. The more things they know about you, the easier it will be to be like them.

• Getting the Environment Right

The environment that we are in has a huge impact on our behaviour, emotions, our mindset, and also our learning effectiveness.

If a room is too cold, then you are going to be distracted by that cold. If you are sitting too far away from the trainer, then you won't be able to hear what they say. And if the lighting is poor, you may not even be able to see the person sitting next to you!

I have a checklist that I go through whenever I enter a training room. It is as follows:
- **Temperate Temperature**
- **Easy Entry**
- **Light for Sight**
- **Tech Set**
- **Shareable Deliverables**
- **Visible Visuals**
- **Speaking Seating**
- **No Noise**
- **Charts Charted**
- **Labelled Learners**

Environment Checklist

Temperate Temperature?	❑
Easy Entry?	❑
Light for Sight?	❑
Tech Set?	❑
Shareable Deliverables?	❑
Visible Visuals?	❑
Speaking Seating?	❑
No Noise?	❑
Charts Charted?	❑
Labelled Learners?	❑

Taking the time to go through each one of these before the training will help a lot, but it also means you should arrive at the venue early. I always try to arrive an hour early, although given the unpredictable nature of traffic in China where I primarily work, I find it difficult to arrive at a desired time. Nonetheless, the earlier you arrive, the more control you will have over your environment.

Let's have a look at each of these, one by one.

Temperate Temperature

Too cold and everyone wants to switch the heating on. Too hot and everyone falls asleep. Open the windows and the temperature adjusts, but then quickly drops too low. Bring in a fan and people cool down, but the sound drowns out everything else. Oh, the joys of temperature!

As a general rule of thumb, room temperature is good. You can find various research online that talks about what the optimum temperature is for cognitive performance, but the reality is that this will vary for each room and each participant.

As another general rule of thumb is: don't touch the thermostat. Get an expert to do it. You know how it goes. You turn the knob down a few degrees but nothing seems to happen. So you turn it down even more. Then, an hour later, suddenly the whole room is freezing and you need to go back and tweak it again. Don't waste your time playing around with thermostats. Get someone who knows what they are doing to adjust them.

I always aim to get the temperature sorted first thing on arrival and that is why it is at the top of the list. Temperature can often take time to adjust, so get someone to change it early on (if it needs changing) so you have time for the room to reach the right temperature.

Easy Entry

There will always be latecomers. As the training gets in full swing, a dozen more people will walk through the door. As inconvenient as that is alone, the inconvenience increases exponentially when these latecomers have to walk past everyone to get to their seats.

To avoid this sort of situation, we want to make sure that an easy path to their seats has been prepared beforehand… a path that will minimise the inconvenience to everyone else who was able to arrive on time.

In some rooms, there are multiple entrances. For example, maybe there is an entrance at the front of the classroom, and an entrance at the back. When latecomers arrive, it will be better if they can arrive through the back entrance. This way, they don't have to walk past any visual aids or other participants.

Something else to do is to leave empty seats closer to the entrance. This way, latecomers don't have to walk past everyone. They just open the door, enter, and sit down.

Another thing to keep in mind with regards to entry is any hazards lying around. There might be flip charts, computers, tables, or even a whole array of crazy tangled cables. If people have to walk past these to get to their seats, it can cause a lot of trouble. Flip charts might fall over, someone might knock a hot cup of coffee over, or another person can trip over the cables. Try to move these things as far away from the entrance as possible.

Light for Sight

Changes in light can create significant biological, mental, and behavioural changes in both humans and animals alike.

For example, melatonin is a hormone that induces sleep, modifies mood and mental agility, and does a number of other things. When light hits our retinas, the production of melatonin is suppressed. But once light stops hitting our retinas, melatonin starts to work its magic. Our mental functions start to shut down, our energy levels drop, and we become sleepy. In the interior of buildings where daylight and artificial lighting are inadequate, the suppression of melatonin production during the day can drop. This can lead to feelings of depression.

Seasonal Affective Disorder, or SAD for short, is a mood disorder in which people who are happy throughout most of the year become more depressed during winter time. Symptoms of this include tendencies to oversleep and overeat, a lack of energy, and poor concentration. I can wholly relate to this disorder. At the time of this writing, it has been about one week since I returned from a nice holiday to Thailand. I was on a tropical island with plenty of sunshine and very warm weather. Now, I am back in Shanghai where it is freezing cold and the evenings get dark very quickly. My energy levels have decreased dramatically, I am waking up later in the morning, and have even taken to napping in the afternoons.

Our bodies have evolved to make the most of sunlight. From the wavelength of sunlight to the times in which we are exposed to it, the regulation of our biological processes are optimised when exposed to natural light. So, for the best results, make sure your training is in a room that allows sunlight to shine through, and make sure to open the curtains.

Tech Set

Technology problems are incredibly annoying. Crashing computers, dying projectors, and flickering light bulbs can all have an impact. Yet technology problems are easily minimised with good preparation.

Technology is another good reason to turn up early. Get everything set up as early as possible. Check connections to make sure everything works. If it doesn't work, call an expert to come have a look, or prepare a backup solution.

Another good principle is to depend on as little technology as you can. Reduce your dependency on PPT and you may reduce stress for everyone.

Shareable Deliverables

Throughout the course of your training, you may have various handouts to deliver to people. Make sure these are prepared as early as possible. There is nothing more annoying than having to pause for a few minutes whilst you shuffle through stacks of paper to find the handouts you require for the next activity, or to have to make photocopies at the last moment, which could cause you more grief (especially if the photocopier runs out of paper or toner and no replacements are available!).

A general principle I employ is to use as few deliverables as possible. I either put them all together into one booklet (so I only need to hand things out once), or I just reduce the amount of handouts in general.

Visible Visuals

If you do an Internet search for 'Classroom seating arrangements', you'll inevitably find lots, with lists of the pros and cons for the different types. Yet, sometimes, the room we're in doesn't allow for our preferred seating arrangement. Instead of giving you a long list of seating arrangements, let me give you two principles to help you decide how best to arrange your seating.

The first principle is all about visible visuals. **Consider what learners need to be able to see throughout the training.** It might be the PPT, the flip charts, you standing at the front, or being able to see another person sitting in the far corner.

Move the seating so every participant will be able to see everything they need to see whenever they need to see it. Go around and sit in the different seats to check if you can see things clearly or not.

Aim to avoid having to change the seating more than once. Ideally, you should be able to get it all set up at the beginning of the training and then never have to touch it again.

And for the second principle…

Speaking Seating

This is the second principle of seating arrangements. **Make sure that where people sit, they can easily speak with each other.**

If they need to turn around to speak with each other, then that's going to limit the amount they speak with each other. This is a big disadvantage of using rows to layout seating like in a traditional lecture theatre. Straight away, this will be a big mental barrier to any interaction.

Also, consider how splitting people into groups would affect their interactions. If each group has their own table, then they're going to find it easy to speak to the people in their group, but have a big mental barrier to speaking to people in other groups.

Consider who they need to interact with throughout the training, and how you can make it as physically simple as possible to carry out those interactions.

This is a big reason that I tend to use a 'U' layout with smaller groups, with no tables. Everyone can see everyone without having to turn around. They can interact with each other all the time, and the energy tends to remain quite high.

Seating Principles

A really good tip with using 'U' layouts is to do away with tables. When people have tables, it is much easier for them to get out phones and laptops and distract themselves. Remove the tables and you remove the potential for distractions, allowing them to be much more focussed throughout.

No Noise

Noise can be really distracting. Construction works outside, the buzzing and hooting of rush hour traffic, and even the constant hum of an air conditioning unit can all be incredibly distracting.

Our brains have learned to spot differences in our surrounding environment. So when a noise is consistent, our brain registers it as safe and filters it out. But when it constantly changes, our brain registers it as a threat and directs our attention towards it.

The most annoying kind of noise is the inconsistent noise. An air conditioning hum, for example, is quite consistent, and our brains will easily filter it out, eventually. But an annoying mosquito buzzing around can drive us insane.

Whilst there are a lot of noises that you can't control, the earlier you arrive, the more you will be able to control. Somethings you can put a stop to the problem on the spot. And other times you may conclude that the noise renders a training room inadequate so you can ask to move to another one.

Charts Charted

You may have certain visual aids that need to be put up on a flip chart. As helpful as visual aids are, they can be a bit distracting when you need to interrupt the flow of the training to write or draw them.

To reduce the potential for distraction of your visual aids, prepare them in advance. This is yet another reason to turn up early. Do all your writing and drawing early on, and put them somewhere they can be easily accessed at the time of need.

An even simpler thing to do is to print out any visual aids in advance. This saves you time in drawing them!

Labelled Learners

Find a way of labelling everyone's names. You might use a name tent, stickers, or even name badges on a neck chain.

This is for everyone's benefit, not just yours. In the past, I found some fancy ways of memorising everybody's names (my record was 48 names in 15 minutes). But it's also helpful for the learners themselves to be able to clearly identify each other. The easier they can remember each other's names, the easier they will feel closely connected.

Make sure that when they write down their names, they do so using big, clear letters. Ideally, give them a marker to do so. Printed names in CAPITAL LETTERS are best. If you are working with people from different countries, then make sure you use a language everyone can read.

- ## Goodwill towards All Learners

How you think of your learners will affect how you treat them. At times, we might encounter learners (or their behaviour) we don't particularly like. If you think they are useless, lazy, or stupid, then you will probably end up treating them that way. No matter how hard you try to hide it, it will still come out in subtle ways such as your facial expressions, your gestures, and your tone. We don't want to be doing any of that.

We need to keep a positive mindset towards our learners. We need to think the best of them. Most importantly, we need to care about them.

That should be easy, right? But sometimes it's not. Sometimes, it's not just a case of us losing our patience with our learners, it might simply be a case of being too distracted. At times, we lose interest in what we are doing, or our minds are too focussed on other things. We forget to care. And that's perfectly natural, but we should try to change that.

Here are some things we can do cultivate a mindset of goodwill towards our learners.

Appreciate them.

As they walk into the room, force yourself to find three things you appreciate about them. It could be a simple thing such as turning up on time, or even just smiling at you, or maybe how they purposely tried not to disturb anyone as they walked to their seat. It's interesting how our feelings towards them change once we notice what we appreciate about them. And it's equally interesting to notice how little attention we normally pay to what we appreciate about people.

Believe in them.

They have all the resources they need to handle their problems. This is not just my opinion. This is a fact. Everyone is capable of either solving their problems, influencing their problems, or accepting their problems. Sometimes they need a bit of guidance in doing any one of those things, and that's typically why they come to the training. But, at the end of the day, they are capable.

As they share their problems and challenges, as they ask questions, and as they express their fears and concerns, remind yourself that they are capable of dealing with it all. Even if they don't know they are capable, remind yourself that they are capable, and treat them like they are.

Value them.

We can all learn from each other. Just because you have more experience than them, more knowledge than them, and maybe more abilities than them, that does not mean there is nothing you can learn from them. They will always have a new insight, suggestion, or tip that you can learn from as well. This simple shift in thinking will show itself in subtle yet profound ways. Instead of saying 'Tell me the answer' you'll say 'What do you think about that?' Instead of responding with 'Yes, well done', you'll say 'That's interesting, tell me more'. Instead of them worrying you'll judge their answer, they'll feel you are genuinely interested in what they think.

Wish them well.

This is an interesting exercise I learnt from practicing meditation. If you are out and about, maybe on a crowded subway, in a shopping mall, or just walking through town, stop and look at the people around you. As you notice each individual, just think 'I wish you well'. It's that simple. Spend a few minutes doing this and notice how differently you feel.

Whenever I do this, it always brings a smile to my face. Not a huge clown smile, but a smile of genuine warmth and care. I find this really raises my mood.

You can do this anytime with your learners—when they first walk in, when they share their thoughts, when they are in the middle of an activity, when they're eating cake at tea break, and so on. Take some time to secretly wish them well.

They're doing their best.

They can always do better. But, given the resources they currently have, they are doing the absolute best they can. Given all the knowledge, motivation, and clarity they have regarding their situations, they are doing their best.

Anytime you find yourself wondering why they don't do things differently, or find yourself mentally judging them or wanting to criticise them, stop and think. Remind yourself that, with everything they have at the moment, this is the best they have been able to do. And their desire to want to do even better is admirable.

Some of the above can seem a bit touchy-feely, but try them and see what happens.

Building Goodwill Toward All Learners

Appreciate Them

Believe in Them

Value Them

Wish Them Well

Remember, They're Doing Their Best

- ## Building Confidence

Your level of confidence impacts their learning experience. If you are nervous and lack confidence, they may start to doubt what you say and the effectiveness of your training. This can be very distracting.

Conversely if you are confident, they will relax. They will trust that you know what you are talking about, know what you are doing, and are perfectly capable of delivering a training that meets their expectations.

How do we build confidence? Let's have a look.

Proper Planning Prevents Piss-Poor Performance

It also builds confidence.

The enemy of confidence is doubt. Once a little doubt soldier pops up in your mind, your reaction is to feel worried. You feel worried that something bad is going to happen and you haven't got it under control yet. So the easiest way to prevent feeling worried is to prevent any doubt.

The easiest way to prevent any doubt is to plan really well.

Sometimes I go into stupid detail to plan my trainings. I plan my explanations, the guiding questions I will use, the activities I will use, the timings of each activities, the instructions I will use to initiate each activity, the areas my feedback should focus on in different sections, and so on.

I even plan what I need to prepare when I arrive, what I need to prepare during the breaks, what I need to write and draw on the flip charts, and on and on and on.

Furthermore, I typically put into a checklist all of this preparation. The beauty of a checklist is that it turns plans into actions. Once I have completed each action, I can tick it off. And once I've ticked it off, that's one more doubt that has been killed.

The better prepared you are, the less you have to worry about. The earlier you arrive, and the earlier in advance you start planning, the better prepared you will be.

They Love You, Really

Remember that your learners want you to succeed. They don't want to walk out of your training then go online and write nasty things about you on your LinkedIn profile. They genuinely want you to succeed, because if you succeed, then they will as well.

Use Anchoring

Have you ever noticed how football players have special rituals they follow before they play a game? Some of them might look up to the sky and pray, others might jump up and down several times, and a few others might kiss the grass with their hand as they run onto the field. As strange as these rituals seem, there is some logic to them.

The idea is that you create a certain ritual, or pattern, that makes you feel a certain way. Then, whenever you perform that ritual, or initiate that pattern, you bring on that feeling. This is called anchoring.

For example, I have certain music that I listen to whenever I go running or work out. I use the playlist 'You Can Do It' on Spotify. Every time I hear that music, I start to feel energised. Now, sometimes I will listen to it before I go into a training so I feel energised for it.

I also have music I listen to when I need to focus. For this I use the playlist 'Music for Concentration', also on Spotify. In fact, I am listening to it right now as I type. Whenever I hear this music, I instantly find it much easier to concentrate.

If you do an Internet search for 'Morning Rituals', you will see that some very famous and successful people have shared what they do first thing in the morning. These rituals typically include meditation, exercise, and even cold showers. Morning rituals are a bit of a craze right now because people have recognised that, if you start the day in the right way, then it will help make you more productive throughout the whole day. It's all about priming yourself to have the right mindset to take on the day.

We should approach our work in the same way. If we develop special rituals that we can perform on our way to the training venue, or as we arrive, or even as we begin the training, then this will help anchor us into a better state of confidence and get off to a much better start. Here are some examples of possible rituals:

- Go for a ten-minute walk before the training
- Listen to a special music playlist
- Combine the first two together!
- Follow a checklist to get the room set up in a specific order
- Always start every training with the same few activities (e.g. an icebreaker, a warm-up discussion, etc.)

Prime Your Mind

If you are feeling really nervous, take a few minutes to prime your mind using this awesome little tool I found in Caroline Webb's book, *How to Have a Good Day*. It's called AAA and stands for:

- **Aim**
- **Attitude**
- **Attention**

The logic is quite simple: set your intention for the day (Aim), affirm the mindset you need to achieve this aim (Attitude), and identify what things you need to focus on to strengthen this mindset (Attention).

For example, a few years ago, I panicked when I saw the list of attendees for my training the next day. They were all very senior people, the most senior team in the Asia Pacific Region for this company. And it was my first time delivering that topic. I was well out of my comfort zone and when I saw how senior everyone was, I started to have a meltdown.

After a few minutes of panic, I calmed down enough to remind myself to use this AAA tool. And I primed my mind in the following way:
- Aim—to encourage them to share more of their experience
- Attitude—I am not their teacher; I am their facilitator, here to help them reflect
- Attention—focus on making them comfortable enough to share, and then encourage them to reflect and share

I probably spent 5 minutes on that, but it put my mind into a much more useful state. Rather than panicking by focussing on the idea that they were all so senior and scary, it helped me clarify a decent goal for the day and focussed my mind on the things that I could control that would help me achieve that goal.

You don't need to wait until you have a meltdown to use this. Priming your mind is a fantastic habit to get into before you go into the room. Taking just a few minutes to clarify your focus for the day will help you spend the day being much more focussed.

If you do, indeed, have a meltdown, then don't worry, because that's what we're going to look at next!

AAA Model

What's my **<u>Aim?</u>**

What **<u>Attitude</u>** will help me achieve my aim?

What should I pay **<u>Attention</u>** to in order to strengthen my attitude?

● Why We Get Nervous

Every single trainer has felt nervous at some point in their career. Nerves don't have to be a big issue, and they can easily be managed if we just understand a bit more about how they work.

Our Monkey Brain on Fear

Picture this scene: You are a monkey, hundreds of thousands of years ago, standing by a tree, just minding your own business. In the distance, there is a dinosaur (yes, I know they didn't exist hundreds of thousands of years ago… but in my story, they did, so there!). It is hungry. It sees you. And it starts to run towards you. As you notice it getting closer, how do you feel?

You're going to feel scared, so your heart is going to beat faster. Your jaw is probably going to drop and your eyes will open wide. All you want to do is get as far away from that dinosaur as possible. Your limbs will receive an increased flow of blood, to prepare you to run. This means blood will drain from your brain, which means you become somewhat stupid. All you can think about is running and you certainly don't have the cognitive resources to ponder the meaning of life.

Fast forward a few million years, and you are in a training room. Your brain still has some of the same parts as that monkey. Whilst there are no dinosaurs in the room, there are other people looking at you, and your brain registers them just the same way a monkey would register a dinosaur.

Your body will react in the same way that monkey's body did. Your heart will beat faster. As a result, your breathing will become faster as well. As your breathing gets faster, it will become shallower and cause you to start to get light-headed. Blood will drain from your brain to your limbs. This means your brain will become stupid. You will forget what you were going to say next. Your mind will go blank.

Furthermore, with all of this extra blood in your arms and legs, and all the adrenaline pumping around in your body telling you to get the hell out of there, how do you think your arms and legs will respond? They'll start to shake. The shaking means that you are primed to run for your life. Except you can't, because that's not socially acceptable in a training room. So you will stand there, with all this extra energy, and continue to shake.

Furthermore, it's not socially acceptable (at least in your nervous mind) to stand there, shaking and looking nervous. So you try to hide it. Your brain starts to focus on where your nervousness is showing, in order to hide it. But, ironically, the more attention you pay to your nervous reactions, the stronger they get. And the stronger they get, the more ashamed and awkward you feel. And so on.

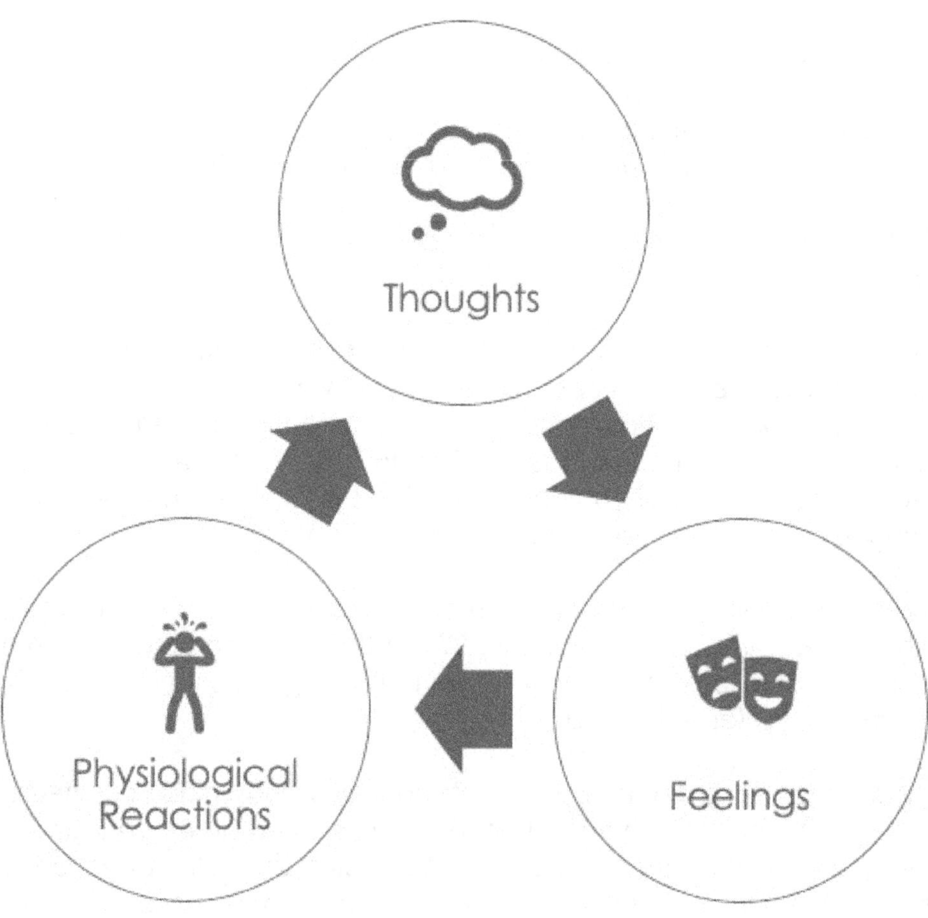

Congratulations. You have now entered the monkey brain's cycle of anxiety. So how the hell do we get out of it?

- ## Breaking the Nervous Cycle

First of all, accept that you are nervous. You might think this is easier said than done, but it's actually pretty easy. Here is why. The reason feeling nervous becomes a cycle is because we stigmatise it. We deem it socially unacceptable for the situation we are in. We are the trainer and we should look confident, but we don't, so we think this is bad. But this just adds an extra layer of negativity to an already negative feeling.

If you deem your nervous reactions as bad and unacceptable, then your brain will be focussed on stopping them, which first involves identifying those nervous reactions, and then involves an incredibly stupid self-dialogue of 'Stop shaking!'

This kind of self-dialogue is very ironic. For example, if I say, 'Don't think of chocolate ice cream', then you're probably going to think of chocolate ice cream. I know that I told you not to think of chocolate ice cream, but you're probably going to think of chocolate ice cream anyway because by saying 'Don't think of chocolate ice cream', I've put the words 'chocolate ice cream' into your mind.

By telling yourself to 'Stop shaking!' you've put the word 'Shaking' into your mind. What's in your mind is more likely to come out in your behaviour. So put a stop to the ironic self-dialogue.

The easiest way to stop the ironic self-dialogue is to replace it with useful self-dialogue. Either focus on observing your reactions ('My legs are shaking') or tell yourself what you should be doing ('Calm down').

Secondly, remember that it is perfectly OK to be nervous. In fact, it's in your best interest.

Think back to that monkey. Let's change the situation a little. The monkey is smoking marijuana and thoroughly enjoying it. As the dinosaur runs towards the monkey, the monkey doesn't care. In fact, he laughs. He's perfectly calm. And so the dinosaur kills and eats the monkey very easily!

Those nerves are there to help you. Yes, they might not be very helpful right now, but they have a good intention anyway. So thank them. Appreciate them. Because telling them to go away is going to have the exact opposite effect. But appreciating your nerves is also, ironically, going to have the opposite effect as well. The more you appreciate them, the more they will go away.

The reason they will go away is because everything comes and goes in the end. Your pet dog, Christmas day, and your hair. That's just the laws of the universe at work. If you let your nerves run their natural cycle, then they will go, too. They will probably go quite quickly, as well. Whereas, if you tell them to go away, they will just extend their cycle.

As an example, a few years ago, I had to deliver a keynote speech to 200 people. The venue was circular, which meant I stood in the middle and was surrounded by the audience. Furthermore, I had to speak in Mandarin, not English. Oh, and I only had 20 minutes to prepare for it. As I approached the stage, my legs started to shake.

What did I do? I let them shake. In my mind, I mentally noted that my legs were shaking. 'That's interesting', I thought, and then let them shake. I did not try to stop them. After about one minute, they stopped shaking. That cycle of nervous energy lived out its short life and then moved on to another realm.

So, accept this survival instinct. It is your friend (albeit a very embarrassing friend that you'd prefer not to hang out with), but it really does care about you.

And remember, you are not the only person to have ever felt nervous before. Every single person sitting in the room has felt nervous before. Right now, there are billions of other people who feel nervous as well. It is a natural feeling and you are not alone. So accept it and let it move on.

Get into the Flow

Because it takes a little while for the nervous energy to live out its life, try to get into the flow of things as quickly as possible. This means several things.

Firstly, with speaking, just speak and get those awkward, croaky frogs out of your throat. Once your voice is warmed up, it will sound calm and confident. But if you don't give it a chance to warm up, then the frogs won't go away. Sure, you might sound a bit strange for a minute or two, but the sooner you get your voice warmed up, the better.

Secondly, move. Move your arms and your legs. Not in a crazy madman manner, but just enough to get the energy out. Walk around a little, and use gestures as you talk. Remember that your limbs are primed to run for your life, so there's a lot of excess energy in them. It's not going to go anywhere by just standing still.

Thirdly, start interacting with your learners as soon as possible. Once you interact with them and notice that they are actually nice and fun people (and not dinosaurs), you will start to forget about your worries. You will start to remember that this is actually going to be really fun. Your nerves will suddenly vanish and you'll start to remember why you do this job.

• Projecting Authority

Part of being confident is looking, sounding, and behaving confidently. Even when you don't feel confident, it is surprisingly easy to still act confident. The skills I'll describe below are really worth practicing because, once they become a habit, they will have a huge impact on how your learners will feel in your presence.

Vocal Authority

It's very, very easy to make our voice sound more authoritative. Just remember these four words:
- Throw
- Slow
- Low
- Flow

Throw

Can you throw your voice so that the people of the back of the room can hear you clearly? If no one can hear, then speaking is pointless.

This is a bit trickier for some more than others because not everyone's volume is well-developed. But this is definitely something to practice. All it involves is making sure you speak loud enough so that the people at the back of the room can hear you.

When I first started training, I went to karaoke, one evening, shortly afterwards. I didn't really think much of that particular night, but what struck me was what I noticed when I went back to karaoke about a year after I started training. By that time, I had delivered so much training that my volume had naturally developed. And when I went to karaoke, I could suddenly sing much, much louder. I'm still not a great singer, but I am definitely a loud singer. In fact, I am so loud my wife refuses to go with me now!

Slow

Slow down when you are speaking. If you speak fast, then very soon you will run out of words and the only sounds that come out are 'Umm…' and 'Errr…', which will make you look nervous. Also, think about your words before you say them. This will reduce the amount of times you say 'Umm' and 'Errr'.

Imagine for a second that we have two people who are about to give a presentation:
- One is Barrack Obama.
- The other is a 12-year-old boy who has never done any public speaking before in his life.

Which one of those do you think will speak slower? (I can't imagine the 12-year-old boy speaking very slowly. Either he's going to be very nervous and speak desperately fast so he can get it over and done with, or he's going to be overly excited and unable to control the words that come out of his mouth.)

Obama, on the other hand, will be very confident. He's been seen as the most powerful man on the planet. He is very much aware of his achievements. And he knows that he is more important than anyone else in that room. He doesn't need to worry and get things over with. Furthermore, he's calm and controlled, so he will speak at a much more controlled speed.

It's surprisingly easy to speak slowly. Just remember to think clearly about what you're going to say before saying it, and pause more after saying every few words and in between sentences.

If you want to check your speaking speed, then read these sentences and time how long it takes you to read them. Keep practicing until you can match the target.
- *Read this in two seconds*
- *It takes three seconds to read this sentence*
- *And, for this third sentence, it takes five to six seconds*

Now try reading all of these together in ten to eleven seconds.

Low

Do you sound confident and authoritative? If the answer is yes, then you can skip this and move on to Flow. But if the answer is no, then lowering your tone will help.

For example, try reading this sentence and finishing the last few words with a rising tone: 'Can everybody stand up, please?' Now try saying it again, but this time lowering the tone on the last few words. Which one sounds more authoritative? The rising or lowering tone?

You probably noticed that the lowering tone sounds more authoritative, because that's probably how you have heard senior people speak before. When we are uncertain, that'll come out in a rising tone. But when we are certain, it comes out in a lowering tone. So, lower your tone more frequently to sound more authoritative.

If you struggle to do that, then think of your voice as having three different levels. At the highest level, the pitch comes from your mouth. If it is slightly deeper, it comes from your throat. The deepest is from your chest, so you should aim to speak from your chest. This might take a bit of getting used to, but it is very easy to do. It's just a case of getting into the habit.

Flow

Do your tone, volume, and speed vary over time? Varying our tone, volume, and speed helps our voice flow better and makes it naturally more engaging. In fact, you can try this simple experiment: Record yourself talking about what you did this morning. First, say it out loud, and focus on keeping the tone, volume, and speed the same throughout. Then record it again, varying the tone, volume, and speed. Have some fun as well and make yourself sound overly dramatic if you want! Which one sounds more engaging?

A good flow in your voice can make even the most mundane topics (such as what you did this morning) sound so much more engaging. So if you are already confident with throwing your voice, slowing down, and lowering your tone, then focus on making your voice flow.

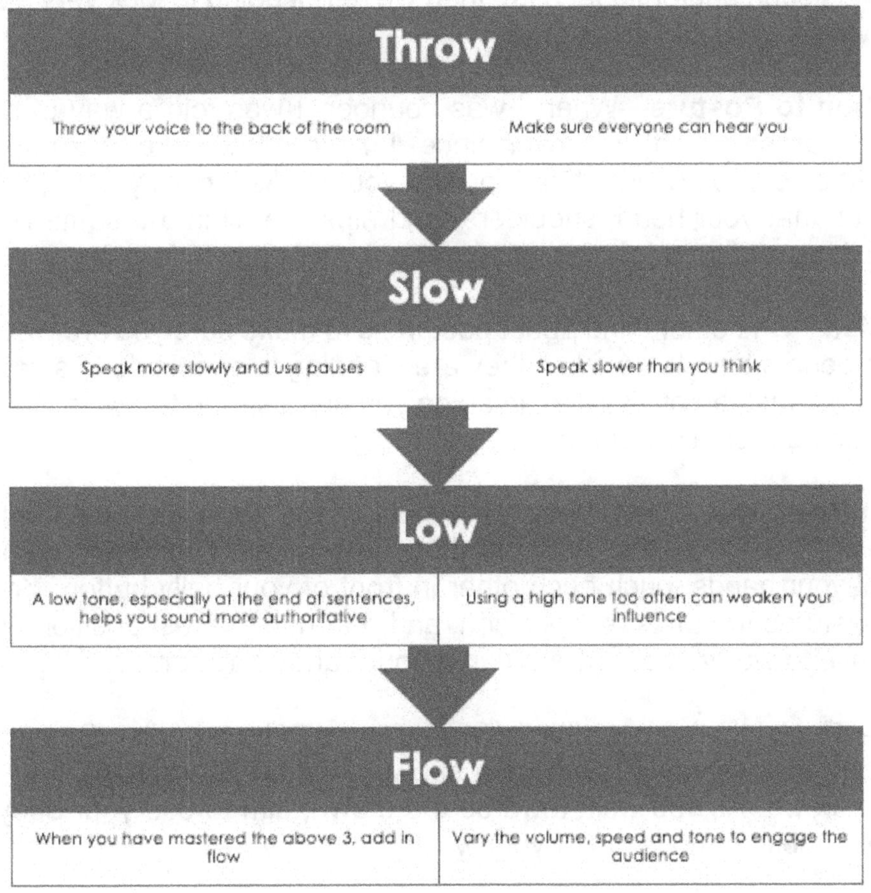

Non-Verbal Authority

Communication is 55% body language, 38% tone of voice, and 7% words. In theory, that means I could more effectively deliver all of the ideas in this book through the art of mime…

I hope you realise I am being sarcastic. Those statistics are famous but are commonly abused. They are based on research conducted by Albert Mehrabian, whose original research concluded that, when we communicate about our feelings, 55% of that is done through body language, 38% through tone of voice, and 7% through words. If those 3 elements are not congruent (e.g. I say 'I like you' whilst trying desperately not to make eye contact with you), then the other person is more likely to decode our body language and tone of voice than our words.

And the body language we project to our learners communicates a lot about how we feel and what we are thinking. It also significantly impacts on how much authority we project. If we slouch and/or fidget a lot, then we're not going to look very authoritative. So here is what we should do instead.

Pay Attention to Posture—When I was younger, I was told a way to manage my posture that has stuck with me ever since. Imagine that there is a piece of string attached to the very top of your head, pulling you up. As it pulls you up, it straightens your spine so that your head, shoulders, and hips are all in the same line. It's very simple, but does require a few reminders, as it's very easy to forget.

Be Grounded—One other thing about posture is to make sure you are well grounded. What some people tend to do when they are standing is sway side to side, a bit like a tree in the wind. Instead of swaying, imagine you are a strong tree with deep roots. As you talk, your legs remain planted solidly in the ground.

Use a Rest Position—A lot of people have asked me 'Where should I put my hands when I speak?' I tell them 'Lay your hands by your sides. Then bend naturally at the elbows until your hands touch each other in front of your belly button. You can then initiate all gestures from this rest position, and return to the rest position as well. And you don't have to worry about where to put your hands anymore.'

Think Big—Think big, like a gorilla. In fact, pretend to be a gorilla. Go out to a public space, somewhere crowded, such as a subway station during rush hour, then walk towards the crowd. As you walk towards the crowd, aim to use your body language alone to get people to move out of your way.

This is quite a fun experiment to do if you are in a bad mood. But it's also great for developing confident body language. The idea is to take up as much space as possible, like a gorilla does. Gorillas show their authority by taking up space, and we can do that, too. That doesn't mean of course that you should be pushing people out of their seats and blocking the doorways, just use gestures and walk around confidently, taking up as much space as you can.

I got this idea from Olivia Fox Cabane's book *The Charisma Myth*. This book actually had a massive impact on my confidence and the presence I am now able to project in the room, so if this is an area you are interested in developing more, then I strongly recommend you check it out.

One thing that some people struggle with when they try this is figuring out how to use their arms effectively. They try to make big gestures with their arms, but keep their elbows stuck to their rib cages and end up doing something that looks more like 'jazz hands'. Remember to relax your arms whenever you make a gesture and keep your elbows unstuck from your ribs.

Eye Contact—Eye contact is a great way of projecting authority, as well as warmth, to your learners. It also subconsciously builds a connection with them.

Remember to spread your eye contact around to everyone in the room, not just the good-looking people sitting immediately to your left. This will mean you have to stand in a position where you can easily see everyone. It also means that you will need to adjust your eye contact every few seconds, to share it evenly. You can easily do this by scanning the room from left to right and then back again, so you look at everyone in the room.

Keep repeating this process, while staying grounded, so you are only moving your head. This will also help you control your arms. You will be so focussed on making sure your eyes have contact with everyone that you will not think about them, and you'll be seen as a confident person who projects authority.

Body Language

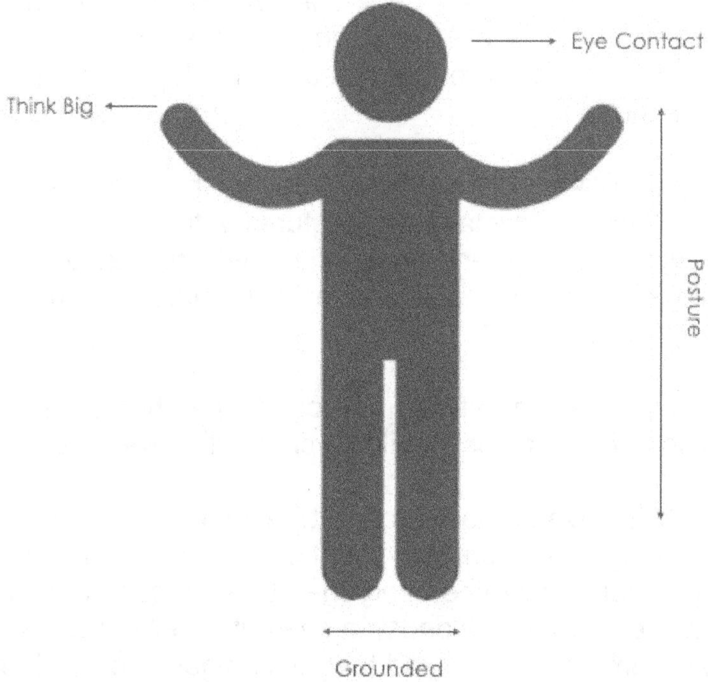

• Dealing with Resistance

Resistance from participants is not pleasant to deal with, and can come in many forms, such as direct challenges, disruptive behaviour, or even just being distracted. But, as unpleasant as it is, it is easily managed, and just as easily prevented.

Predicting Resistance

As you design your training, the more you focus on your learners' needs, the less resistance you will encounter. Take the time to understand what motivates them about this training. Learn about their expectations. If you can, enquire about the potential attitudes they will be bringing to this training.

Sometimes learners come to training in a bad mood. Maybe their team has just been downsized. Maybe the company is going through a crisis. Maybe they're being forced to attend this training. As you find out the reasons for them attending this training, you will pick up on any likely resistance you may encounter.

Preventing Resistance

Most resistance can be dealt with before it even begins. If you get the training off to the right start, then you will be less likely to encounter resistance later on.

As you start the day, take some time to set up the environment properly. Ensure it is comfortable and distraction-free. Allow everyone to introduce themselves to help build rapport amongst the group. And work together to agree on some ground rules everyone can hold each other accountable to.

I view the ground rules as a chance to express expectations. I share my expectations of the group, and allow them some time to reflect on their expectations of each other. This is especially effective if you do it after introducing the objectives for the course. You can then ask them what behaviours will help us achieve these objectives. If you get everyone to commit to these expectations by taking a piece of paper and signing their name below a sentence that reads 'I agree to abide by the expectations outlined', then people are more likely to take them seriously for the rest of the course. You will not have to deal with much resistance because you can simply hold up the sheets of paper you have collected to remind them to get their behaviour back on track.

Embracing Resistance

Sometimes people resist because they disagree with the content that is being shared. Maybe they have found a flaw in the theory, or pointed out a time when they tried using it but found it didn't work, or maybe they think it won't apply to their situation.

When you encounter these situations, avoid getting defensive. Instead, embrace their challenge because, normally, they will have a point. But so will you.

Embracing it doesn't mean you should accept that you are wrong, call it a day, and pack up your bags. It means embracing their point. If you think their point is valid, then share what you agree with. But also point out what they have overlooked.

I was once delivering a management training where we were talking about coaching employees. One participant said they didn't agree with coaching because it took too much time. I agreed that it can take a lot of time, and there are situations where we don't need to coach, such as the situations they just described. But I also explained that, in the long run, when we coach, it helps keep our staff more motivated.

As I dealt with the resistance this way, a lot of participants were nodding their heads at me. And after I'd finished talking, a few others even chimed in, to back me up.

Four Steps to Managing Disruptive Behaviour

Whenever disruptive behaviour shows itself, follow these four simple steps to get things back on track:
1. Calm Down
2. Hint
3. One-to-One
4. Go Public

1. Calm Down

Disruptive behaviour can be pretty frustrating at times, but getting angry only makes things worse. You risk damaging your rapport with the learners and give them more reasons to be disruptive.

The same goes for the participants. If they are getting emotional, then we need to give them some space to calm down. If we push things on without waiting for them to calm down, then they will struggle to focus and may even get more emotional.

If you can, take a break. Call a time-out, and give everybody a chance to catch a breath of fresh air and calm down. Sometimes that is all that's needed and, fifteen minutes later, participants return in a much calmer state.

If you are struggling to calm yourself down, then remind yourself that this disruptive behaviour probably isn't personal. The learners may be behaving this way for reasons unknown to you. Maybe their dog died, they just got a divorce, or their boss called them during the break to tell them they need to work overtime tonight. Maybe it's just their personality. Some people are naturally loud and boisterous, others are natural jokers, and some may naturally have a negative disposition. Just because they are behaving in a way you don't like doesn't mean they are doing it to spite you.

One way that disruptive behaviour tends to get out of hand is when it becomes personal. Either you say something to offend someone, or they say something to offend someone. When this happens, it is important to redirect everyone's attention to the disruptive behaviour, not to the person.

I once had two people start a very big argument in the middle of a game. We had to stop the game because it got too out of hand. So we took some time to calm down. Then we came back to debrief what had just happened, as it was a bit too big to pretend it hadn't.

As we got into the debriefing, one of the people in the argument started to point out everything that was wrong with the other person, and tried to get me to agree with her. I let them both vent for a while, to get rid of some steam, but I avoided getting drawn into their personal arguments. Once they both had their turns to vent for a little while, I pointed out that it wasn't the people that had caused the argument, but the difference in behaviour. Other people in the group agreed with me on this. Eventually, the two arguing participants agreed as well. Then I asked them to state what behaviour offended them, and what behaviour of theirs they thought offended the other. Once this was out, I then asked them to share what they might do differently next time they interact with each other. It started to calm down a lot from there and, in the end, they shook hands and we continued as if nothing had happened.

2. Give Them a Hint

One of the most common disruptive behaviours I encounter is two people continuing on a conversation amongst themselves whilst someone else is sharing with the whole group. It can be hard for people to listen to the person sharing when there's all this whispering going on.

In a situation like this, sometimes a simple hint will suffice. Something as simple as eye contact, a cough, or even a subtle shift in your body language will be enough of a signal to encourage them to change their behaviour.

A lot of disruptive behaviour occurs because people are unaware of it. So rather than just hoping they will stop, address it head on. But do so in the most subtle way you can, which should ideally be through a simple hint.

Occasionally, though, hints won't work and we need to address it a bit more directly.

3. One-to-One

You've tried giving hints yet their behaviour is on the verge of getting out of hand. What do you do?

Take them aside and ask them to stop it. Explain to them what you have observed and how it is affecting the group. Then ask them kindly if they would be able to stop it. Framing it this way avoids making you sound like you are telling them off and gives them the power to take responsibility over their behaviour. Doing this in private also avoids embarrassing them in front of the group.

4. Go Public

Maybe you've tried a one-to-one already and nothing has changed. Or maybe you didn't have the opportunity to take them aside before it got out of hand. Because they don't seem to be getting your hints, the only thing left to do is go public.

Stop what you are doing, make sure you have everyone's attention, and then speak directly to the disruptive participants, telling them to stop. You don't need to do this in an embarrassing way. Saying something as simple as 'Guys' and pairing it with an appropriate facial expression can be enough to get the message through.

So, remember, the next time you encounter some resistance, tackle it step by step.

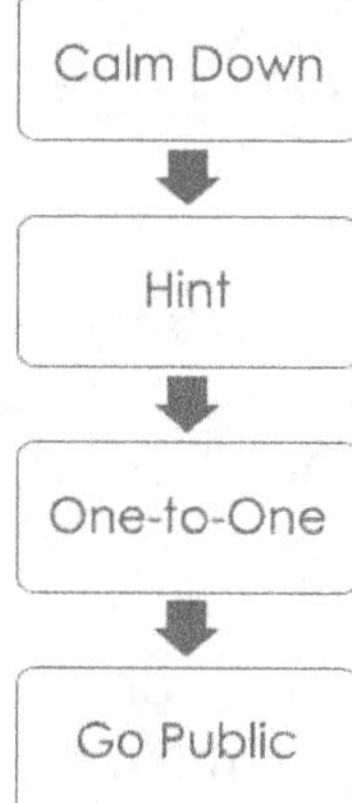

- ## The Who, Why, How Template

To make this section easier to remember, I've created a simple template for you. Really, all you need to remember to prime people for learning are the following:

Who: Introduce who you are to build rapport and trust
Why: Help them see the benefits for them
How: Agree with them on the process to help them deal with any concerns they might have

Who

Whether you like it or not, you will have a major impact on their training experience. The more they trust you, the more they will accept what you say and cooperate. And the more they like you, the more easily they will open up to you.

So, when preparing a self-introduction at the beginning, consider the following questions:
- **What do you have in common with them?**
- **Why are you the trainer and not someone else?**
- **What examples do you have of previous times you successfully ran this training?**
- **What is the story of how you got here?**
- **What special ability do you have that can help them?**

Remember, you are not the only person in the room they don't know. They probably don't know all of their fellow learners, so they need a chance to get to know each other. This is where icebreaker activities come in, which we have already discussed.

As a reminder, recall the following principles when designing your icebreaker activity:
- **Each individual should interact with as many people as possible**
- **Individuals should share personal details, their working backgrounds, and their reasons for attending the training**
- **Through the sharing, they should be able to identify things they have in common with each other**

Why

It can be really valuable to dig deep into the 'why' at the very beginning. Help the learners realise the benefits they will get and only move on from this when you are very certain they have a deep enough awareness of how this training can help them.

It is generally better if the Why comes from them, as opposed to you. So here are some suggestions:

- **Ask them to share common challenges or problems related to the topic of the training**
- **Give them some time to write clear and specific goals for this training and share them with the rest of the group**
- **Give them some time to create their own case study that they can use throughout the training**
- **Give them a role-play or simulation at the start to test their current abilities, and follow up with a debrief**
- **Get them to do their own Gap Analysis (ask them to describe where they would like to be and where they currently are, and what's holding them back)**

How

Remember that your learners might have certain questions on their mind or pressing concerns from the very beginning. They may have urgent work that they need to find a spare moment to do or they may have an early flight to catch. Maybe their canteen has long queues during your scheduled lunch times and they are worried about buying and eating their lunch in the time given.

They may also be curious about what will happen in the training. They may wonder if they'll get a chance to practice, if there will be relevant case studies, or if they'll even have a chance to share their own experiences with each other.

So besides Who and Why, the final thing we need to align on before we start our training is How. And here are some suggestions:

- **Give them a rough agenda for the day and ask them what good times for the breaks are**
- **Share with them the types of activities they'll be doing, and the benefits of those activities**
- **Ask them what rules they hope everyone will follow for the training**
- **Ask them to share what things might distract them during the training (e.g. urgent meetings, phone calls) and how they plan to deal with those**
- **Start a discussion about learning and elicit key learning principles (e.g. reflection, practice, feedforward, etc.) and then link those to how the training has been designed**

The Who, Why, How Template

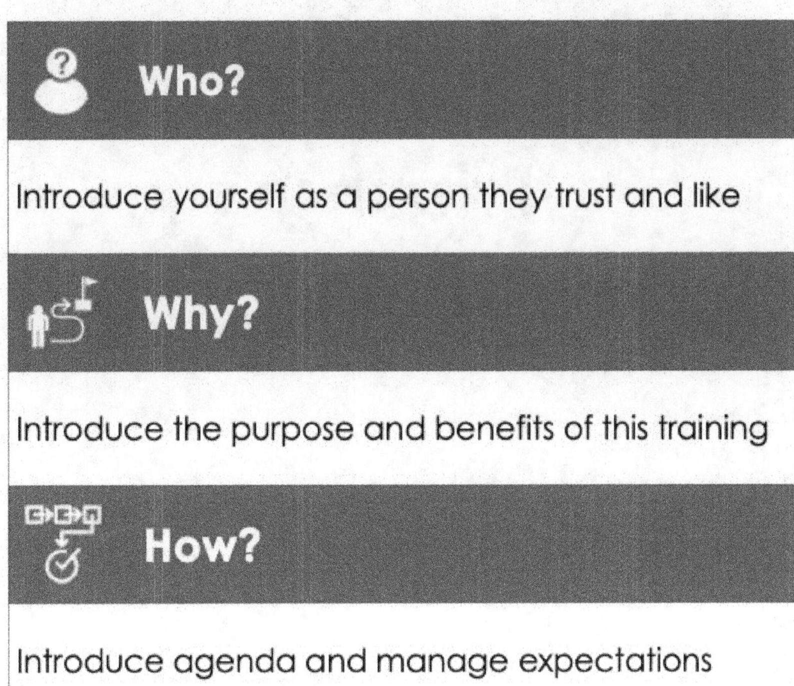

Priming Summary

The following flowchart is a summary of everything we have looked at in this section:

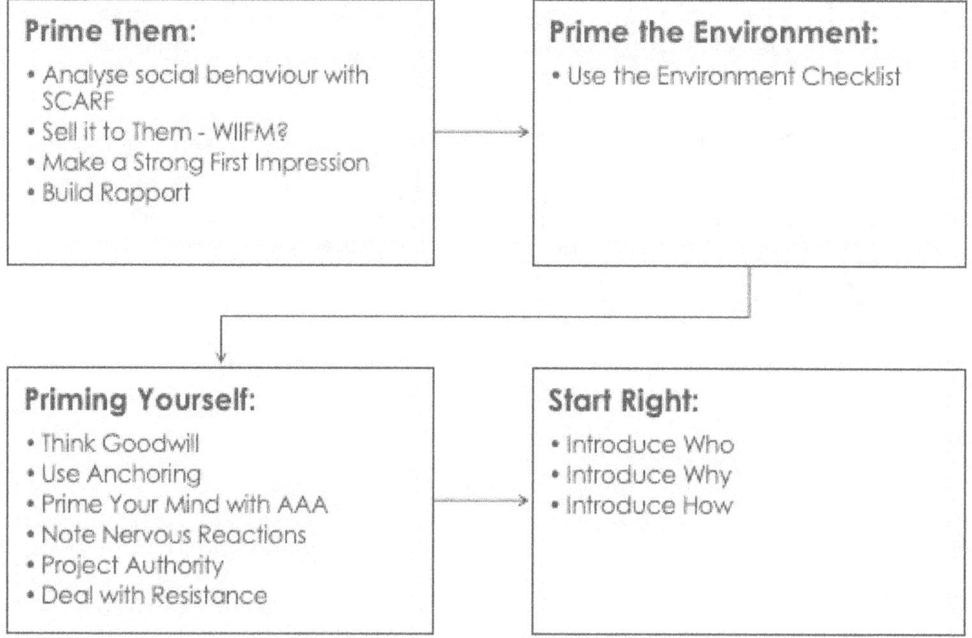

Guiding

Part of the value of training is in being able to get new ideas faster than learning by chance, so there is inevitably some amount of input involved in training.

A lot of the time, learners are coming to listen to specific ideas. They want to hear and see specific solutions to their problems. They expect these solutions to be something they've never heard before, and something that they can try using immediately.

The challenge is in getting these ideas through effectively. This is where less experienced trainers tend to go overboard because they overwhelm learners with copious amounts of information and don't even bother to package it in a digestible form.

Here is where much debate happens in the training world. Many people believe lectures are ineffective. Many fear death by PowerPoint. Many believe facilitation is superior to training. There are many opinions on how this should be delivered best.

In my opinion, the best solution is the one that works, which typically involves a combination of facilitation and training.

Facilitation involves putting more responsibility for learning into the learner's hands. This involves stepping back as a trainer, asking lots of questions, encouraging discussions, drawing out ideas from the group, and involving them as much as possible. Pure facilitation involves almost no input from the trainer whatsoever; we simply ask the right questions and set up activities to enable learners to learn by themselves. When a learner asks a question, the facilitator should not supply the answer. Instead, it should come from the rest of the group.

Training, on the other hand, requires the trainer to have and share expertise. It involves you, as the trainer, stepping in and showing the way, providing the knowledge, and having the solutions. When a learner asks a question, you have an answer.

But we have to be careful with both training and facilitation. Too much lecturing and presenting can cause learners get bored. But too much facilitating can cause learners to get frustrated.

I have seen people go overboard with facilitating. Every time someone asks a question, they throw it back to the group, and the group starts to get impatient and lose trust with the facilitator. But I have also seen people rely too much on the presentation and bore the group instead.

In reality, most of what we do in the classroom is a combination of Training and Facilitation, or Facilitative Training. We have the answers but, rather than showing them the answers, we set up experiences to help them discover the answers by themselves. We try to encourage them to learn as much as possible by themselves, but we step in when we sense they need us.

To be a great trainer, you need to learn a variety of techniques and keep them in your 'toolbox'. You can have techniques for presenting, telling stories, asking questions, running activities, and drawing out knowledge from the group. If you can pull out the right technique (or tool) at the right time, then you can adapt to the group perfectly and keep them fully engaged all the time.

In this Guiding section, I will show you how to explain things clearly, how to tell stories, and how to use questions. With all of this knowledge in mind, you will have a toolbox that will allow you to adapt to the needs of the room.

- ## From Lecturing to Storytelling

Reflect back to your school and university days for a moment. How often were you not paying attention when the teacher lectured?

According to John Medina, author of *Brain Rules—12 Principles for Surviving and Thriving at Work, Home, and School*, when listening to lectures, most people's attention spans last for about 10 minutes. After 10 minutes, people mentally check out. And that's a serious problem if you are lecturing for more than 10 minutes.

Think of attention like a door to a room. When you have people's attention, the door is open and everything you say can get in. But once that door shuts, nothing gets in. If you lecture for an hour, that's basically 50 minutes of shut-door time, and a complete waste.

But beyond the 10-minute limit of attention, there are other problems with lectures as well.

From Attention to Understanding

Just because I say something does not mean you understand it. If poorly packaged, information can be incredibly challenging and, at times, impossible to take in. Have a look at the following two examples and note which one is easier for you to understand and remember:

1. *Information that does not engage the audience on an emotional level will most likely fail to grab attention. There must also be context to the information because, without it, the brain must put in extra effort interpreting the meaning of the incoming information. Information must also be presented in a logical manner by summarising it into key concepts and ensuring only information relevant to the concepts are presented and linked back to the concept.*

2. *An audience of eager faces are staring at you, waiting for you to impart your pearls of wisdom for the next hour. Speak well, and this customer will invite you back. Make a mess of it, and you might not get paid. But it's after lunch, and you know everyone's feeling sleepy. How do you make sure you keep them awake and do a good job?*

Start by making them scared or excited. Their company's business model is about to become outdated and only you know what to do. Or maybe you're about to tell them how they can enjoy more time at home with their families without taking a pay-cut. If you can start by scaring or exciting them, you've got their attention.

So now you've got their attention and it's time to impart your pearls of wisdom. But slow down a minute. We all know you've got lots to share, but it's probably too much. Much like a suitcase, there's a limit to how much you can put in. How much are they really going to remember, after your talk?

Only share a handful of key points with them. 1 point is perfect, 3 is fairly good, and 5 points might only just get through. The less you share, the easier it is for them to remember.

But one hour to share only a handful of points? Surely, I can cover each point in just a few seconds…

Unfortunately, that's not how our brains work. A point is an abstract concept, and our brains don't like abstract concepts. Our brains need to see, hear, feel, and experience what these points mean. Our brains need to experience why and how we can use this point to solve our problems. Let me give you an example of how this works.

Maybe the point you want to share is that virtual working is the future. But what does that mean? Give an example of how more and more people are working from home. Give another example of companies that are benefitting from adopting virtual working. Give another example of companies that are starting to lose staff and customers because they weren't adopting virtual working.

Those examples will show why virtual working is important to your audience. Your audience will pay attention and they will care. You can then share examples of other companies that have successfully adopted virtual working to show your audience how they can do the same.

So, to summarise how to keep an audience's attention throughout your presentation:
1. ***Start by scaring or exciting them to grab their attention***
2. ***Condense your presentation into a handful of key points***
3. ***Put each of those points in context by showing the audience why and how they should apply them to their life***

I'm betting the second example was much easier to understand, quite simply because it is brain-friendly. Sure, it's longer than the first example, but this also shows just how much effort it takes on our part to help the audience understand.

What the second example does well is that it puts everything into a context that is meaningful for you, and guides you through each point, step by step. In other words, it uses storytelling techniques, which, as we'll learn in the next few sections, are extremely useful for us in the classroom.

• The Ladder of Explanation

At some point in our training (in fact, probably at many points), we're going to be explaining things. We'll be explaining new concepts, the set-up for activities, or maybe how to use what they've just learnt.

Sometimes, however, our explanations just fall flat. Our learners might have zero interest or take nothing in. Sometimes, it feels a bit like talking to a brick wall.

I had this experience once when I was running an Influencing Skills training for a group of very introverted engineers. One of the activities was called 'Moving Chairs'. It's actually a very useful activity to help develop empathy for others, and is something I learnt in an NLP course I attended. But these engineers didn't take to it as well as I had hoped, and I was left feeling a bit stupid.

Put simply, Moving Chairs is an activity that encourages us to look at a challenging situation (normally involving a disagreement or conflict with someone else) and analysing it from three different perspectives.

The first perspective is our own perspective, of how we think and feel about the situation. The second perspective is from the other person's view. And the third perspective is more like a CCTV camera objectively watching the situation unfold.

As we do this activity, we want to physically move to different seats to represent the different perspectives. At the end, we'll get new insights about the situation, which will help us find solutions.

Is that clear? I'm going to assume that's not very clear, because that's about as much as I explained to the engineers in that Influencing Skills training, and they did not enjoy the activity at all.

So the next time I found a group of introverted engineers that I thought this would be useful for, I used a model I call 'The Ladder of Explanation' to explain it to them. And this time, the result was exponentially better. They took to it with a lot of enthusiasm, and actually got some really useful insights they hadn't thought of before.

So how did I explain it?

The Ladder of Explanation

This is how I structured my explanation. I took them up each step of the ladder. By the end, they were ready to go.

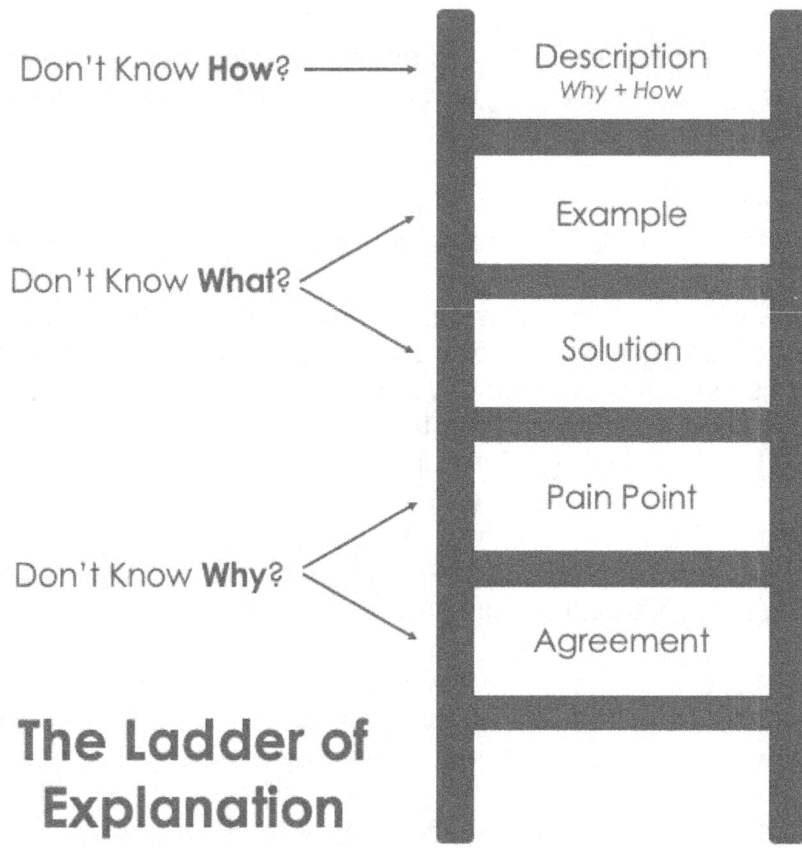

But we have to be careful which step we start from. Different people have different understanding levels, and we can classify these different understanding levels with the words Why, What, and How.

Why, What, and How

People at the Why level don't care. They have no reason to care. So if we want to explain things to them, we have to spend more time at the beginning explaining Why this is important. Once they care, they're ready to hear more.

The group of engineers were at the Why level. They were introverted, shy, and highly cerebral. When that first group watched me demonstrate the activity, they were probably thinking 'Why on Earth do we need to move to different chairs? This is stupid.' And as you can probably guess, once they started doing the activity, a lot of them refused to move chairs!

People at the What level already care. They know what problems our explanation is relevant to, and they really want to solve these problems! But they don't know what the solution is.

For example, when it comes to website loading speeds, I am at the What level. Recently, I have been trying to set up a nice website that runs smoothly in China. But after all the effort I put into designing it, it runs so slowly that no one can open it! I care very much about making this website speed up, but I don't know what to do. Do I change the WordPress theme? Delete some plugins? Change my host? Hire a professional? I have no clue!

And the highest level of understanding is How. These people already care, and they already know what to do. But they still struggle to do it! For example, people who know they need to lose weight, but can't, are definitely at the How level, much like smokers who know they need to quit, but can't. They already know what they need to do, but haven't quite figured out how to do it yet.

Making the Whys Care

People at the Why level (like my introverted, highly cerebral, and sceptical engineers) can lose interest very, very quickly, unless they see a reason to care.

A safe place to start with them is by saying things they can agree with. Get their heads nodding, and you know you're all staying on the same page. Once their heads have been nodding enough, you can start talking about their pain points.

With this second group of engineers, I started by saying things they could agree with. I gestured towards one of the learners, a Taiwanese man called Alan and said 'Yesterday, Alan shared an example of a colleague he doesn't like and has always struggled to get along with.'

Alan nodded his head. I continued.

'We've all encountered colleagues we don't like, right?'

Now everyone nodded their heads.

Then I drew a picture on the board of an iceberg floating in the sea. At the top of the iceberg, just above the surface, I wrote the word 'Behaviour'.

Then I said, 'These people do or say things that drive us crazy. But they don't do this because they were put on Earth to make our lives a living hell. There are reasons people behave in certain ways, and we can call these reasons "Driving Forces"'.

I added that to the part of the iceberg beneath the sea.

Then I gave an example of a previous participant I'd met, who was obsessed with safety. I explained how, on the surface, his behaviour looked extremely strict and obsessive to his colleagues. But there was a good reason for it. Earlier on in this person's career, an accident had killed someone during a project he was working on and it had a big impact on him. That's why he became obsessed with safety.

So I wrote the word 'Experience' under Driving Forces. I asked the group to brainstorm other types of Driving Forces. They shared words such as 'Values', 'Beliefs', 'Education', etc. I felt, at this point, we'd kept on the same page long enough that I could take them up to the next level: Pain Points.

'But the biggest challenge for us in dealing with these people is understanding these driving forces. Once we understand these driving forces, their behaviour seems more reasonable, and we can even think of new ways of dealing with them. But how do we understand these driving forces when we don't know much about them?'

Several members of the group nodded, so it was now time to take them to the What level.

Giving the Whats a Solution

At the What level, we need to tell them the solution, and give them examples to help them understand and accept it.

So I explained to the group that there is an activity that I use in situations like this called 'Moving Chairs'. I said a key benefit of this activity is that it helps us generate reliable insights about people when we don't know much about them.

And I gave them an example. I chose an example of a situation I had from the week before with a customer who had irritated me. They sent me a message just when I was about to go to bed, asking to arrange a call with me for the next day when I already had a full schedule.

I sat down in the first chair and explained my perspective. Then went through the other two chairs. Each time I generated a new insight, I made sure to make it very obvious so they could clearly see the benefit of this activity.

As I went through each perspective, I even shared some questions on the slide to show what we should be analysing when we sit in these chairs. I did everything I could to make this demonstration as understandable as possible.

With the Whats, we're showing them the solution, to help them see the value and want to learn more about it. When they're ready to go into detail, we can then move up to the next level.

Describing to the Hows

When people are ready to learn How, we can help them by describing each step in just the right amount of detail.

As I was demonstrating that activity, I also broke it down into vital steps, and described very clearly Why we did each step and How to do each step. And that is what describing is all about: showing the Why and How of each step.

So, as I sat down in the first chair, I explained that the first step is to visualise the situation. I explained the Why of visualising: we want to stimulate our imagination in order to generate more insight than we currently have. I talked a bit more about the power of imagination for helping us with situations like this, and showed the insights my now-stimulated imagination was generating.

Then I explained the How of this step: 'All you need to do is describe what you see, as this person, at this time.' So I described what I was seeing, how I was seeing my mobile phone, the message, the words the client had written in the message, how the room was dark and I was in my pyjamas ready to go to sleep.

Then I moved to describing the next step: 'Now think of the body language of that person, at that time. Are they sitting? Are they standing? How are they breathing?'

This is the How of this step. But Why?

'Because when we do this, we stimulate our imagination even more. When we are angry and when we are happy, our breathing and our body language will be different. If we know their body language, we can guess their feelings, and then we can guess why they are feeling that way'. Now they knew the Why of this step.

I took them through a few more key steps, explaining very clearly the Why and How of each step. I stopped frequently, to check for understanding. Then I let them get to it.

In total, this explanation took me about 10 minutes. But during the whole explanation, I was involving them all the time and, as I was gradually moving them up the ladder, I kept their interest throughout. Once they started the activity, they went really deep into it. I was very pleased when they came back afterwards and shared all the new insights they got from it. This was 10 minutes extremely well spent.

Think Differently

Whenever I train people in using this model, I find it forces some people to think in a way they're not used to. Rather than focussing on what they want to say, they now spend more time focussing on how to help the audience understand.

This can be a difficult habit to break for some people, because it is naturally much easier to just think about what we want to say. But if we can spend more time thinking about how to structure information in a way that helps our learners stay interested, find solutions to their problems, and grasp each step, then we'll be providing a much more valuable service to them every time we open our mouths.

- ## Talk to Their Emotions

When you were a child, you probably heard a lot of fairy tales and saw a lot of children's movies. I bet that you can still remember some of those stories to this day.

Take, for example, *The Lion King*. I've watched it twice in my life, but I can still remember what happens. Simba is going to grow up to be a great King. But then, his uncle kills his father and takes the throne. So Simba runs away to the jungle to keep safe and forget his past. Then one day, Simba is reunited with a lioness whom he then falls in love with. She persuades him to return to his father's Kingdom, and so he does, where he takes the throne back from his uncle and restores peace to the Kingdom.

As can be seen from *The Lion King*, stories are easy to remember, and that's what makes them powerful.

But why are they so easy to remember, exactly?

To understand that, let's take a look at some of the things most people can remember very clearly.

Flashbulb Memories

Throughout our lifetimes there are events we experience that leave a deep impression on us. To this day, we can still remember vivid details about what we were doing at that time.

For example, my mum still remembers exactly where she was when she heard JFK had been assassinated (she was working in Boots in Bournemouth). I remember exactly where I was when I first heard about the September 11th terrorist attacks (I was standing outside Haywards Heath railway station, talking on the phone to my sister). And you can probably remember similar details from similar events. Scientists call these 'Flashbulb Memories'.

You can probably remember vivid details about what clothes you were wearing on your wedding day, or the time you woke up on the day your child was born. That's because all of these events had an emotional impact on you.

Earlier, when I talked about Memory through Visualisation, I mentioned these points. I said: **These kinds of memories are called flashbulb memories, and the reason they are so strong is because of the emotion associated with them.**

Emotion is like superglue for memory. It relates to our evolution, and that is why the emotional aspect makes storytelling powerful.

Meaning

Something else about emotions that makes stories powerful is 'meaning'.

Meaning comes from the emotional side of our brains, not the rational side. We think of things as good or bad because they have an emotional impact on us. For example, I like chocolate because of the emotions I get from the sugar rush it gives me. And I know why stories are important for training because I've always felt good when I see how much they help trainees understand.

Stories both help us remember things and help us understand the meaning of things. In the next section, we'll look at how to craft a story.

- ## **Crafting Stories**

According to Lisa Cron, author of *Wired for Story*, stories are the language of experience. What a beautiful and entirely accurate definition! If we look at the basic structure of a story, we can clearly see why this is the case.

Any story can be summarised into these 4 basic words:
- **Someone**
- **Wants**
- **But**
- **So**

Those words pretty much sum up the human experience.

Firstly, it's always someone's experience. Experience happens to individuals, because individuals have feelings and can tell you what that experience means to them. And because they can tell you, you can relate to it as well.

For example, let's take the story about a Commercial Airlines Pilot called Chesley. He's a good, old-fashioned family man who's been flying planes for over 40 years. Today's flight should be just like any other, and he's looking forward to getting back home to seeing his family.

Secondly, the thing that helps us relate to the individual's experience is knowing what they want and why they want it.

For example, Chesley wants to land his plane. (Okay, that doesn't sound interesting, that just sounds normal. But why does he want to land his plane?) The plane was struck by some birds shortly after take-off and has now lost power in both engines. He needs to land it within the next 2 minutes. Otherwise, it will crash. And there are 155 people on board. Now, this is more likely to get your attention.

Thirdly, the BUT! A good story will always have something get in the way of the main character getting what they want. For example, Chesley wants to land his plane within the next 2 minutes. Air Traffic Control has cleared him to land at the nearest airport, BUT it's too far away and he won't be able to get the plane there before it hits the ground.

And finally, the solution, the SO. So what does Chesley do? He lines his plane up with the river below, and glides it down. It lands on the water, safely, and all passengers and crew on board survive.

I actually didn't make that story up. This is a real story, famously known as *The Miracle on the Hudson.* The Captain's name was Chesley Sullenberger, more famously known as Captain Sully. It happened in 2009, and you may have seen it on the news at that time. I definitely recommend you read his book, *Sully: My Search for What Really Matters,* because there are lot of lessons that come out from this story.

Story Structure

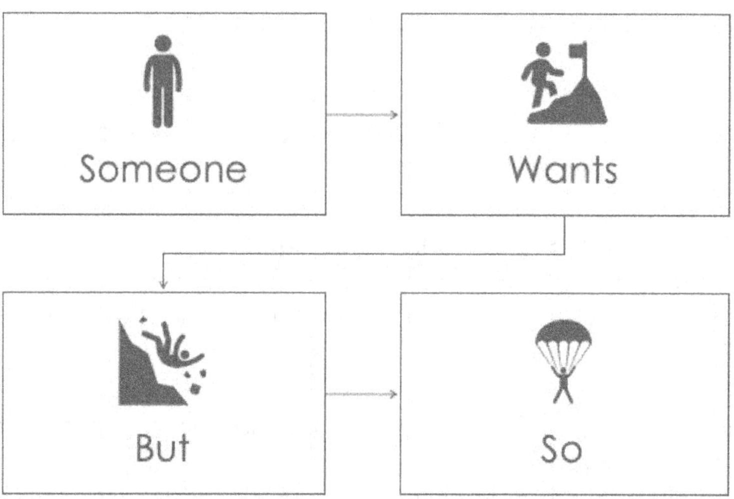

What's the Point?

In training, any story you share should make a point. It should be directly relevant to the topic you are training and your objectives. And it should help learners understand your point clearly enough to be able to start putting it into action.

So what's the point of *The Miracle on the Hudson* story? In the way I told it above, it was to show an example of the Someone, Wants, But, So structure of stories. But there are a lot more points that can be taken from that story.

If you look at Captain Sully's reflections on this event, he summarises the story as a lesson on the value of experience. In one interview he said: 'One way of looking at this might be that for 42 years, I've been making small, regular deposits in this bank of experience, education and training. And on January 15, the balance was sufficient so that I could make a very large withdrawal.' (This quote can be found in many places on the Internet!)

If I wanted to demonstrate Sully's point in that story, I could emphasise more of the details. I could share a bit more of his background—for example, his experience of working in the Air Force. During that time, some of his friends died in horrific accidents. Sully always reflected deeply on what happened in those instances, and what lessons he could take from those experiences and apply to his own life.

I could also emphasise how much his experience helped him in that moment. I could talk about how calm and professional he and his co-pilot acted when faced with immediate danger. I could talk about his decision-making process that led him to land on the Hudson River, and how, in later investigations, it was revealed that Captain Sully's judgement was actually the best decision given the circumstances (it was proven in simulators that they wouldn't have been able to make it to the nearest airport in time).

As you can see, the same story can be used to demonstrate multiple points. It all depends on what details you highlight.

Experiment

The first time you tell your story, it might not go down as well as you hoped. It can sometimes take several refinements before you get a story that both resonates with your audience and helps make your point. So don't give up. Keep refining it until you finally get it right.

Next, we'll look at some more ways of how you can refine it.

- ## Show, Don't Tell

Some types of information are just difficult to take in. For example, technical specifications can seem like a foreign language, big numbers can be difficult to relate to, and legal terminology can be mind-numbingly dull.

But what if we have something important to say that will be difficult for our learners to take in? How can we help them understand?

Well, we can use a principle from storytelling to make even the most complex, vague, and dull concepts more relatable, which is: Show, Don't Tell.

At the heart of this principle is a handy and simple bit of brain science.

Consider for a moment where you are. How do you know where you are? And how do you know what's around you? How do you know you're in a quiet or a noisy place? How do you know you are drinking coffee or tea? How do you know the seat you're sitting on is comfortable or uncomfortable?

You know all the answers to those questions because of your five senses. You can see, hear, smell, taste, and feel the world around you. It is through the five senses that our brains take in information about the world around us.

When we try to describe things with language, there are some words that connect very strongly to the five senses. As soon as the other person hears these words, straight away, like a 4D cinema, their brains will start projecting images, sounds, scents, tastes, or feelings in their mind. We call this type of language 'vivid language'.

The opposite of vivid language is abstract language. When people hear abstract language they don't have pictures, sounds, etc. in their minds. Instead, they have to think about what those words mean.

For example, don't think of chocolate ice cream.

What are you thinking of now? I bet you are thinking of chocolate ice cream! As soon as you saw those words, your mind probably started projecting images of chocolate ice cream. You could probably smell and taste it, you might have had the sounds of an ice cream shop come to mind, and maybe even the feeling of eating chocolate ice cream on a hot summer's day. But the words 'Don't think of' had zero impact on you, because those words are abstract words.

As can be seen from this example, vivid language trumps abstract language.

So how do we use this? When I train behaviour change in things like productivity, change management, or even train the trainer courses, one of the things I share is the importance of giving clear rules for helping people make better decisions. And I do so with a vivid example, which I also mentioned earlier, in the section called **Require No Decision-Making in the Moment of Action:**

'Imagine you want to start living a healthier life. So you decide that from now on you are going to only eat healthy foods. And that is now your rule for deciding what to eat whenever it's time to choose food: "Eat Healthy Foods".

So you go to the convenience store for a mid-morning snack. You look at the options around you. You see chocolate bars, yoghurt, sports drinks, sandwiches, and dried fruits. Then you think, which ones are healthy foods? Chocolate definitely isn't. Is yoghurt healthy? Are sports drinks healthy? Are those sandwiches healthy? Are those dried fruits healthy? You get confused and eventually run out of time, then your old habits kick in and so you decide to buy a chocolate bar. This "Eat Healthy Foods" rule is not useful enough.

Instead, we can change the rule to something more actionable. We could use "Eat Natural Foods".

Then the next time you go to the convenience store you don't get confused. Is chocolate natural? Nope. Neither are those yoghurts, sports drinks, sandwiches or dried fruits. So you walk out of the store and go to the fruit shop across the road! Lots of natural foods there!'

With this simple example, you can probably picture the selection of food available in the convenience store. You can probably feel the confusion you'd experience trying to make that decision yourself.

Not only is it a vivid example, but again it's showing how (set a rule that helps you make quick decisions when you need to act) and why (because otherwise you get confused and easily revert back to old habits).

Numerous Applications

The Show, Don't Tell principle can be applied in almost any communication context. Not only will it make you an effective trainer, but it can also make you an effective presenter, sales person, and leader. Have a look at the examples below and consider how you could use vivid language to make them easier for other people to understand.

Example 1: You are a real estate agent trying to sell an apartment. You know the following about this apartment:

- It is 200 square meters
- It has 3 bedrooms, 2 bathrooms, and 2 living room areas
- It is 500 meters away from the nearest subway station

How could you use vivid language to help potential buyers more easily picture them living in this apartment?

Answer: You could describe how many of their family members could live in it, the activities they could do in each of the rooms (e.g. you can watch TV in one living room and then play ping pong in another!), and you can even describe their short, 10-minute walk to the subway station every morning for their commute.

Example 2: You are a bicycle manufacturer and have just made a brand-new, portable bicycle. It has the following features:
- It has a GPS device on the handlebars
- It weighs less than one pound
- It can be folded up into the size of a cereal box
-

How could you use vivid language to help customers more easily picture their day to day life with this bicycle?

Answer: You could describe how they'd never get lost again, because they'd always have GPS with them. They'd never have to get their phones out to check the way. Instead, they just look at their handlebars. And it's so lightweight and small they can easily fit it into a backpack!

Always Show, Never Tell

To always be making an impact, use vivid language whenever you tell a story or give an example. It will help engage your learners, help them understand, and also help them remember.

Show, Don't Tell

Talk to the senses

• Using Analogies

When introducing something your learners *don't* know, use something they *do* know. This is what analogies are for.

Analogies are amazing learning tools. They are also amazing persuasion tools.

What, exactly, are analogies? Simply put, they are connections between something they don't know and something they do know. As you stand on a cliff face with your idea, they stand on another cliff face off in the distance with their ideas. The analogy is the bridge between your two cliff faces, linking your ideas together. In fact, one of the most famous movies in history exists because of a production team's use of analogy.

In the 1970s, a filmmaking team had a great idea for a horror movie involving an alien. Their one challenge was getting the studios to accept their idea. So they thought about how they could make their pitch as appealing as possible, and the movie *Jaws* kept on coming to mind. *Jaws* had been a big hit in 1975, millions had seen it, and its success could not be denied. So, when pitching their idea, they simply said '*Jaws*, in Space'.

And so, in 1979, the movie *Alien* was released. Its success speaks for itself. I am sure you have at least heard of it, and have probably seen it. All the producers did was connect their new idea (terrifying alien in space) to a very successful, well established idea ('*Jaws*').

Brian Clark, who owns the website *Copyblogger*, offers this definition of an analogy:

'An analogy is comparable to a metaphor and simile in that it shows how two different things are similar, but it's a bit more complex.

Rather than a figure of speech, an analogy is more of a logical argument. The structure of the argument leads to a new understanding for the audience.

When you deliver an analogy, you demonstrate how two things are alike by pointing out shared characteristics (a hunter with an unloaded umbrella and an elderly man who is "firing blanks" sexually). The goal is to show that if two things are similar in some ways, they are similar in other ways as well.'

(Source: https://www.copyblogger.com/persuasive-analogies/)

To use analogies, just think of what your learners can relate to. Think of these things when you create your own analogy:

- **Things everyone does every day (e.g. brush teeth, read the news, take the subway, etc.)**
- **Everyday objects (e.g. doors, boxes, tables, keys, mobile phones, etc.)**
- **Famous things and people (e.g. movies, songs, landmarks, holidays, celebrities, politicians, etc.)**
- **Common life experiences (e.g. breaking up with a loved one, buying a house, the birth of a child, etc.)**
- **Jobs or industries (e.g. plumber, banking, scientist, astronaut)**
- **Animals (e.g. parrots, lions, ants, etc.)**
- **Environmental elements (e.g. weather, natural disasters, landscapes)**
- **Places (e.g. The Sahara Desert, Paris, your backyard)**

Using Analogies

Things everyone does everyday
- brush teeth, read the news, take the subway, etc.

Everyday objects
- doors, boxes, tables, keys, mobile phones, etc.

Famous things and people
- movies, songs, landmarks, holidays, celebrities, politicians, etc.

Common life experiences
- breaking up with a loved one, buying a house, the birth of a child, etc.

Jobs or industries
- plumber, banking, scientist, astronaut, etc.

Animals
- parrots, lions, ants, etc.

Environmental elements
- weather, natural disasters, landscapes, etc.

Places
- The Sahara Desert, Paris, your backyard, etc.

For example, in the next section, I am going to make the point about how all the different learners in our training room already have so much experience they don't need to listen to us explain everything. I came up with an analogy to more clearly represent this idea.

I tried to think of things that represent the variety of experiences different people bring to the room. I looked at the above list, and Everyday Objects brought to mind the idea of puzzles. We, as trainers, are trying to paint a complete picture for them, but a lot of the time they already have different pieces of the picture, like a puzzle. Rather than paint the picture for them, invite them to share their different puzzle pieces and put them all together themselves.

- ## From Showing to Asking

Adults already know a lot of stuff, so having to patiently sit down and listen to us talking about stuff they already know can get quite boring. Instead, we should ask questions.

A good analogy is that of a puzzle. Learners come to training to solve a puzzle. Each learner already has certain pieces of the puzzle, and all learners in the room, combined, have all the pieces they need to solve it. We can use questions to draw out their individual puzzle pieces, and then use more questions to link those pieces together. After enough questions are asked and answered, the puzzle is complete.

There are several key benefits to using questions.

Firstly, it raises engagement levels. One of the definitions of the word 'engage' is to involve someone in a discussion. And, quite naturally, the simplest way of involving someone in a discussion is to ask a question. You'll notice that, when you do so, you will have grabbed their attention and they will be actively reflecting.

This brings me to the next benefit. Remember, learning involves reflecting. Our questions direct our learners to reflect on specific things. Instead of passively absorbing information, questions help our learners actively learn.

Another benefit is that you get immediate feedback. Questions help you to gauge how well they are keeping up. If they can answer your question correctly, then you know they are following along. If they struggle to answer, then you know you need to take it back a few steps.

The most interesting benefit is that you can learn new things. If you ask an open question, you can get any answer, including answers you weren't expecting.

As fun as storytelling techniques are, however, we really shouldn't overdo them. **As a general rule, if you think you can get learners to make your point just by asking questions, then ask questions. Questions make for a far more powerful learning experience.**

So, let's have a look at how to use questions effectively.

- ## How Not to Put People on the Spot

The biggest challenge with asking questions occurs when no one answers. Once you throw your question out there, and are met with silence, you will feel very uncomfortable. For a lot of less experienced trainers, this can put them off from asking questions again.

But these problems are easily overcome if we ask questions in the right way. If you ask a question in the wrong way, you risk putting learners on the spot. As a result, they will feel uncomfortable and close down, and no one else will want to answer your questions again. But if you do it in the right way, you'll make them feel safe enough to open up and share.

There are 3 different ways of asking a question to a group. Each way has its pros and cons, and therefore needs to be used at the right time.

Three Phases of Questioning

As we progress through a topic, we should ask questions in different ways at different phases:
1. **Ask, Then Wait**
2. **Ask, Then Direct**
3. **Direct, Then Ask**

Ask, Then Wait

Ask a question, then wait for someone to answer. The implication here is that we open the question to everyone in the group, and we wait for someone who is comfortable with answering.

This type of questioning is best suited for use close to the beginning of a topic. At the beginning, we are assuming our learners don't know much. We don't expect anyone to have an answer, so it is unreasonable to pick on people.

We don't want to pick on people if they don't yet have an answer. This makes learners feel uncomfortable. If we think back to the SCARF model, then we can see why it makes learners feel uncomfortable. It can reduce their status, they might feel it's unfair, and there might even be uncertainty about what happens if they answer incorrectly.

At this stage, as well, we are asking more questions about things the learners knew before this training. We want to draw out the knowledge they have already, and then link it to whatever new knowledge we have to share with them.

One particular challenge of this phase of questioning can be getting people to feel comfortable sharing answers. As we finish asking the question, we may be greeted by silence. Silence can make us feel incredibly awkward. As a result of that awkwardness, less experienced trainers tend to just answer the question themselves.

Consider the process learners must go through to answer a question. It's somewhat like this:
1. Take in the question.
2. Check that they understand the question.
3. Search for an answer.
4. Evaluate the answer.
5. Judge if they want to share the answer or not.
6. Plan how to share it.

All of that can take a long time, especially for less confident learners, so be prepared to wait for an answer.

Whenever I ask a question, I open my arms out wide to signal to the audience that it's in their hands now. I work with a lot of Chinese learners, and they are sometimes reluctant to be the first to speak out, especially if they are introverted (like my engineers were). But I simply tell them 'I can wait here all day' and, eventually, someone always answers. So, be patient, wait for them to go through the process of answering, and encourage them to answer.

Ask, Then Direct

Ask your question, then direct it at a particular person. The implication of this technique is that it should be used at a time when learners should already know certain things.

However, there is another implication. We are not directing first. We are asking the question, then pausing, and *then* directing it at a particular person. The advantage of pausing before directing is that we are still involving all learners.

Once I direct a question to a particular learner, everyone else will switch off. They know the question does not involve them, so there's no need to pay attention. The focus is all on that one person in particular.

And it may seem that we are giving that person a bit too much pressure. But, at this stage of the training, it should be reasonable to expect them to know the answer. We should have covered enough content already, and given them enough reflection and practice opportunities to reasonably expect them to have an answer.

With 'Ask, Then Direct' we are about halfway through the topic, but not quite there yet.

We might be at the 'Practice' or 'Reflect' stages. We might be asking them to share their plans for practice or their insights from reflection with everyone. With everyone focussed on the same question, it can be interesting for them to hear other people's answers and compare them to their own.

Direct, Then Ask

Point to one particular person, then ask the question.

This technique is used more as a test, and should be reserved for the final stages of the topic. Typically, I use this technique more during the 'Commit' phase. Here, their plan of commitment is not always relevant to other learners, but it's important that they have a plan. It is here that I start to pick on people and challenge them. I want to make sure that they are committing to something they will genuinely see through.

Where a lot of less experienced trainers go wrong is that they use 'Direct, Then Ask' too early into the session. When you ask someone who doesn't have or know the answer, then you put them on the spot and make them feel uncomfortable. This phase of questioning should only be reserved for later stages when people should have answers.

Now that we have looked at the different ways of presenting a question to a group, let's look at how to actually construct questions that gets answers.

3 Phases of Questioning

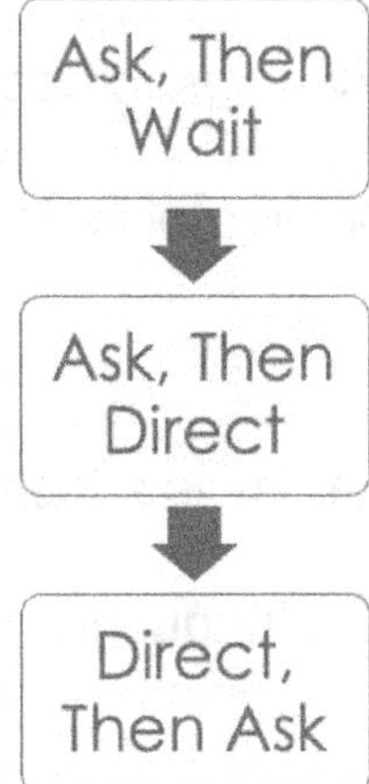

• Constructing Questions

If you've done everything you can to avoid putting people on the spot and you are still not getting answers, then it's probably because they don't understand the question or because you have not framed or constructed the question properly.

There are certain building blocks we can use when constructing our questions to ensure our questions get understood and get answers. These building blocks are:
- **Context**
- **Open Question**
- **Clue**
- **Closed Question**

But before we get to the building blocks, there is an important starting point.

What's Your Point?

Questions in training can be used as a way of making a point. During the 'Guiding' phase, you are probably going to have lots of points that you want to make, so it makes sense to know what the point is before asking your questions.

I'll be using an example to introduce these simple building blocks. First of all, let me clarify what the point is that I am trying to make in this example.

This point is something I normally share during any communication skills related training (and is something I shared in the 'Show, Don't Tell' section earlier). It is simply that, to make your words easier to understand and have a deeper impact, we need to use vivid language, which describes things that our five senses can relate to (things we can see, touch, hear, etc.). If you are describing something overly theoretical, abstract, or complicated, then it really helps to describe it in a vivid way.

Let's see how we can use these building blocks to make the above point.

Context

The biggest cause of confusing questions is a lack of context.

For example, with my point about vivid language, I could start with the question: 'How do we take in information?'

But this question has little context. As a result, I would get a wide range of answers that are far from my point. People would suggest things like TV, email, radio waves, etc. These answers aren't what I'm looking for, so I need to give more context.

So instead I could ask: 'How do you take in information about the world around you? How do you know that's coffee you're drinking? How do you know I am speaking? How do you know if that chair you're sitting on is plastic or leather?'

Whenever I ask the question in this way, I almost instantly get the answer 'Through the five senses', and that is the answer I am looking for.

It's always useful to add more context to your question. Think of context a bit like using a marker to highlight an area on a 'Where's Wally?' picture. Without marking that particular area, you'll scan the whole picture. You'll waste a lot of time looking in the wrong areas for Wally. But if I use a marker to highlight the rough area where Wally is, then you'll look in the right area and will find him faster.

Open Questions

Open questions have many benefits. The most interesting benefit is that we are more likely to hear answers that we hadn't considered before. Another benefit is that open questions really make our learners think.

The right answer to an open question is not always obvious. There is no list of answers to choose from. Learners must choose by themselves how to find the answer, so it forces them to reflect deeply, to dig through what they already know, and form new connections.

Another benefit is that open questions are easy for us to use. All we need to do is remember the six wives and one husband:
- **Who**
- **What**
- **Where**
- **When**
- **Why**
- **Which**
- **How**

With my point about using vivid language, I've already brought to learners' minds the idea of the five senses. Now I can go on and ask another question to start forming those new connections. So I could ask them: 'How can we use the five senses in our language when we are communicating with other people?'

The answer to this question is not obvious, and forces learners to sit back and think a little. Normally, after a few seconds, someone will say something like: 'We can use words that paint a picture.'

Our goal is to keep on asking open questions until learners start to realise how they can apply this point to their problems. So I might go on to ask the following questions:
- What's the benefit of using the five senses in our language?
- Could someone give me an example of using this to make something clearer?
- How could you use this in your work?

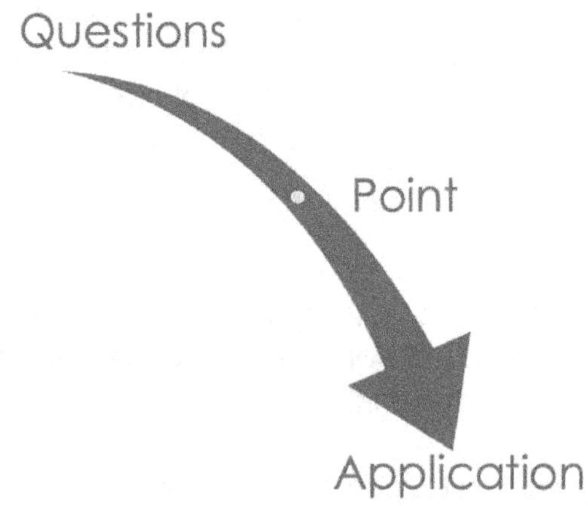

As you use open questions, you can do so for different purposes:
- Simplify terminology
- Share examples
- Use the point to analyse an example
- Use the point to solve a challenge
- Describe how they can apply it to their work

Firstly, you could collectively add some terminology to the concept you are talking about. It's not very efficient to always say 'Using the five senses in our language', so by questioning my learners on what word we could use to describe this, they would probably agree on 'vivid'. Maybe they will agree on another word, and that's OK as well. Accuracy of vocabulary is not important; what's important is that they understand it. And once we've got that word, we can now talk about that concept more efficiently.

Secondly, we could add in some examples to make the point clearer. It's good to ask learners for their own examples. When they can share their own examples, this helps increase participation and keeps everyone engaged. However, a downside of asking learners for their own examples is that they don't always have them. So it's always best to come prepared with examples that you're ready to share in case they do not have any.

Thirdly, we can give them some 'analysis questions' to see how the concept works. With my point about vivid language, I use the example of 'Don't think of chocolate ice cream'. After I say that sentence, I ask them what they're thinking of. Most people are thinking of chocolate ice cream. Then I ask them why. Eventually, someone realises that the only vivid words in that sentence were 'chocolate' and 'ice cream'. Now they've seen how impactful vivid words are.

Different Types of Questions

Terminology Questions
- Ask them to simplify the language they use to make their point easier for others to understand.

Example Questions
- Ask them to change their abstract point into a concrete example.

Analysis Questions
- Give them an example that demonstrates the point and ask them to analyse how the point works.

Challenge Questions
- Give them a challenge or puzzle and ask them to use the point to solve it.

Application Questions
- Ask them to explain how they could use this point to solve their own problems.

Fourthly, we can give them some challenges to get them reflecting on how they can use this. Here, I normally give an example and say '571,231,000 pounds of paper towels could be saved every year if each person only used one paper towel every time they washed their hands'. I first ask them to analyse that statistic, and tell me what makes it difficult to understand. Normally, someone will come out and say that it's a big number and it means nothing because it's too big to understand. So then I ask them how they could use vivid language to make it easier to understand. Eventually, someone will come out and say something like 'We could describe how many football stadiums that many paper towels could fit into'.

Finally, we can ask them to think about how they can use this concept to solve their own problems. They may have shared examples earlier of challenges they are facing, and so now we could ask them to think about how they could use this concept to solve that challenge. But now we are verging into the territory of 'practice and reflection', and those tend to require more structured approaches to get the most out of them. So whilst you are still in the 'guide' phase, it's best to avoid going too deep here, and instead only attempt this when the answer is quite obvious.

Using a steady flow of open questions to take our learners through the 'guide' phase is our ultimate goal. However, sometimes open questions fail and we need to take a step back to get back on track again. To do that we can use 'Clues' and 'Closed Questions'.

Clues

Using clues is basically the same as building more context, but is something we do when our open questions fail and we want to get them back on track again.

For example, maybe I ask the question 'What's the benefit of using vivid language?' and I am met with a room full of blank faces. So I know I need to change things up and add a clue.

I could then say 'What's the benefit of using vivid language? How does it impact people's understanding of what we say?' Adding that section on understanding has given a pretty big clue and, hopefully, they will then respond by saying 'It makes things easier to understand' or 'It helps leave a deeper impact'.

If our clues don't work, we need to change things up yet again. That is when we turn to closed questions.

Closed Questions

Closed questions are easy for everyone. They are especially easy for our learners because they have a 50% chance of getting it right.

They are very useful for us because they help us check people's understanding and guide them in the right direction.

I've just asked 'What's the benefit of using vivid language? How does it impact people's understanding of what we say?' and no one has responded. So now I could try something else. I could use my chocolate ice cream example and say 'Don't think of chocolate ice cream'. I can then ask them the following questions:

- Are you now thinking of chocolate ice cream? Yes or no?
- Are the words chocolate and ice cream vivid? Yes or no?
- What about the words 'Don't think of a'? Are those words vivid? Yes or no?

Once I've got them back on track again with a string of closed questions, I can then go back and ask them some open questions again.

Always Ask

Remember, if you think you can get your learners to make your point for you by asking questions, then ask questions.

Questions have so many more benefits than lectures and even storytelling. They involve everyone, they force people to think, and ultimately help people learn better.

So, where you can, replace *telling* with *asking*.

Constructing Questions

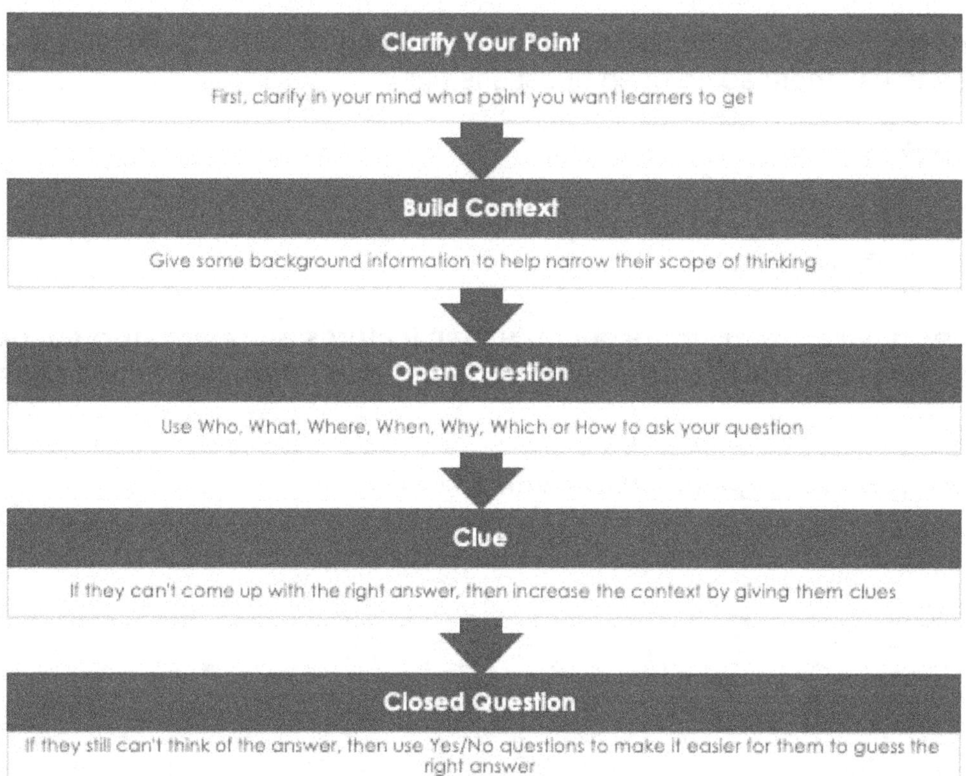

- ## Experiential Learning Activities

Different learners come into the training with different understanding levels. Some of our learners may be at the Why level, whereas others may already be ahead of them at the What or How levels. And some may even think they are at How, but are actually at Why!

Not everyone is going to have the patience to listen to explanations about things they already know, or run through a series of questions for which they know all the answers. So, a great way of getting everyone on the same page is to use experiential learning activities.

An experiential learning activity is simply an activity that has been designed to give learners an experience that they can learn from.

Experiential learning activities are different from practice activities. Practice activities give learners a chance to practice using what they have already learnt and improve. Experiential learning activities don't require that learners have learnt anything yet. They typically involve following the instructions and seeing what happens.

In a way, experiential learning activities serve the same purpose as lectures. Lectures try to convey information. Experiential learning activities provide an experience through which learners can discover or realise that same information by themselves. But in order for an experiential learning activity to achieve that purpose, it needs to be followed up with a debrief.

A debrief is where we use questions to draw out that information. We ask learners to reflect on that experience and share what they learned. We then take that information and link it back to the points that we wanted them to learn from that activity. If you structure the activity and the debrief correctly, then those points will come out naturally and there is no need for us trainers to share them.

The debrief is where we move into the realm of 'Reflection', which we'll look at in a few sections. But for now let's look at how to choose and use experiential activities.

- ## Choosing Experiential Learning Activities

The topic you are training is probably something other people have trained before. If that is the case, then there are probably pre-made experiential learning activities relevant to that topic. Because they are pre-made, this means you don't have to go through the hassle of designing them from scratch.

Designing an experiential learning activity is more a case of getting it wrong enough times to get it right. It can be very tricky to get an activity that creates the exact experience required to help learners realise your desired learning points. Nonetheless, once you get it right, it can be very rewarding having an experiential activity that you designed yourself.

Most of the experiential activities I use have been taken from elsewhere. I've either read them in books, participated in them in other trainings myself, or have been taught them by someone else. As I learn how to run these activities, I start tweaking them to find a way that works for my purpose.

To find experiential learning activities, you can do a quick web search, which will reveal a few. But some of the best ones are found in pre-made training materials, so try to get access to those. A great website for experiential activities is the following website (also by the same author as the *Barnga* book, Thiagi, who is a well-known facilitator and expert on experiential learning): http://www.thiagi.com/gameblog/.

If you want to design your own, you can use the tips in the next section to do so.

• Designing Experiential Learning Activities

To design an experiential learning activity from the ground up, you can use the following process:

1. **Summarise your desired learning points.**
2. **Think of situations where those learning points apply.**
3. **Think of the specific challenges in those situations. Make sure those challenges are still relevant to the learning points.**
4. **Consider how you could recreate those challenges in the classroom.**
5. **Take what ideas you have and simplify them.**

For example, let's say we want to create an experiential learning activity to compare the difference between designing something from scratch and using something pre-made. If I follow the above steps, then I might come out with the following ideas:

1. Summarise desired learning points:
   - Designing takes time
   - Getting it right happens through trial and error
   - Borrowing is faster
2. Think of situations where those learning points apply:
   - Designing a kitchen
   - Designing a website
   - Designing a garden
3. Specific challenges in those situations:
   - Coming up with a design.
   - Having a time limit.
   - Matching the design to the budget and resources they have.
4. Recreating those challenges in the classroom:
   - Divide the class into groups. Give each group a set number of cardboard boxes, a set of specifications, and ask them to build a model kitchen using those resources according to the specifications. Then give only some groups a few design samples. Give all groups the same time limit and see what happens. (Do the groups that have the samples perform better than the groups that don't have samples?)
   - Give two groups a Lego kit for making a helicopter (or any other pre-designed model). Give one group the instructions and another group no instructions. Give them a set time to complete it and see how long it takes.
5. Simplify those ideas:
   - Use resources that are already available in the classroom (e.g. paper and pens)
   - Use a smaller and cheaper Lego kit

You might have to go through the above process several times to get an idea you are happy with. Then, once you have it, you probably have to go through a lot of trial and error to enable learners to come out with the learning points you desire.

A Word about Time

In my opinion, experiential learning activities should not take much time. The most important parts of training are the Practice, Reflection, and Commitment sections. This 'Guide' section exists to input knowledge so that people can practice using it.

Some training I see sells itself as highly experiential. From an engagement point of view, that is really good. But, from a learning effectiveness point of view, it's lacking. More time in training needs to be spent reflecting on 'How can I use this?' as opposed to 'What did I just learn from that?' So, think of experiential learning activities as a stepping stone to get your learners to discussing 'How can I use this?' faster. If you have another way of getting to that discussion faster, then use that other way.

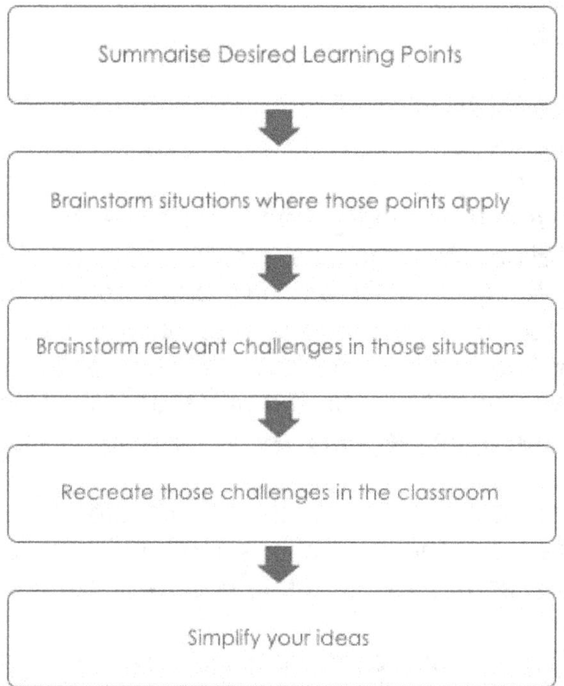

• Sample Experiential Learning Activities

Here, I'll share a few examples of experiential learning activities I frequently use:
- The Communication Gap Game
- Barnga
- Card Triangles

The Communication Gap Game

This game is great for anything communication-related. Its purpose is to help learners realise the barriers to verbal communication and discover effective strategies for overcoming those barriers.

Learners are split into pairs. Each learner is then given a different picture. They cannot show their pictures to each other. They must then describe their picture to their partner without showing them the picture. The partner must listen and draw that picture, according to the instructions. Once one partner has finished drawing, they then swap and the other person has to listen and draw.

I typically give them a 12-minute time limit to finish drawing both pictures. Once the time is up, I ask them to compare the picture they drew with their partner's original copy.

For the debrief, I normally ask them:
- What were the challenges they encountered?
- What effective strategies did they use?
- How is this similar to communicating at work?

Barnga

Barnga is a fantastic game for any course related to cross-cultural communication. Its purpose is to help learners realise how they react when they encounter cultural differences and to discover more effective ways of responding and managing their behaviour.

Learners are split into groups of 4. I first explain to the group that this game will test their ability to learn quickly as a group. This is actually a lie to mask the real purpose of the game (which I'll get to in a little while). Each group is then given instructions for a card game called Five Tricks. They have 10 minutes to learn this card game before the real competition begins.

After 10 minutes, I take the instructions away and inform each group that they can no longer talk with each other. They can only communicate through body language.

We then start the competition. The competition has 5 rounds, each lasting 5 minutes. At the end of each round, the person who got the highest score must move to the group to their right. The person with the lowest score moves to the group to their left. All others must remain seated. There is still no communication allowed, until the end of the game.

What they don't know is that each team was given slightly different instructions. They all assume everyone was given the same instructions, so this creates big challenges for them. For example, for one team, an Ace is the highest card whereas, for another team, an Ace is the lowest. As the players move into different groups, they suddenly find people playing differently. This creates misunderstandings and sometimes even conflict.

This game does a fantastic job of simulating the reality of working with different cultures. It's hard to communicate and everyone is playing by different rules. We see a lot of different ways of reacting to these circumstances. Some are effective and some are ineffective.

When I come to debrief, I typically ask:
- What assumptions did people make when playing this game?
- What reactions did people have?
- What is the most effective way of thinking when encountering cultural differences?
- What is the most effective way of behaving?
- How is this similar to real life?

For a much more detailed explanation on how to play this game, along with all of the instruction sheets that you need, I strongly recommend reading the book, *Barnga: A Simulation Game on Cultural Clashes* by Sivasailam 'Thiagi' Thiagarajan.

Card Triangles

This is a really fun game for simulating a negotiation situation. Its purpose is for learners to discover the challenges of and effective solutions for planning and executing a negotiation strategy and adapting to sudden changes.

Using a deck of playing cards, cut each card into 4 triangles (this requires about half an hour of preparation time!). Divide your learners into groups, then randomly distribute the card triangles evenly between each group.

Explain to each group that soon they must negotiate with other groups to exchange cards. Their goal is to have the most amount of complete cards by the end of the time limit. This means they will need to find which teams have the triangles they need, and negotiate on an acceptable exchange for those triangles. The team with the highest amount of complete cards wins.

Give them 15 minutes to prepare their strategy. This will involve analysing the triangles they already have and planning on which cards they want to complete and which triangles they are willing to exchange. It may also involve deciding on roles for each player. After 15 minutes, give them 25 minutes to go and exchange with other groups.

This game is really fun, and does a surprisingly good job of simulating a market economy. Sometimes they will find they have a golden triangle that is worth a lot to another group. Some teams will try to be sneaky and lie to the other groups about which cards they have. Some may even try to steal. And as the timer gets closer to zero, suddenly everyone goes a bit crazy as they get desperate to complete their cards.

When I debrief this, I typically ask:
- How effective were you at planning? Why?
- How effective was your strategy?
- Which groups were you more willing to exchange with? Why?
- Which groups were you less willing to exchange with? Why?
- What things happened that you didn't predict?
- If you were to play this again, what would you do differently next time?
- How is this similar to real life?

Guiding Summary

The following flowchart is a summary of everything we have looked at in this section:

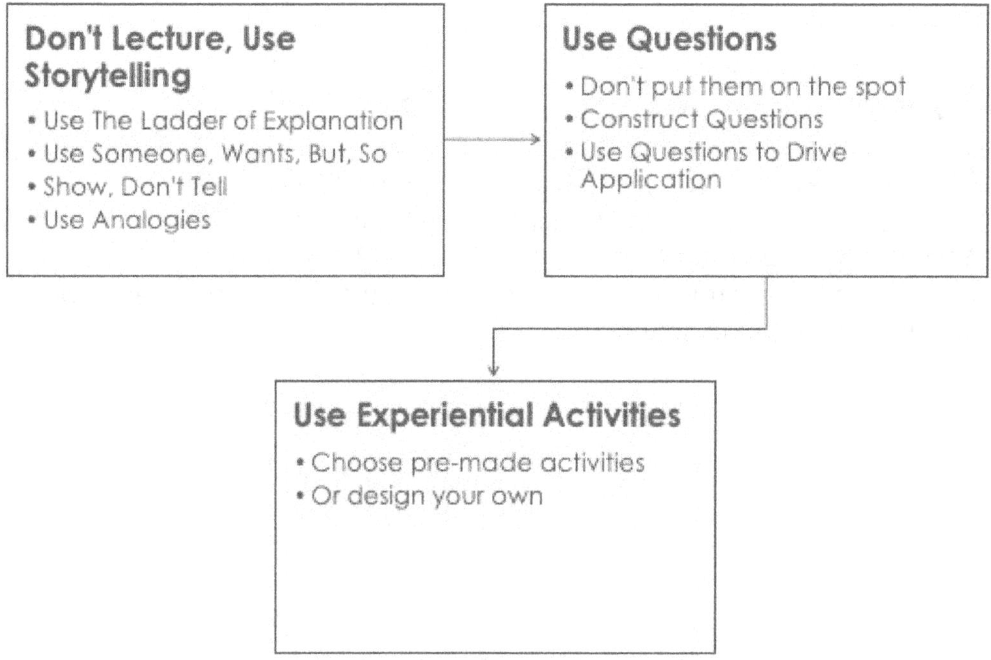

Practicing

Practice helps us improve. It gives us a platform to make mistakes and learn from those mistakes. Through practice, we can eventually master our skills.

In training, practice tests whether or not the learner can achieve the training objective. Testing them should provide plenty of feedback opportunities. This way, if they don't achieve it first time, they will, at least, gain valuable feedback to help them improve the next time.

The challenge lies in designing effective practice activities. Much training out there is littered with ineffective practice, or even worse, has no practice at all.

I have seen numerous examples of technical 'training' that was instead just a lecture—two hours of bombarding learners with information and expecting them to absorb it. Once the time is up, learners still don't know what they are supposed to do with this information. They return to work and forget everything.

I have also seen numerous examples of learners being overwhelmed through practice. For example, in Presentation Skills training, learners may learn skills such as voice control and how to use body language. Then, when it comes to practice, they are asked to stand up and deliver a full presentation using those skills they just learnt. However, they struggle to remember what to present, and spend so much time focussing on remembering what to present that they completely forget to use the skills they just learnt. They are overwhelmed and don't have the cognitive capacity to focus on actually practicing.

I've also seen many examples where practice is considered as a grand finale and nothing more. Learners spend three days listening to lectures and discussing concepts. Then, at the end of the last day, they finally get to come up and practice for the first time. But, instead of practicing, they are asked to demonstrate what they've learnt. They have no chance to make mistakes and gain feedback, and no chance to reflect either. They are simply expected to have learnt by listening alone. We all know that those words that have been going into their ears will not magically transform into skills without practice!

So, in this section, we'll look at how to design practice, how to optimise practice, and how to help learners get the most out of practice.

- ## Start with Objectives

If we want to design effective practice activities, then where exactly do we start?

The starting point is where some people go off-track with practice. I say some people, but I have also been guilty of this in the past. Before I started working more systematically, I'd spend most of my time trying to think of fun games to play. I'd focus more on getting people up and moving about and laughing. I thought that's what good practice was all about. But it's not.

Good practice is about applying focussed effort towards achieving specific results. Give learners a goal to achieve, show them how to achieve it, give them a chance to try achieving it and, if they don't achieve it, then keep on helping them until they do achieve it.

Logically, if we want our learners to achieve specific results, then we need to start by defining those specific results. We do this this by writing training objectives, which I'll show you how to do in the next few sections.

In my experience of training people on this, it is so, so easy to overlook the importance of objectives. Writing objectives can seem a bit boring, and is far less fun than finding good games to play or designing fancy PPTs. So it tends to get left out. But it is absolutely essential you do this, and here is why.

Why Write Training Objectives?

A good objective can do a lot of your instructional design work for you. For example, I set a really useful objective for a module on voice control that I designed for a basic Presentation Skills training. A problem that a lot of people have when presenting is they get nervous and so speak too fast. To present more effectively, they need to speak at a more controlled speed. So I set the following objective:

'Deliver a 20-word presentation in 10-15 seconds.'

This objective is pretty much an activity in itself. All I needed to do is write a 20-word script, and ask learners to take their phones or watches out and time themselves reading the script.

Not only is it an effective activity, it's also a great reference. Learners have a standard to adhere to (20 words in 10-15 seconds), and so know the exact speaking speed they need to be aiming for. They can even use their feedback (the time on their phone's timer) to compare their performance against this standard.

It also helps me focus the content of my training. Any content I introduce in that module should be specifically aimed at helping them achieve that speaking speed and overcoming the barriers to achieving that speaking speed.

It helps me evaluate all of the content I have collected during my research. I can judge the content against this objective and decide if it's a 'need to know' or a 'nice to know', and if it's a vital 20% or a not-so-vital 80%.

Setting a good training objective makes your training easier to measure and therefore more effective, and it also makes the rest of the design process easier and faster.

Another great advantage is that, if you are selling training to a customer and you are competing with other trainers and training companies, then you can stand out as the only one that can tell your customer exactly how they can measure the success of the training and exactly what their learners will be able to do afterwards. I am constantly amazed at the number of training providers that either don't do this at all, or do it wrong.

Sometimes it might take a long time to write the objectives, and other times it won't take long at all. But one thing is for certain: a good training objective will be a big help and save you a lot of time further down the line.

What do Training Objectives Look Like?

You've probably heard of the SMART acronym, which stands for Specific, Measurable, Achievable, Relevant, and Timely. This is the standard for setting most objectives, but it is not the standard for setting training objectives.

For training objectives, we have something a little different, and a lot more specific. Good training objectives simply consist of 3 key components:
- **Behaviour**
- **Standard**
- **Condition**

This means that our training objectives must describe what the learner should do (behaviour), what results they should achieve (standard), and in what kind of situation they need to be doing this in (condition).

In the following sections, we'll look at how to get each of these just right as well as how to get the most out of our objectives.

Training Objectives

Behaviour

- What they must do to achieve the objective.
- Observable action.

Standard

- How well they must perform.
- Set standards that are both measurable (either quantitative or qualitative) and achievable.

Condition

- Under what conditions must they achieve the objective.
- Clarify When, Where or How.

- ## Defining the Behaviour

The behaviour is simply what the learner must do. Maybe they need to give a presentation, complete a task, or demonstrate something.

There are 3 key conditions this behavioural description must fit:
1. Time-based
2. Action-based
3. Observable

The 1st Condition—Time-based Behaviour

Training objectives answer the following question: *What will the learner be able to do by the end of the training?*

This is a simple question, but it provides excellent guidance. It reminds us that the time frame for achieving this objective is by the end of the training. To ensure every objective answers that question, a fantastic habit is to start each objective with the sentence: *'By the end of the training the learner will be able to…'*

This might look silly, but it is incredibly easy to forget what our training objectives are about. I have reviewed numerous training objectives that fail to answer this question. And even on reviewing my own training objectives, from time to time, I notice that I have steered away as well. At the very least, write this sentence once, then list all training objectives underneath it.

2nd Condition—Action-based Behaviour

Training objectives are all about *doing*. So we need to identify the action that they need to do.

For example, we want to train sales people on how to learn about a customer's needs. Some of the actions they might need to take include:
- Demonstrate active listening
- Use open questions
- Summarise and paraphrase customer responses to check understanding

Some actions are actually a combination of actions. For example:
- Write and review a training objective that includes the 3 Key Components of Effective Training Objectives

The above example includes writing an objective then reviewing it, to be sure it includes all 3 key components (behaviour, standard, and condition). We could write each of the 3 components out in our objective, but that would be a bit more time-consuming. This is another advantage of using tools. Tools condense actions into a package and so, instead of writing all of the actions out, we can just reference the tool that they should use.

3rd Condition—Observable Behaviour

What a lot of trainers and instructional designers forget to do when writing training objectives is ensure that the trainer can actually observe the action in the training room.

For example, think about what's wrong with the following objectives:
- Know the 6-step process…
- Understand the importance of…

How will a trainer know if a learner knows or understands something? **'Know' and 'understand' are two verbs that should NEVER appear in any training objectives.** Knowing and understanding are pretty broad 'actions' (if you can call them that) that take place in the learner's head. Because trainers cannot see knowing and understanding taking place, these words are useless to us.

If you find yourself wanting to write these words, then ask yourself the following question: *What will the learner be able to do as a result of knowing or understanding?*

Maybe they will do one of the following:
- List
- Recall
- State
- Explain
- Give examples of
- Compare
- Define
- Recognise

And so on.

If, as a result of knowing something, they will be able to list something, then use the word 'list' in your objective instead. **Always replace 'know' or 'understand' with verbs that can actually be observed.**

The field of soft skills (communication, emotional intelligence, leadership, etc.) meets a lot of challenges when it comes to observable actions. A lot of soft actions take place in the head, behind closed doors.

Meditation, or mindfulness, is a good example of a skill with unobservable actions. Take a look at the following actions:
- Focus on your breath for a count of 10
- When distracted, note the distraction as a thought or feeling
- Identify where in the body an emotion is felt

How is it possible to observe these actions? Well, we can't. But, if the action is required in order to successfully complete a task, then we *kind of* can. If the task is completed successfully, then they did the action.

Take, for example, the action 'Focus on your breath for a count of 10'. The action here is really just 'focus'. So, we could replace counting the breath with a task that requires focussing on something. The trick is to find a task that can only be successfully completed by doing the desired action, not by any other means.

For example, there is an interesting app available on the iPhone called 'Pause'. This app is designed for the practice of mindfulness. All you need to do is hold your thumb on the screen and follow a dot around at a slow pace. After a little while, it tells you to close your eyes and continue following the dot. This requires a great deal of focus because, once you stop focussing, your thumb relaxes and gets out of sync with the dot. The app then freezes and the peaceful music stops, letting you know you broke your focus.

Let's take another example of the hidden action of decision-making. Now, this one is a bit easier to measure because if I make a decision, then I can show you what decision I made. I can even tell you how I made that decision. And the reason it's easy to measure is because of exactly the same thing I described above. You are using a task (in this case, sharing a decision, or explaining and justifying a decision) that requires the desired action to be performed in order to be done successfully.

Going back to mindfulness, we could find an even simpler task that requires the application of mindfulness techniques to be successfully completed. That simple task would be to follow the instructions for a meditation exercise (e.g. focus on your breath for a count of 10) and then explain how they followed the instructions, or share their experience of following those instructions.

With a simple explanation or justification, however, there's still a little room for cheating to go on here. It is possible to just remember a suitable explanation, and then use that without having even performed the action. Of course, there are ways of managing that, and people who write exam papers are masters of overcoming these sorts of issues. (But I won't go into that here.)

Think of it this way. It's OK to start with something simple that can be cheated on. If we have a group of intrinsically motivated learners in our group, they're not going to see the benefit of cheating anyway. And then, after the simple stuff, move from just being able to explain to actually being able to complete a challenging task (like the ones I described above).

- ## Defining the Standards

Standards allow us to measure goals, track progress, and give us a base level to reference learner performance against when we give them feedback.

There are 4 conditions for writing good standards:
1.   **Measurable**
2.   **Achievable**
3.   **Efficient**
4.   **Relevant**

1st Condition—Measurable Standards

If we set a goal, then we should be able to measure it. We should be able to see how close we are and how much more we have to do. This is different from observable. Observable is just about whether or not the trainer in the room can see the action being done. Measurable is about how well the action should be done.

Generally, this involves the use of numbers to clarify what standard of performance is desired. For example:
- 10 times
- 80% of the time
- with an accuracy of 95%

2nd Condition—Achievable Standards

If the objective is too difficult, then our learners won't achieve it, and they will leave the training feeling frustrated. If it's too easy, then our learners will get bored.

Look for that sweet spot between too difficult and too easy, at just the right level for your learners to get into a state of flow.

It is vital that learners will be able to achieve the objective by the end of training, so objectives need to be achievable within that time frame.

But we can't forget what our learners must be able to do in order to perform effectively on the job. If our training objectives do not prepare learners for their required on-the-job performance, then our training will be a waste of time. So, if it is necessary to set a difficult training objective, we need to focus on one thing at a time.

For example, say we want to help them improve their presentation skills. There are so many things to improve on. They're not making enough eye contact, they're spending too much time talking to the PPT, they haven't used a logical structure, and so on. For this, we just need to focus on one issue at a time. Set a standard for having better eye contact and get them to deliver a presentation with most of their focus on doing this, and all of our feedback directed on that. Then, next time, focus on spending less time talking to the PPT, and so on.

Or, even better, focus on the one thing that will have the biggest impact. In the above example, we could encourage them to use questions to guide the audience to their points. This both helps the audience understand better (achieving the goal of the logical structure), and means they have to actually make eye contact with the audience. Focus on the 20% that will lead to 80% of improvement.

3rd Condition—Efficient Standards

We want to make the best use of the time available in the training because a lot of the time it will feel like there is not enough time. The way we do this is by making our training objectives efficient.

For a start, when you were preparing your tools earlier, you should have filtered out all nonessential content, so, by now, all of the actions you will have identified are absolutely essential. As you write your training objectives, always question if this objective is essential or not. If not, then it is probably a waste. By removing it, you could free up more time for learners to focus on more important things.

But even if all of your objectives are absolutely essential, there is still something else we can do to increase efficiency, and it simply involves asking this question: *If written in a different way, could it be achieved faster?*

An example I use when training this is the action of controlling speaking speed whilst delivering a presentation. To do this, I could set the following objective:
- Deliver a 200-word presentation in 100 seconds.

That is an action that is observable, measurable, and achievable. But it can create a bit of a headache for the trainer in the room.

Imagine there are 30 people in this training (which does happen, at times, when budgets are low). 30 people speaking for 100 seconds each means about 3000 seconds. Now I'm pretty bad at math, but 3000 seconds worth of practice time is a lot for just one little objective. That's almost a whole hour!

There are two main ways of simplifying this particular objective:
- Reduce the standard from 200 words in 100 seconds to 20 words in 10 seconds
- Ensure that it can be measured by the learner themselves, or a partner, removing the need for the trainer to measure it

If we reduce the time from 100 seconds to 10 seconds, we've cut the time down to a tenth of the original. This is still the same action, and actually still the same standard (just divided). The time saved allows for more practice opportunities. Furthermore, the shorter time means they get feedback faster. At the end of the activity, they can check if they achieved the target or not, and if they can do that in 10 seconds, then they are getting that valuable feedback ten times faster.

If the standard is very clear, then the learner can measure themselves, saving the trainer a great deal of time during the training. With the above example, it's possible for learners to use a timer to see how long they took. The trainer can then focus on checking everyone in the room and occasionally stepping in to offer feedback.

• Defining the Conditions

Finally, we want to check that the objective is as close to real life conditions as possible. Practicing in context leads to performing in context.

Take the example of self-defence classes. A lot of these do not practice in context. Your partner throws a punch at you and then freezes whilst you take some time to figure out how to apply the technique you've just learnt. But, in reality, when someone attacks you, they don't freeze after they punch you. They follow through with more attacks! If the self-defence class is to be effective, it must allow learners to practice under realistic conditions.

Here we focus on the conditions the learner will be performing this action under in real life. So, consider the following:
- **Who—Who would they do this with in real life?**
- **What—What would they actually have to do at work?**
- **Where—What kind of environment will they do this in in real life?**
- **When—In what sort of situation would they do this? Are there certain preceding events or following actions?**
- **Why—What kind of purpose would they do this for in real life? What kind of reward or penalty would they get? What motivation would there be?**
- **How—How should they perform the action? Is there a specific kind of methodology, technique, or process they should use?**

For example, say our objective is to train a sales person to consult a customer on their needs. If we use the above guidelines to review the relevant conditions, then we might identify the following key points:
- Who—They'd be doing this with a customer.
- What—They should use a sequence of questioning techniques (for example, the funnelling technique).
- Where—They'd probably do this in a meeting room, probably with only one person or several other people present.
- When—They'd probably have already spoken to the customer on the phone before and so will have a basic understanding of their needs. They'd probably have already spent a little time in the meeting trying to build rapport.
- Why—They'd probably do this to gain more information before putting together a proposal for the client.
- How—The company might have its own particular process or methodology it uses.

- ## Training Objective Template

To make training objectives easier to design, simply follow the guiding questions below and then use the checklist to make sure your objective is the best it can be:

What is the behaviour they need to do?
What standard do they need to perform this behaviour to?
Under what conditions do they need to perform this behaviour?

Checklist:

- **Does it include a verb to describe the action the learner must do?**
- **Is the action observable?**
- **Is it measurable?**
- **Can you, the learner themselves, or another participant, easily measure it during the practice activity?**
- **Can all the learners realistically achieve this goal within the time limit available for the practice activity?**
- **Is the challenge level of the objective engaging for the learner (e.g. not too easy and not too difficult)?**
- **Does it specify the conditions (where, where, or how) the learner must do it under)?**
- **Are these conditions realistic (e.g. do they reflect the conditions the learner will have to face in real life)?**
- **Can you create these conditions during the practice activity?**
- **Does the training objective you a clear idea of how to start designing your practice activity?**

Training Objectives Checklist

Does it include a verb to describe the action the learner must do?	❏
Is the action observable?	❏
Is it measurable?	❏
Can you, the trainee themselves, or another participant, easily measure it during the practice activity?	❏
Can all the trainees realistically achieve this goal within the time limit available for the practice activity?	❏
Is the challenge level of the objective engaging for the trainee (e.g. not too easy and not too difficult)?	❏
Does it specify the condition/s (where, when or how) the trainee must do it under?	❏
Are these conditions realistic (e.g. do they reflect the conditions the trainee will have to face in real life)?	❏
Can you create these conditions during the practice activity?	❏
Does the training objective give you a clear idea of how to start designing your practice activity?	❏

• The Stages of Mastery

When we practice new skills, we don't just suddenly master them. There is a process we go through. We usually fail a lot, at first. Then, as we practice more, we start to get better. Eventually, we get to a stage where we can pull off the skill with barely any effort.

Recently, a friend of mine taught me how to juggle. I say 'taught', although there isn't really much to teach. He showed me the proper technique for juggling, explained it, then let me try it. I tried it and failed. He gave me a bit of feedback. So I tried it again, and got the hand motions and order of movements down better, but still failed. He encouraged me to keep going.

Eventually, I got to 5 catches in a row. That took me maybe 30 minutes to reach. But it was pretty hard. Every time I threw the balls up in the air, I didn't feel fully in control. I felt like catching the balls was more a matter of luck than skill.

Fast forward several weeks to the day that I am writing this, and I am now a much better juggler. My record, so far, is 125 catches, which is quite an improvement on 5! Now, it doesn't feel like so much effort. In fact, I can start to do other things whilst I'm juggling. I can watch TV or chat with my wife at the same time (although normally only for a few seconds before I drop everything!). It feels more like skill than luck now. Pretty soon, I'll take it up a level and go from 3 balls to 4.

The process I experienced with practicing juggling matches most peoples' experiences with learning most skills. When we talked about skill gaps earlier on, we learned about the 4 stages of going from unskilled to skilled. Let's revisit this now using my example of juggling and also look at the implications of these stages in training.

1. **Unconscious Incompetence—Where someone doesn't know what they should be doing.**
2. **Conscious Incompetence—They know what they should be doing, but can't do it.**
3. **Conscious Competence—They know what they should be doing, and can finally do it. But they haven't mastered it, so need to use a lot of conscious effort to perform the actions effectively.**
4. **Unconscious Competence—They can finally perform the actions without the need for conscious effort. They can will the action into life and focus their conscious attention elsewhere.**

1. Unconscious Incompetence—When I first attempted to juggle, I just threw one ball in the air and then threw the other ball horizontally to my other hand. This was the wrong technique, so my friend corrected me and taught me the right technique.

2. Conscious Incompetence—My friend showed me the right technique and explained it to me clearly. Then I tried it. I did a bit better this time around, but I still couldn't catch the balls in the right way. However, my hand-eye coordination soon improved and I was able to start catching the balls, so I then moved to the next stage.

3. Conscious Competence—I can catch the balls (and sometimes do so several times in a row), but it's pretty messy and doesn't feel natural. I still drop the balls frequently, and don't feel fully in control. As I mentioned earlier, here it felt more like luck than skill. But after several weeks of practice, the luck to skill ratio started to change.

4. Unconscious Competence—At this stage, I can perform effortlessly. I feel much more in control, and it feels less like luck and more like skill. I can even start to do other things at the same time, such as watch TV or chat with my wife. This is because I no longer need to direct a huge amount of cognitive energy to this task. That energy is now freed up and can be used for other tasks.

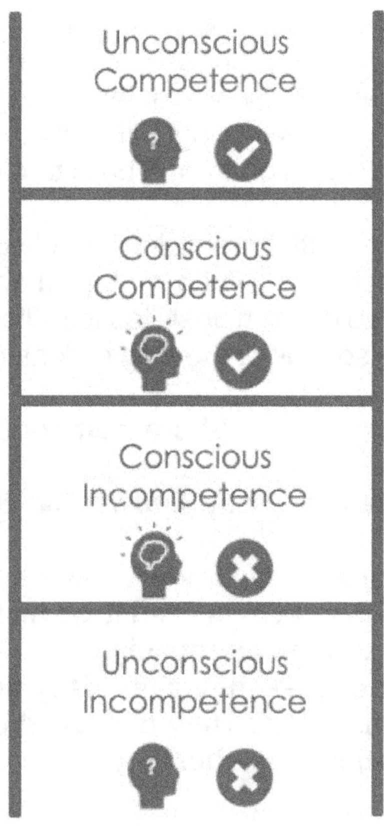

Implications for Practice in Training

When it comes to training skills, you will find different people are at different levels, so you need to tailor your approach to suit these different levels in order to get the most out of the time spent practicing.

For Unconscious Incompetence—Start with lots of demonstrating and explaining. Break the skill into little chunks, explain the reasoning behind each step, describe the thinking process, mention what they might be paying attention to, and include what they might see or hear or feel when they perform those steps. Use a lot of guided questioning here to get them to form those mental connections so they can approach the task with the right mindset.

But don't overwhelm them with information here. When my friend taught me juggling, he showed me one technique, explained it, and then let me try. He spent a grand total of about 1 minute teaching me. Give them only as much information as they need to start.

For Conscious Incompetence—At this point, feedback (or 'feedforward', as we'll see a bit later) is really important. When we first practice new skills, there is a chance that we can pick up bad habits. We do not want to spend a lot of time practicing the wrong thing because we will master the wrong thing! So, observe your learners performing, and correct them as soon as possible.

But also remember what this step is like for learners. It's frustrating and can result in a lot of self-criticism. When I started juggling, I had a voice in my head cursing me for doing it wrong. It really wouldn't have helped things if my friend joined that voice and started telling me I was doing it wrong. Instead, he stepped back and gave me space to make the mistakes I needed to make. So, let your learners fail as many times as is necessary to succeed.

For Conscious Competence—Leave them to it. At this stage, I didn't really need my friend's intervention. I practiced alone at home. And just kept practicing. It took several weeks of multiple practices a day to finally up my skill to the next level.

One way of leaving them to it is to reduce the amount of focus they need to put on other things. For example, my wife learnt how to drive a few years ago. But, after passing her test, it was still very difficult for her. She needed to stay on small roads during quiet times of the day, not busy highways, because she would easily get overwhelmed. By taking the space and time to get comfortable with driving, she was gradually able to up her skill level and take on higher challenges.

For Unconscious Competence—Now, they are pretty much masters. They're confident as well. They know they can perform effectively without any effort.

One challenge for people here is that they become so good they don't actually realise how they are doing things. If I were to teach you how to juggle, I'd actually have to stop and look at myself in a mirror first because I've completely forgotten the techniques I learnt.

This means people at this level (and for your training topic, this may very well include you) are not conscious of how they perform, which can make them highly ineffective trainers. But if you can raise your awareness of how you perform and articulate it clearly to others, then you'll be able to both demonstrate and explain, which are two key steps to helping people go from unconscious incompetence to conscious incompetence.

• Planning Transfer Activities

Simply put, transfer activities are a list of activities that the learner must complete after the training by certain times. Their purpose is to reinforce what was trained.

Poor transfer planning is the biggest cause of training waste. Without transfer planning, the newly trained habits can quickly fade away, bad habits can emerge, and old habits can creep back in.

Why do this now and not later?

If you clarify the transfer activities now, then you have time to check with the relevant stakeholders (e.g. supervisors, or the learners themselves) if these activities are practical or not, giving you time to amend them.

Furthermore, with these done before you start designing, you will design with these objectives in mind. This can help you identify more efficient ways of delivering the course. For example, there may be some activities that are not necessary during the training itself, helping us free up time to focus on more important things.

Also, the tools you designed earlier will probably be used in the transfer plan. So, now is a good time to look back at those tools and see if they need to be amended in any way to make them more suitable for transfer. You want to be doing this before you start designing the course because, after you've designed things, you might have a lot of material to go back and revise.

Three Types of Transfer Activities

Remember, transfer activities are simply lists of activities the learner must complete after the training in order to reinforce the training.

There are three types of transfer activities:
1. **Peer Observations**
2. **Peer Shadowing**
3. **Learner Observation**

1. Peer Observation

This is the least demanding of all the activities. It requires learners to simply observe others performing what was trained.

But we don't want them to just passively observe others. They need to be actively observing others. What this means is that learners need to be actively looking out for certain things.

For example, our learners could be looking out for the following:
- the order of certain actions
- specific details of each action
- the intention behind the action
- the benefit the action achieves

The purpose of observing peers is to reinforce the conscious side of competence. It should help strengthen the thinking processes, the intentions, and the decisions that drive the actions.

2. Peer Shadowing

This is a bit more demanding on both the learner and the peer. The learner should follow a peer performing in the real world, but with plenty of interaction between each other.

A great example is that of plane spotters during World War 2. As German bombers flew over the British coast, the spotters would listen to the hum of each plane and use their experience to identify which type of plane it was. Such information helped cities take adequate precautions to minimise hostilities.

But there was a challenge. The spotters were only able to do so with an unconscious level of competence. They couldn't explain *how* they could distinguish the different types of planes; they just did it.

So, to develop new spotters, a shadowing system was used. The learners would stand next to the spotters and, as the planes would fly in, the spotters would first ask the learners to guess which planes they were. After sharing their guess, the spotters would then reveal the answer. Through this feedback, the learners themselves gradually developed the same level of competence. It proved to be a highly effective way of pushing learners directly from unconscious incompetence to unconscious competence.

Shadowing is a fantastic way of developing learners. But it can't be done passively. It needs to include lots of interaction between learner and peer, with plenty of feedback.

3. Learner Observation

This is the most demanding on the learner because it involves them performing the action in the real world whilst being observed by an expert.

This is a perfect opportunity to use a tool that can measure the learner against the standard evaluation criteria, but shouldn't be done by surprise. The learner should be clearly reminded what the standards are and what they will be evaluated against. This way, they will perform the action with more accurate intentions, rather than carrying on with misguided intentions and only receiving feedback after it's all done.

Furthermore, learners should feel comfortable making mistakes and expressing their uncertainty. They should feel comfortable appealing for help, especially at the time of need (if convenient). The more comfortable they are asking for feedback, the faster they will learn. Here, the expert can also offer some on-the-spot coaching during their performance, but only so far as providing simple reminders and pointers.

Finally, any feedback should be geared towards what they should do differently the next time, which shouldn't focus too much on the mistakes they made but, instead, point them towards better future performance. This actually means our feedback becomes more like 'feedforward', as it is focussed on what learners must do going forward.

Reality is Not This Simple

In reality, we won't always need to go through all 3 steps. Sometimes, it's just not practical. Other times, it's just not necessary. Sometimes, they are already quite high on the competency ladder or the conscious level.

But we should always have a plan. And we should always implement a plan of action that will push learners to take accountability for their own development.

Maybe you can't engage all relevant stakeholders in your transfer plan. That can be pretty frustrating, but that doesn't mean we can't do anything. At the very least, we can provide learners with a suggested transfer plan. We could even offer to check in with them every so often. Something is better than nothing.

Transfer Activities

 Peer Observations

 Peer Shadowing

 Learner Observation

• Design Practice by Testing Objectives

When I hear the word 'test', it sends shivers down my spine. It has the same impact on lots of other people and probably you as well. We hear that word and think back to sitting in a school exam hall. All we can hear is the sound of a clock ticking. Then we have to wait a long time to learn if we passed or failed.

In schools, it seems that the point of a test is to give people labels that helps the education system decide where to place them. **Grade A**s go to this class. **Fails** get kicked out. I'm not really sure how any of this is related to learning.

In training, we also want to test people. And we also want to give them a passing mark to, in a way, see if they pass or fail. But, in training, practice shouldn't stop with a pass or fail. It should simply be one step in the cycle of learning. It should give learners an opportunity to discover what they should continue doing, and what they should start doing.

So, think of practice as a test, but a friendly kind of test. Learners shouldn't feel under pressure to pass or fail. They should simply approach it with the intention to perform the required behaviour, to the desired standard, under the required conditions. And as they try that, they should know that they will have access to guidance on how to improve.

Objectives Do Half the Work

If you've written a good training objective, then most of the design for your practice is done. You will have the behaviour, standard, and conditions. All you need to do is create a way of testing learners to see if they can perform the required behaviour, to the desired standard, under the required conditions.

For example, maybe we want to design a practice activity for using the Why, What, How Scale from The Ladder of Explanation that we looked at in the previous Guiding section. So our objective may be: *Referring to the examples provided by the instructor, correctly identify the audience's understanding level using the Why, What, How Scale.*

We know we need to provide examples. We also know that these examples should describe an audience and a topic, and give some indication as to what their understanding of that topic is.

Ideally, those examples should be relevant to audiences the learners are likely to encounter in real life. And the information given should also be at a similar level of detail to what learners would have access to in real life. Once those examples are made, it's then a case of deciding on the logistics of the activity such as timing and so on.

Once you have a clear objective, the activity pretty much comes naturally. It's just a case of designing some context for the activity, such as providing examples, case studies or certain resources, and then planning some logistics around all that.

Testing Means Feedback

In our training objectives, we should have included a standard. This standard gives us guidance on how to provide feedback in the activity.

In the above example, the standard is 'correctly identify', which implies there is a correct answer. This means we should clearly define the correct answer before giving our learners the activity. Then, as they share their answers, we can compare them against the standard and give them feedback as to whether they are correct or not.

Remember, the purpose of practice is not to tell learners if they have passed or failed. It is to tell them if they are doing well enough, or what they need to do more of. This feedback will help them improve.

As I mentioned earlier in this book, feedback is a very misleading word. Feedforward is far more appropriate, because the information from 'feedback' should give them guidance on what they need to do going forward. I'll go into this in more detail in a little while.

• Describe and Model Before Practice

Practicing comes after guiding for a reason. In guiding, we guide learners to the required knowledge to perform effectively. In practice, they take that knowledge and turn it into action. This means that before learners practice, they should know how to practice.

There are two key things that we must do before we ask our learners to practice: describe and model. This is especially essential for learners who are at the level of unconscious incompetence, but is also essential for showing how an activity should be done. Let's see how we can do these effectively.

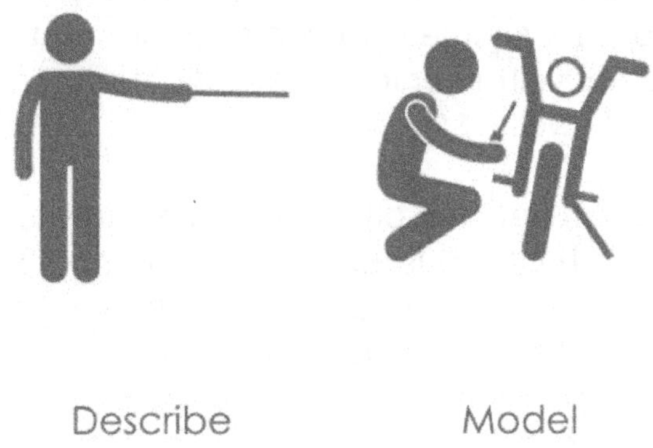

Describe   Model

Describing

In describing, we go into detail about the actions learners need to perform. These are actions that they should be performing back at work after the training, but also actions that they will shortly be attempting to perform in the practice itself.

This is another reason we want to have clearly defined training objectives. In those objectives, we will have clarified the behaviour, standard, and condition, and these are the details we want to be communicating to our learners.

Behaviours, standards, and conditions are more for our own benefit as instructional designers and trainers. Simply communicating the training objectives to our learners won't really help them much. Training objectives are difficult for them to understand.

This is where The Ladder of Explanation comes in handy. If you introduce the actions in a meaningful and digestible manner, you will have set them up with a good foundation for practice, especially when you describe the how and why of each step. And the next part will make it even clearer for them.

Modelling

Modelling is where we actually perform the actions for our learners' benefit. They then have an example that they can see first-hand, and you, as the trainer, can call their attention to certain areas.

For example, a few weeks ago I delivered a Train the Trainer session to a group of financial consultants. During one section on questioning techniques, I explained the how and why of the techniques, and gave them lots of examples. But I felt they didn't fully grasp it, so I invited one volunteer to come to the front of the room and be the trainer. I then invited another volunteer to come and pretend to be someone who didn't understand technology very well.

The trainer's objective was to train the other person on how to use a map app on their smartphone to find a route home, but they could only do so by asking their trainee questions. Everyone else would sit around and observe goldfish-bowl style, and I would jump in, at times, to steer it in the right direction.

The trainer started by going back into old habits and just telling them. I paused after a little while and asked the trainee how they felt. The trainee said they felt overwhelmed, so I asked the trainer what kind of questions they could use to convey the same learning points. After they came up with some questions, I got them to repeat what they just did, but using the questions this time. Then we paused again and checked to see how the trainee felt this time, which was much better.

That goldfish-bowl observation was extremely useful for everyone in the room. The role-playing trainer and trainee got first-hand experience of it, whilst everyone else got to witness what good techniques were and what happens when they are and aren't used. This was far more impacting than a simple explanation.

Modelling is a fantastic way of helping people learn. It is a far more comprehensive training tool than a simple story, video, or case study. It is a fully interactive example.

Think of it a bit like a 4D movie, where we can pause, rewind, and fast forward. We can move around and view it from different angles. We can analyse details over and over again. We can even get into people's heads and ask them what they're thinking and why they're doing things that way.

A more advanced way of modelling is Super Modelling. **Super Modelling is where you, as the trainer, continuously model everything they should be doing.** For example, if you are delivering training on presentation skills, then every technique you share should be modelled all the time. If you share vocal techniques, then you should model those every time you talk. If you share The Ladder of Explanation, then you should model that whenever you explain something. And so on.

Super Modelling is something we, as trainers, do whether we intend to or not. And whether we intend it or not, it is extremely influential. Learners will notice your habits over time, and may even subconsciously start to copy some of the things you do.

I once delivered a training in business writing. This training had two objectives. One was to help learners improve their business writing skills. The other was to show them how to deliver a training in that topic. The learners were not only trying to learn this topic, they were also learning how to train this topic.

At the end of the day, there was a group discussion to share their observations and new insights on how to deliver this training. I was quite surprised by some of the things they observed, such as the way I stood, the way I used my gestures, the way I described examples, and so on. These were all naturalised habits for me and I was no longer aware of them. Thankfully, nothing bad came out! But it was interesting to note that they had observed things I was no longer aware of.

So, as you deliver training in your topic, take care to super model effectively.

- **Practice in Context**

Practice like you play and you will play like you practice. This is a fantastic saying that I picked up from a fantastic book on learning called *Make It Stick—The Science of Successful Learning* by Peter C. Brown, Henry L. Roediger III, and Mark A. McDaniel. I strongly recommend you check this book out.

It describes, quite efficiently, the value of practicing in context.

For example, imagine you are practicing a skill in football. You run into the penalty area whilst someone passes the ball to you from the left-hand side. Once you get to the ball, you then shoot for a goal. You do this over and over and over again, until you can finally score a goal each time. Does this make you a better football player?

No, it doesn't. It makes you better at shooting a ball into an empty goal when it's passed to you in the penalty area from the left-hand side. It might help you in other areas of football. It may give you better spacial awareness, it may help you time your run-ups, and improve your shooting accuracy. But this isn't enough to become a better football player.

So what is the best way of practicing to be a better football player?

Quite simply, practice playing football. Play in a team, against another team, on a pitch for 90 minutes.

To truly benefit from practice, the practice should be exactly like the real thing. This means the practice should mirror realistic conditions, provide the same levels of complexity, stimulate the same emotional reactions, and so on.

Real life is complex. To perform effectively in real life, our learners must be able to perform under the exact same levels of complexity. And to demonstrate true mastery, our learners need to demonstrate creativity at that exact same level of complexity.

Coming back to football, think about how creative some of the true masters are. They pull off tricks their opponents couldn't predict. As they are chased down by four defenders from all angles, they pull off a dazzling spin in a split second and leave those defenders ten yards behind.

Consider a doctor giving a patient a consultation. When they're surrounded by screaming children and agitated patients, the pressure is high. But they remain focussed on diagnosing the problem. Furthermore, as they are diagnosing the problem, they find magical ways of soothing the patient's anxiety and calming the children down.

Creativity happens when we become so good at something we no longer need to think about it. We can relax, focus more, and allocate more conscious energy to other things. **The purpose of practice is to minimise the conscious effort involved in performing a skill so as to free up cognitive function, allowing the learner to focus on other and more complex actions.**

Practice Simple First

When a learner is making too many mistakes under complex conditions, we need to break things down for them and give them a chance to master the basics in a vacuum before using them in the real world.

Whilst our ultimate goal is complex practice, we may sometimes need to start with more simple practice, otherwise known as isolated practice.

Isolated practice means exactly that. The skill is isolated in a vacuum. There are no other factors that require concentration. You are free to concentrate on just that skill. If you struggle to shoot a crossed ball in the penalty area, then we need to remove anything that could distract you from that skill. In a real match, you'll be distracted by all of the defenders around you, the roar of the crowd, and the shouts of all the other players. Get rid of all that and you are free to focus on just shooting a crossed ball.

When you do complex practice without having the basics, you don't know what you are doing. The ball comes to you in the area and you are not sure where to run to, or when to start your run, and which direction to kick the ball from. **But when you have practiced the basics in isolated practice, then you know what you need to do.** You know where to run to, when to start your run and which direction to kick the ball from.

Shifting from isolated practice to more complex practice is a struggle, but you will shift to it with the benefit of clearer direction. You won't be confused anymore; you'll just be slow. And that's OK. With enough complex practice, you will get faster.

The Goal Is Success in Complex Practice

For training to be effective, learners must leave with the ability to perform to the required standard under realistic conditions. So, before the training finishes, we must ensure our learners have proven they can perform to the required standard under those conditions. As the course progresses, it may start with isolated practice, and more isolated practice, before jumping to complex practice. **But the goal is to give them enough complex practice to demonstrate the required level of**

competence.

The key is to start at their exact level of competence. If they've already mastered the basics, then we don't need simple isolated practice. Maybe they need more practice making better decisions on how to use their skills under these realistic conditions. But if they haven't even mastered the basics, then we need to ease them in to it.

Start with isolated and gradually build up. Go from simple to semi-complex before going to full-on complex. What this means is that, as they master the basics of separate skills, give them an activity that combines those separate skills before moving on to a fully complex activity. Gradually increase the level of complexity to suit them.

Another advantage of practicing in increasing levels of complexity is that you can use previously practiced skills when practicing new ones. This leads to optimum repetition and optimum retention.

Practice is a numbers game. It's all about spending the most time practicing the most important skills under the most realistic conditions.

- ## Focussed Practice

What should learners be focussed on? Consider this question when designing your practice. There will be specific things they need to do, to a required standard, under certain conditions. They should spend as much time focussing on those specific things as they possibly can.

But in practice there are a number of things that can distract learners. We want to minimise those distractions as much as possible.

Content Should Not Distract

A big part of many practice activities is the content. If they are practicing presenting, then they need some content to present. If they are practicing using the Why, What, How Scale to evaluate an audience's understanding level, then they need an audience to evaluate. If they are practicing sales skills, then they need a product to sell.

The content to present, the audience to evaluate, and the product to sell are all examples of content in practice activities.

Content is important because, without it, they sometimes have no way of practicing. But, ultimately, the practice is more important than the content.

Consider the potential distractions each of these types of practice content might create:
- The content to present—Might be too long and difficult to remember, meaning the learners spend more time trying to remember it than actually presenting it.
- Audience to evaluate—These are probably going to be written examples for the learners to read. But if they're poorly written and too long, then learners will spend too much time trying to understand the examples.
- Product to sell—If this is too vague, then the learner will be unsure of how to sell it and have lots of questions. If it's too detailed, then the learner will spend too much time trying to understand it.

I have heard other books recommending that the learners create the content themselves. Their reasoning is that the act of creating is engaging. But there is a big risk to letting learners do this if it takes too long to create. If they spend more time creating the content than practicing, then that is just another distraction. Whilst creating content might be engaging, it can take valuable time away from practice.

Here are some principles I follow when creating content:
- Stick to things they are familiar with
- Written examples should be clear enough for a ten-year-old to read

- Spend no more than a tenth of the practice time learning the content

How could we apply these principles to the previous examples of content? Let's have a look.

Content to Present

If the goal is to practice presentation skills such as eye contact, voice control, and body language, etc., then the content needs to be something simple. Or, even better, something they already know.

Whenever I run activities like this, I sometimes ask learners to talk about their favourite hobbies, their last holiday, or what they did last week. These require almost no thinking at all, freeing their minds to focus on using the skills.

Other times, I will ask them to present something they prepared earlier. Normally, I split my Presentation Skills training into several sections. During the first morning, we focus on structure, logic, and storytelling. They then use what they have learnt to prepare a short presentation and present it to everyone. Once they've prepared and presented it, they are able to remember more clearly, so now they can use that same presentation to practice other presentation skills.

Audience to Evaluate

Here, I write brief case studies. I select situations the learners can easily relate to. I think of situations they might encounter in their daily lives or their work. I stay away from situations they have little to no experience with.

As I write these examples, I take care to write them clearly. I use simple, everyday words to describe the situations, staying away from abbreviations or anything overly technical. I write short sentences and short paragraphs. I even try to keep them within 1-3 paragraphs, in total.

Product to Sell

Here, I would select a product and customer they have first-hand experience with (for example, selling their mobile phone to a classmate who just so happens to be looking for a new mobile phone or, even better, actually selling one of their company's products to a classmate who acts as a customer).

They need to be very familiar with the product to practice selling it, so it needs to be something they definitely have first-hand experience with.

Control Their Focus

For example, if I told you to deliver a presentation in which I would be evaluating your use of eye contact, then you would feel a bit of pressure about using eye contact effectively.

However, if I told you that I would be evaluating only the content of your presentation, then you would feel more pressure to focus on delivering good content.

We can use evaluation as a way of controlling what learners focus on. If you give them something to aim for, and tell them how you will evaluate that, they will be more likely to focus on that.

We can also let learners know what they don't need to worry about. Using the example of presenting, maybe they are very self-conscious of their body language and don't know how to use that. If we want them to focus on something else (for example, their use of eye contact), then we can explain to them that they don't need to worry about their body language for now and we can get to that later. If we make it very clear that we are going to be taking notes and scoring them on eye contact and nothing else, then they are more likely to relax about their body language.

Sometimes I even ask learners to tell me what they are going to focus on and what they would like to be evaluated on before they practice. Just a few moments spent reflecting on this question means they are more likely to practice with that particular focus.

Another advantage of asking them to select a focus is that sometimes they can only focus on that one thing. Going back to the example of the learner who is conscious of body language, maybe we tell them not to worry about that but they're still worried about it. In that case, let's switch the focus to what they are most concerned about. If we can't direct their focus away from that concern, then let's use that as the focus point during the practice, because they're going to be focussed on that anyway.

Redirect Focus before They Build Bad Habits

Just because we clarify what they should focus on doesn't mean they are guaranteed to focus on that throughout the practice. Their attention will wander and, before we know it, they've completely forgotten what they should be doing.

If you've ever practiced meditation before, you will know very clearly how often your mind wanders. You focus on your breath and then, suddenly, you realise you've spent the last few minutes thinking about what to have for dinner tonight. But meditation isn't about preventing our minds from wandering, it's about recognising when our minds have wandered and redirecting our attention to where it should be.

Using the example of presentation skills again, we've agreed they'll focus on their use of eye contact. As they start off, they do a good job. But a little while into the presentation they seem to forget about eye contact, and end up just making eye contact with the people to their left, completely missing out on everyone else in the room.

If we, as trainers, ignore that, then we are actually reinforcing bad habits. The longer they spend doing that, the more it will become a habit, so we need to redirect their attention as soon as possible. So, call a time-out.

As you call the time-out, don't tell them directly that they've forgotten about the eye contact. Use questions. Ask them what their focus point was. Ask them how they think they're doing. Use guiding questions to help them realise by themselves, and redirect their attention by themselves. By guiding instead of telling, you are helping them reflect, and thus helping them burn those learning pathways deep into their mind.

This is the beauty of practice. It can be stopped. Whether it's simple or complex doesn't matter. If it's practice, then you can call a time-out, redirect their attention, and correct them before they build bad habits.

● Efficient Practice

Time is a luxury that we don't have enough of, both in life and in the world of corporate training. We may complain about that, there really isn't much we can do to change it. But what we can change is how we use that time. We can look at the time we have and plan to get the absolute most out of it.

Optimising the use of time is essential for getting the most out of practice. There are a lot of factors that can take away valuable practice time. So let's have a look at how to control those factors and optimise learner practice time.

Setting Up

Some activities take time to set up. Maybe you need to distribute handouts, rearrange tables, or move people into their groups. This all needs to take as little time as possible.

The best way of setting up is to do it during the breaks. That way, you are not encroaching on valuable practice time.

The second best way to set up is to do it whilst learners are preparing. Maybe there is a case study they need to read, or they need to plan their group strategy before practicing, or they need to rehearse by themselves. Prepare around this. Get them focussed on their preparation whilst you rearrange things (furniture, handouts, and so on) around them.

Giving Directions

An activity typically involves giving some directions on what they are supposed to do. These directions are another factor that can encroach greatly on valuable practice time if they are not managed effectively.

For a start, maybe the directions are unclear and learners don't get them the first time around, meaning you have to repeat them. Or maybe everyone thought they were clear but, as they start practicing, their misunderstandings become clear, and you have to stop and repeat again. Unnecessarily repeating directions wastes time.

Use Why, What, How to explain the activity, if necessary. Start with Why, give some context to the activity, and let them know their goal. Go to What and tell them briefly what the activity is. Then go to How and start describing the details, step-by-step, making sure to highlight the How and Why of each step.

Clear directions use clear language. Get to the point quickly by forcing yourself to use verbs to describe their actions. Start each sentence with verbs as opposed to useless filler language like 'So, yeah…', 'Basically…', etc.

Avoid overwhelming them. Some activities include multiple steps. Rather than explain all the steps in one go, break them down. Explain Step One, then let them practice Step One. Only explain Step Two when you get to Step Two. If you explain too much at once, they won't remember anything.

Describe then model. After you've given your directions, go ahead and model those directions. Find some participants to model the activity with, or even do it with an imaginary participant.

Finally, use questions to check their understanding. Ask what they should and shouldn't do. Ask how much time they have. And so on. Only when they answer correctly should you go ahead and start the activity.

No Waiting in Line

When there are lots of learners who need to practice, we may end up with a queue of learners waiting to practice. Avoid this situation at all costs. Waiting to practice is an incredible waste of time.

We can avoid this situation in several ways.

Firstly, involve them in evaluating other learners' performance. For example, if I am running a Presentation Skills training, then when one learner is presenting to the group, others will be focussing on that learner's presentation skills. I'll even give different people different things to focus on. One may focus on their content, another on their body language, and so on.

Even though those evaluators aren't practicing, they are, at the very least, reflecting. If you encourage them to evaluate based on the standards that you have trained, then they will be strengthening their awareness of those standards. And if you even ask them to share what they learnt from evaluating their peers, then you are encouraging them to reflect even more.

The key principle here is to keep everyone busy all of the time. Don't have learners sitting by, idly waiting for their turn. Give them something to do or something to focus on. If they can't practice, make them reflect.

If feasible, set the activity up so learners can evaluate their performance on their own (without needing you). This is especially useful for when you are dealing with large groups. The way to do this is to ensure that you have made the standards clear and understandable during the Guiding section. You may want to design a practice activity that tests their comprehension of the standards. And you may even want to design a tool to help them evaluate performance, using those standards.

For example, maybe we are training them in some particular sales skills and they are now practicing using those in a role-play with a partner. We could give their partner a checklist. As they go through the role-play, the partner can check things off to see if that person was doing the right things or not. We could even film them and give them the video footage to review on their own.

You may think that self-evaluation defeats the point of training. It doesn't. Ultimately, we want learners to be able to evaluate themselves. If they can evaluate themselves, they'll be able to use that self-evaluation ability to give their personal development clear direction all by themselves, once the training is over. That independence in learning is what we want for them. It's the difference between giving them a fish and teaching them how to fish.

As you teach them how to self-evaluate, it's important to explain the principles of practice to them so they do it with purpose. I once got groups to practice using eye contact in a Presentation Skills training. I told them that, one at a time, they would give a presentation about their favourite hobby to their group and must focus on making eye contact. Their group members were to focus on showing them the 'no' sign by making a cross with their arms (in an X) every time they broke eye contact. They didn't really get into this at first, but once I explained *why* they were doing the 'no' sign (to help the presenter make more eye contact and improve that skill), they took to it with a lot more purpose.

Maybe you, the trainer, noticed something about their performance that's not within those standards that we are using to evaluate them. Maybe you think that extra observation would be useful for them. But is it part of the vital 20%? Maybe it's helpful, and maybe it's good to know, but if it's not essential, then that might be taking valuable time away from reflecting on essential things. Don't overwhelm them with things they don't need to know. Maximise your time spent by being focussed on things they absolutely need to know.

Fastest Right Version

We want learners to complete the fastest possible right version of a task. The faster they can complete it, the more chances they will have to practice it. And the more they practice doing the right thing, the better they'll get at that right thing.

This involves doing two things. Firstly, make the activity faster and shorter. Secondly, give them more time to practice so they can perform to the highest level of competence they can.

Look at your activity and consider if there is a way of running it faster. If it takes 10 minutes to run, consider how you could do it in 2 minutes. This doesn't mean they spend 8 minutes less practicing. This means they practice doing the right thing 4 more times in those same 8 minutes. Remember, practice is a numbers game. The more times they practice doing the right thing, the more they will tread those vital paths that are what learning is all about.

Activities need to have a high success rate. We don't want learners to practice doing the wrong thing lots of times. That's how we build bad habits. We want them to practice doing the right thing lots of times.

If they are not capable of doing the right thing, then break it down. Go back to simple isolated practice and build them up, step by step, until they are capable of performing the right thing at the required level of complexity.

Targeting the practice at their level is vital to engagement. It if is too easy, they will get bored. If it is too difficult, they will get frustrated. If you get it at just the right level, in that sweet spot between boredom and frustration, they will be in the zone, they will enter a state of flow, and they will be engaged.

Make the Most of the Time Available

In this section, I have shared with you lots of strategies for making practice both efficient and effective. I borrowed many of these strategies from a great book about practice. If you want to learn more about this topic, I strongly recommend you look it up. The book is called *Practice Perfect: 42 Rules for Getting Better at Getting Better,* written by Doug Lemov, Erica Woolway, and Katie Yezzi.

- ## From Feedback to Feedforward

The word 'feedback' is misleading. What's done is done. It's in the past. Telling people they shouldn't have done this or that doesn't help them. Learning is about the future, and that is what we should focus on.

'Feedforward' is about telling them what they should do next time. It doesn't involve telling them what they shouldn't do, which is completely irrelevant and sucks away valuable cognitive resources. Tell yourself not to think of a purple bear and see what happens.

Feedforward focuses on two things: what they should continue doing, and what they should start doing. This is all the information they need in order to improve their performance the next time they practice.

Feedforward examples:

Continue Doing—'Just now, your presentation was very well-structured and used lots of storytelling techniques. Definitely, keep this up!'

Start Doing—'Next time, if you stand more to the middle, you will find it easier to make eye contact with more of the audience, and that will help you engage the audience even more!'

Feedforward

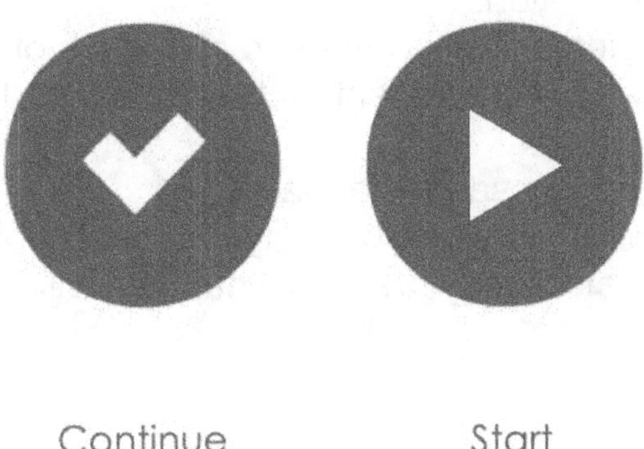

Get Them into a Receptive State

Feedback can be difficult to hear. It can be embarrassing hearing what you did wrong. Because of that, some people don't want to hear it.

And if they don't want to hear it, it doesn't matter if you give it or not. When they don't want to hear it, they won't pay attention to it. Worse still, they may even completely disagree with it.

This is one of the advantages of using a feedforward approach. It's nothing to be embarrassed about because we're not focussed on mistakes. We're just focussed on next time.

There are things we can do to make learners more receptive to receiving feedforward. The easiest way to think about this is to refer back to the SCARF model:

Status
- Frame your feedforward as something they can choose to do. Instead of using the words 'should' and 'must' (which make it sound like a command), let them know what the benefits will be. Say, 'If you do this then…'
- Allow them to share their own self-evaluation before you share yours.

Certainty
- Let them know what you are evaluating them on before they practice. This way, they don't have to worry about all the possible things you might say. They just have to focus on performing that particular thing to a particular standard. By doing this, you may even find that their self-evaluation is the same as yours.

Autonomy
- Teach them how to evaluate themselves and each other. Frame your feedforward as a standard for them to compare their own feedforward against.

Relatedness
- Encourage peer evaluation.
- Pair them into buddies and allow them to give each other feedforward.
- Highlight any areas of improvement that are common to most of the group.

Fairness
- Evaluate everyone to the same standards.
- Provide everyone with the same quantity and quality of feedforward.
- Make it very clear before they practice what they will be evaluated on.

Reduce the Gap

Ideally, there should be as little time as possible between receiving feedforward and applying it.

Where feasible, design your activities so that feedforward can be provided mid-practice. If they are doing a role-play, then step in as soon as they go off track and nudge them in the right direction.

As I mentioned earlier, try to guide them to your suggestions by using guiding questions (as opposed to just giving them your feedforward directly). This encourages greater reflecting and helps them raise awareness of what they should be doing.

Regardless of how you provide your feedforward, the ultimate goal is to have learners spend as much time as possible doing the right thing to their highest level of competence.

Vital Baby Steps

As you observe them practice, you may notice a lot of things they need to do better. Even if all of these things are relevant, we still don't want to overwhelm them. We want to break our feedforward into digestible chunks.

But we don't just want to focus on providing less feedforward, we also want to focus on providing the most valuable feedforward we can. Find the one thing that would require the least amount of effort for them to implement and leads to the most amount of positive results.

For example, when I was delivering a Presentation Skills training, one of the learners came up to deliver their presentation, but they were very nervous as they did it. They stuttered and stammered their way through, making lots of mistakes and looking very uncomfortable. They needed a lot of feedforward, but that amount would have been too overwhelming.

So, I first asked him how he felt about his presentation. He reflected for a moment then said that he felt he wasn't prepared enough. And that was all that he really needed to do. If he spent a little more time preparing, then he wouldn't have felt nervous and he wouldn't have made all of those mistakes. So, we agreed that the next time he was going to present, he should focus on that. Rather than overwhelm him with feedforward on using techniques to deal with nerves, improve his body language, and so on, all he needed to focus on was the one vital baby step of spending more time preparing.

Commitment

For feedforward to be effective, it must be used. Whether or not they use it is up to them. We can't force them to, so we need to see what they can commit to. This means that we should involve them as much as possible in the process of giving feedforward so that they can take ownership over it.

Involve them in identifying what they need to do next time. Encourage them to reflect on their current performance and compare that to the standard they are aiming for. Ask them to identify the gap themselves. And ask them to suggest what they need to do, going forwards.

We can also ask them to reflect on the benefits they could get by doing things differently next time, then to compare those with the results they are getting now. Ask them if they are motivated by those potential benefits.

Remember that we shouldn't tell them what they should do. Instead, we should ask them what they are going to do, because, ultimately, what they do with that feedforward is not up to us. It's up to them.

- ## Practice Activity Template

To make all of the information in this section easier to understand, here is a template you can use to design and prepare your practice activities. Just use these questions:

- **How will you test their ability to achieve the objective?**
- **How will you measure whether or not they have achieved the objective?**
- **What should they focus on during the practice?**
- **How can you reduce any potential distractions?**
- **What (if any) content is needed for the practice?**
- **How long will the activity last?**
- **What do you need to prepare for the activity? How long do you need to prepare?**
- **What do they need to prepare? How long do they need to prepare?**
- **How will you describe and model the activity?**
- **How will you ensure they are following the instructions?**
- **How will you keep them to time during the activity?**

Practice Activity Template

How will you test their ability to achieve the objective?
How will you measure whether or not they have achieved the objective?
What should they focus on during the practice?
How can you reduce any potential distractions?
What (if any) content is needed for the practice?
How long will the activity last?
What do you need to prepare for the activity? How long do you need to prepare?
What do they need to prepare? How long do they need to prepare?
How will you describe and model the activity?
How will you ensure they are following the instructions?
How will you keep them to time during the activity?

Practicing Summary

The following flowchart is a summary of everything we have looked at in this section:

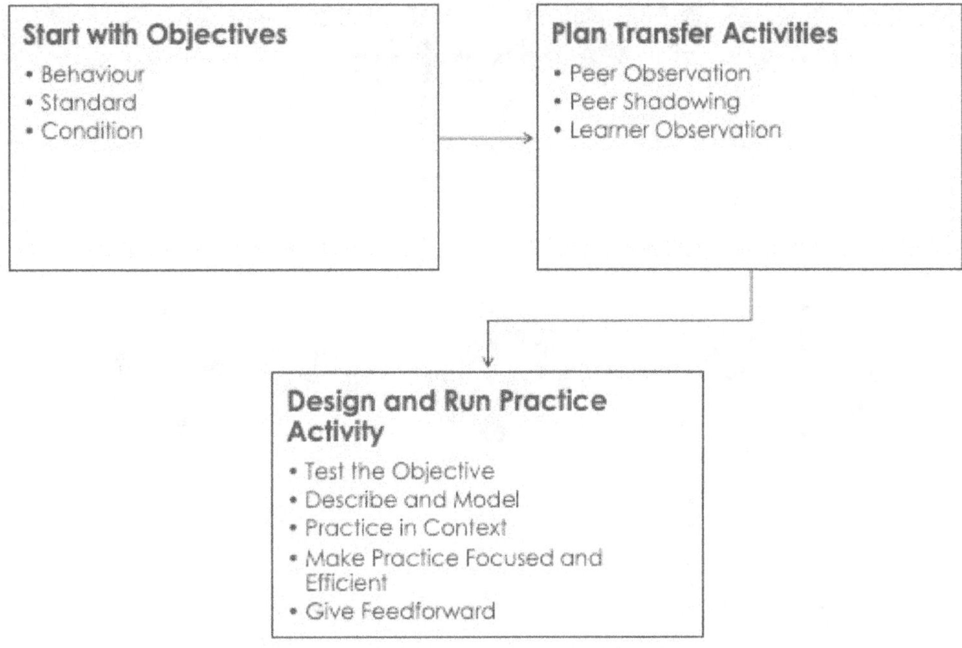

Reflecting

Just because you heard something, or read something, or experienced something, doesn't mean you learnt something. For any of those to result in learning, they need to be combined with reflection, which involves looking back and forwards.

Reflection is where we encourage learners to look back, to see what they learnt, then to look forwards, to see how they could use what they learnt. It's the process of forming those vital connections that eventually lead to the pathways of effective performance.

Reflection

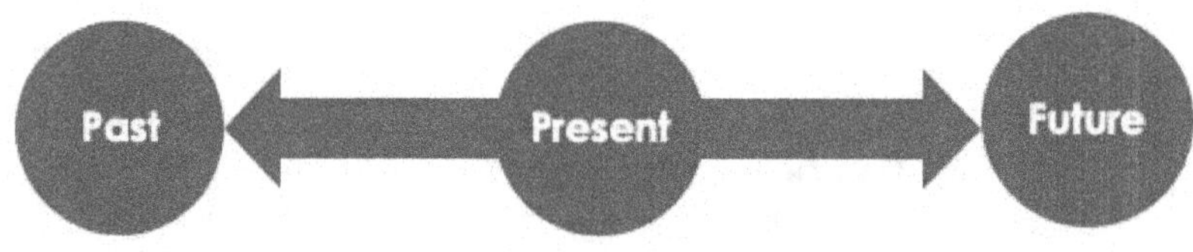

What did you learn?   *How will you use this?*

I believe reflection is one of the major reasons for the existence of corporate training. So often, people are too busy at work to step back and reflect on what they've recently learnt. If you have people who are constantly overworked and overstressed, then how can they have the space to process anything they've learnt and improve?

Training provides both the time and space for busy people to get away from their fast-paced working lives and reflect. This is why reflection is so important for training.

But, in practice, I have witnessed many common issues in incorporating adequate reflection into training, which we will discuss now.

Not Enough Time

Sometimes we spend so much time lecturing and practicing that we run out of time for reflection. It's like finishing a cake without adding the icing!

Learners need time and space to process what has just happened, and recall insights from their training experience. The more often you give them a chance to recall, the better they will remember what they learnt. If the training is several days of cramming information down their throats with no chance to process it, they will very quickly forget most of it. So we need to ensure that opportunities for reflection are spaced throughout the duration of the training.

Incomplete Reflection

There are, at the very least, two key components to reflecting: recalling and applying. In other words, thinking about what they learnt, and thinking about how they can apply that learning.

But what can sometimes happen is (if we even reflect at all) that learners will only focus on recalling. Remember, for training to be successful, it needs to lead to application back into the workplace. The sooner we get learners to think about what they learned, how they could apply it, and when they could apply it, the more likely they are to *actually* apply it.

Poorly-Structured

When groups are reflecting together, structure becomes extremely important. We need to involve them in a meaningful discussion based on recall and application. But discussions can be difficult to manage.

You've probably experienced these issues before: loud people dominating the discussion, quiet people checking out, discussions going off-topic, and some people finishing the discussions before others. All of these issues are a result of poor structure.

If, instead, we focus everyone on specific questions, give them clear time limits, and clarify the expected outputs of discussion, things become much easier to manage. We'll learn how to do this when we look at Designing Reflection Activities.

Shallow and Deep Reflection

I classify reflection as either being shallow or deep.

By shallow, I mean we simply focus on recalling learning points from throughout the day or the previous learning activity, and then think how we can apply them. The reflecting tends to be quick, and there may be more time focussed on sharing what they reflected on, rather than actually reflecting.

With deep reflection, we tend to review certain learning activities (e.g. Experiential Activities). There tends to be a lot of insight that can be gained from these activities—a lot more than initially meets the eye—so it can take a lot of digging to bring out the real learning. For deep reflecting, I will introduce the VACA Model in the next few pages. This helps dig deep, in a well-structured order.

Greenaway and Thiagi

The experts on reflection and experiential learning are Roger Greenaway and Thiagi. I strongly recommend you look them up online. Roger Greenaway has a website (reviewing.co.uk) with lots of free resources dedicated to this subject and Thiagi has a website (Thiagi.com), also with lots of free resources.

Both Dr. Roger Greenaway and Thiagi subscribe to the viewpoint that the reflection (or review, or debrief—whatever terminology you prefer to use) should be just as interesting, if not more interesting than the previous activity that it is debriefing.

I fully agree with this, so I will share the key principles of effective reflection. We'll also look at how to effectively structure reflection activities into our training, and how we can use them throughout it as well.

- ## **Shallow Reflection—Recall and Apply**

As I've already mentioned, two core components of reflection are recalling and applying. Throughout the training, we need to be asking our learners 'What did you learn?' and 'How could you use that at work?'

Common Reflection Questions

Recall	Apply
What did you learn?	How could you use that at work?
What has been most useful to you so far?	When could you use that at work?
What are the top 3 new ideas you have gained?	How can that help you at work?

At certain intervals throughout the day (such as just after lunch or at the end of the day), I'll bring everyone together to stand in a circle. Then I will ask 5 volunteers to step forward and share what they've learnt so far. As they share, I'll then ask them to share how they could use that at work.

In another activity I like to use at similar intervals, I'll spread a selection of pictures on the floor. The pictures are all random and quite abstract. I'll ask the learners to select a picture that represents the most important thing they've learnt so far. I'll then ask them to find a partner and share what that picture represents to them, share what they learnt, and say how they could apply it back at work. Then I'll get them to switch pictures with their partner and find another partner, and share their previous partner's 'recall and apply' points with their new partner. Then I'll repeat this several times, so they mingle with lots of people. At the end, I'll get them all back into a circle and share the learning points of the current picture they're holding.

Another way I ask them to reflect on 'recall and apply' is by opening questions up to the group, at the end of a training section. I will ask 'What did you learn from that?' and I will open my arms up to signal that it's time for someone to step forward. Sometimes I will wait for a while because no one volunteers, so I jokingly tell them that I can wait all day, and so can lunch, and we can finish the class later, if they prefer. Eventually, someone comes forward to share what they've learnt.

There are many ways you can encourage learners to reflect on 'recall and apply', and many opportunities to do so as well. Be creative and do this as often as possible.

Make a habit of finishing each section with a quick 'recall and apply' reflection. Make a habit of starting and finishing mornings and afternoons with a quick 'recall and apply' check. The more often you do this, the more they will remember from their training experience, and the more valuable you will be making it for them.

• Deep Reflection—Reviewing with the VACA Model

Sometimes we want to go a bit deeper with reflection, especially when there is a lot to be reviewed. For example, at the end of an experiential activity or team-building game, many things have probably happened and so there is a lot to learn from. In such instances, we need to make our reflection go into more depth.

As we go into that depth, it's important to structure the reflection in the right way. 'Structure' is a great way of putting it, because the very word implies that there are building blocks to it, which there are. In fact, there are 4.

The 4 building blocks, or elements, of deep reflection, or reviewing, are:
1. **Vent**
2. **Analyse**
3. **Conclude**
4. **Apply**

The VACA Model

I'll go through each of these in detail shortly. Before I do, here are a few pointers on how to get the most out of these elements.

Firstly, reflection will almost always be different. Even if you are running the same activity in the same course (even with the same learners), each time you do it, it may need to be done differently. This all depends on the needs of the learners.

Secondly, to get the most out of these elements, plan an activity that includes all of them but, as you run it, tailor it to the needs of your learners. Maybe you planned 10 minutes for venting but discovered they have nothing to vent. Maybe you planned to do more analysis, but they've already jumped to some conclusions and are already focussing on applying.

Finally, maybe you planned to do the whole thing in 10 minutes, but discover it actually needs 30. This is where training and facilitation becomes more of an art. Knowledge will help you plan for reflection, but instinct will help you run it.

- ## V is for Vent

Whenever I run a really challenging activity, people tend to have very strong emotional reactions. That's what challenge does to people—it brings about emotional reactions. Emotion is a part of the experience that we cannot afford to ignore. If we pretend it isn't there, it will bite us hard. Ignore emotion at your peril.

These emotions could be anything: joy, anger, frustration, confusion, curiosity, and so on. The important thing to know about them is that they need to be allowed to come up to the surface and be released. This is why I call it venting.

Without sufficient venting, learners struggle to focus, and that is why we should allow time for venting in a reflection activity. In fact, I normally don't even need to structure this. I announce the activity is over and BAM, venting just happens.

Time and time again, I have run experiential activities where participants needed to do A LOT of venting. I would stop the activity and, all of a sudden, there is nothing but noise. Every participant has something to share. They release their pent-up emotions, they share their insights, and they find people they had unfinished business with.

Emotions are powerful. If you suppress them, they get stronger and eat away at you. So, allow time for them to be released because, without releasing them, our learners won't focus on anything else. Sometimes, when I have tried to skip venting and move straight into the next part, learners vent anyway. So, structure venting into your reflection.

Learners don't always need to vent. Maybe they just did a simple practice and you ask them how they feel but there's nothing special. That's OK. That means we can move on from venting because they are already in the right frame of mind to move to the next step.

It also depends on the subject you are reflecting on. If you're training them on how to use a new CRM system, then there may not be much emotion because emotion may not be relevant to how they use the system (unless they're really pissed off because it's far more complicated than the older system!).

But if you are training them in conflict management, or another subject where emotion is relevant, then emotion is something they need to discuss. If you ask them how they felt after an activity and they didn't have any strong feelings, in particular, then dig deeper.

At the end of the day, the purpose of venting is to vent. Let them release those pent-up emotions so they are free to focus on the next steps in the reflection process. Once they've done enough venting, they can move comfortably on to the next phase.

- ## A is for Analyse

Things just happened, so there's going to be something to analyse.

For example, maybe we were playing a competitive game and one particular team won. We should analyse why they won and why other teams didn't. What did they do differently to the other teams? What were the factors that helped that team win and made the others lose?

Maybe we were training them on how to code a website using HTML. They entered their code, and then checked what the web page looked like and it was not what they were expecting. What happened there? What was the difference between their expectation and the actual outcome? What caused that difference?

Or maybe we've put them into a role-play with an actor to practice conflict management skills. They try a technique, but the actor responds with more anger. Why is that? What was their intention in trying that technique? What did the actor perceive? Why didn't they achieve what they intended to?

The 'analyse' part is all about cause-and-effect relations. It's all about identifying the factors that contribute to success or failure.

Sometimes these factors will be obvious and not much discussion is required to bring them out. Other times, they are not so obvious. Take plane crash investigations, for example. A lot of things need to be analysed in order to deduce what sequence of events led to the crash. The black box recorder, the wreckage, eyewitness accounts, and so on all need to be analysed in great detail, and assumptions and hypotheses all need to be tested as well in order to come to an accurate conclusion.

During this phase, it is important to remain objective. If not enough venting has been done prior to analysis, then emotions may cloud the analysis. Important factors are ignored and, instead, other people are blamed. It can quickly spiral into a fully-blown argument.

It's also important to draw focus away from people and personalities in discussion. Going back to the example of plane crashes, it is rarely the pilot's fault. In fact, just blaming the pilot would sacrifice a wide range of valuable lessons that could be used to prevent future accidents. Even if it were the pilot's fault, then it might be due to their mental health, their lack of skill in flying, or their inability to communicate effectively. Should we stop the analysis at those factors? No. We should continue our analysis until we find why a pilot with those issues was allowed to fly a plane in the first place. We should look at the system, not the people.

Sometimes it may seem more like a people issue. I once had two participants start an argument in an experiential learning activity that quickly escalated. I stopped the activity and moved to reflection. Throughout the venting phase, there was a lot of blaming of one another. But, through the analysis, it became apparent that their difference in behaviour was what caused the argument. One person suggested something to the other. The other person perceived that suggestion as a command and felt disrespected, so retaliated. And so on. If such a situation happens, get everyone away from personal attacks and blaming as quickly as possible (but don't ignore their need to vent somewhat). Redirect their focus to things that are in their control, such as their own behaviour, their choice of words, and the timing of their communication.

Comparing Expected with Actual Outcomes

In summary, analysing is all about comparing expected and actual outcomes. Was there a difference or not? What caused what? As they start to analyse what happened, they start to generate valuable insights, which brings us on to the next phase: conclude.

• Conclude

Through analysis, we reach conclusions. We summarise the cause-and-effect relationships we identified through analysis, and share what these mean to us. This is where the 'Aha!' moments occur and where insight is generated.

For example, in a negotiation game I sometimes play, we finish with a good reflection. We vent any pent-up emotions from the game. Then we analyse which teams played best and which teams did poorly and why. Generally, they conclude that spending time planning a strategy, allocating roles, and building trust with other teams were vital success factors. These are the conclusions they come to.

In Email Writing training, after people have written emails, I'll get them to share their written samples with one another. They'll then share their first impressions of these emails, and compare that with the impression the email was intended to give. Some conclusions that generally come out are that the structure, choice of words, and level of detail contribute significantly to the impression the email gives.

In Change Management training, normally I will share a model called The Change Curve with my learners. I'll ask them to reflect on recent changes in their organisation, and use The Change Curve to analyse how and why people have reacted the way they did. A general conclusion that comes out is that, during the initial phases of change, it's important to acknowledge people's complaints and show care and concern for those people.

The 'conclusion' part is my favourite part of reflection. It's where the real lessons come out. Even after I've run the same practice or experiential activities, time and time again, I almost always find new insights come out each time. Even as the facilitator, we can always learn something new when learners share their conclusions.

Sometimes 'analyse' and 'conclude' happen at the same time. Sometimes a question to prompt analysis will result in conclusions. Other times, the analysis needs to be a structured process that involves gathering evidence, hearing different viewpoints, and testing different hypotheses. Once that's done, the conclusion comes about in the form of a summary.

But it is at the 'conclude' section that we may be tricked into thinking we have finished reflecting. Those significant 'Aha' moments are what really stands out in the whole learning process. But those 'Aha' insights tend to be abstract ideas. They don't mean anything until they lead to action. So, after concluding, we need to do one more thing: apply.

- ## A is for Apply

At the 'apply' stage, we start planning. We take the conclusions and turn them into a plan of action that we can apply at the next opportunity.

Here, our learners may need to do some filtering. They may have collectively reached a lot of conclusions, but not all of the conclusions will be directly applicable to each individual. Furthermore, it may be impractical for them to apply so many lessons. So, we need to focus their attention on those conclusions that will have the biggest impact on them.

It may be, at this point, that we need to encourage learners to revisit their objectives or the problems they are looking to solve. We should encourage them to find the one lesson that would be easiest to apply and would have the biggest impact.

Sometimes, as well, learners may come up with ideas that need to be parked and revisited later. Maybe reflection is not the time to filter out lessons learnt but just a time to collect lessons that might be relevant. The last phase in the Shaping Paths approach is Commit, which is where we encourage learners to commit to applying certain lessons after the training, and so that may be the time to revisit their lessons and filter them out.

An approach I typically use is to have the learners spend the beginning of the training writing their objectives in a section of the Action Plan template at the back of their books. As we go through different sections and activities and we reflect, I ask them to record any conclusions on Post-it notes and stick those onto their action plans. At the end of the training, they have a big pile of Post-it notes waiting to be reviewed. So, at that point, they then look through for the ones that they think are key, throw away the rest, and then complete their action plan template accordingly.

Other times, we may structure a reflection session just before a practice session. In that case, encourage learners to focus on the lessons they can apply immediately to their next practice.

The essence of this step is in planning how to turn their new insights into actions. So long as learners can take their ideas and turn them into effective actions, then our reflection, at least for now, is over.

If they apply the lessons learnt and realise that those lessons were actually incomplete, that's OK, because we can go through the whole reflection process again and refine those lessons learnt. After all, this is how people learn.

- ## Designing Reflection Activities

We know that a reflection activity can either be shallow and focussed on simply recalling and applying, or needs go deeper and focus on venting, analysing, concluding, and applying. But to design and run an effective reflection activity, there is a bit more to it than those simple steps.

Lots of things can go wrong during reflection, such as:
- running out of time or not even having any time to reflect in the first place
- learners not going into enough depth
- everyone talking about different things or moving through the steps at different paces
- loud participants dominating the discussion
- jumping to false conclusions
- not everyone participating in the reflection
- too much negative or positive focus, and missing out on vital information

There are several things we can do when designing our reflection activities to prevent those problems and get the most out of them:
- Plan Reflection
- Teach Reflection
- Structure Reflection
- Focus Reflection

Let's go through them, one by one.

Plan Reflection

This seems quite obvious, but is so easy to overlook. When designing training, we tend to spend more time focussed on content and practice or experiential activities. Reflection might come in last or, even worse, get completely ignored. Even if we do plan for reflection, we may underestimate just how long it takes.

Not every practice activity needs to be immediately followed by its own reflection activity. Sometimes, we may want to go through several different practice activities and use one reflection to conclude all of them at the end.

Sometimes, we have to get creative in finding ways of scheduling adequate reflection time into our training. This might involve sneakily combining Guiding and Reflecting together, or getting some learners to practice whilst others reflect, or maybe even making the reflection seem like a break.

A good principle to go by is to **schedule as much reflection time as you have**

practice time, so do whatever you can to allocate that much time for reflection.

Teach Reflection

Sometimes learners don't take reflection seriously. Their reasoning may be that they've done the practice already, so there is no more need to discuss. Other times, they may feel discussion is just part of the routine of training and give it as little attention as a routine deserves.

To get the most out of reflection, people need to take it seriously. And to get people to take reflection seriously, we need to teach them the principles of reflection.

A great way of doing this is by getting learners to reflect as early as possible.

At the very start of the training, as part of the Priming section, we can get participants to reflect on and share their most recent experiences with the topic. We can ask them to share what they have learnt and how they learnt it. By structuring a good sharing activity, we may be able to elicit from the learners themselves the very principles of effective reflection.

Another strategy is to include the principles of reflection as part of the Guiding section, earlier in the training, which can actually be content that we include as part of the training.

I have found that there is a very effective way of explaining the importance of reflection in the Chinese language. The word 'experience' has two main translations in Chinese: 经历 (Jing1 Li4) and 经验 (Jing1 Yan4). The first one (Jing1 Li4) means to experience something, or to go through something, whereas the latter (Jing1 Yan4) means to have gained experience. After eliciting these two definitions from the audience, I ask them 'How can we turn Jing1 Li4 into Jing1 Yan4?' The answer is to reflect. Once I've explained it this way, I normally find learners get the concept of reflection and can appreciate why we are doing these discussion activities.

We can even demonstrate the principles of reflection in action by ourselves. As we conclude an activity, we can share our own analysis, the conclusions we reached from that analysis, and give suggestions to certain individuals on how to apply those to future practice.

At the very least, we can describe the principles of reflection as we go through a reflection activity. If you explain more about why you are running this reflection activity, they may take to it with more purpose.

Structure Reflection

Lack of structure in any activity that involves discussion can cause numerous problems.

For a start, people may move through different steps at different paces. Some more vocal individuals may have lots of venting to do, whilst others are ready to jump straight to conclusions. Other times, some people may be talking about applying the lessons learnt whilst others are still testing the validity of those lessons learnt.

Maybe some participants like to think out loud, whilst others need quiet time. Unfortunately, thinking out loud often comes at the expense of those who need to think quietly. Other times, participants may jump through the reflection activity based on their interest but at the expense of missing out on valuable insights that could have otherwise been gained through deeper focus in other areas.

Adding structure to reflection activities can help avoid these problems.

For example, instead of writing a question on the board and asking groups to start discussing, try a slightly different approach. Ask individuals to first reflect on the question on their own and write their ideas down for a few minutes. After those few minutes, get them to share with a partner. Then get them to start discussing as a group.

Structure Reflection Activities

Structuring activities from individual reflection to group reflection can greatly increase the depth we get from reflection. It gives each individual the valuable thinking time they need. It gives each individual a sounding board to share their ideas and hear others ideas, which may even lead to new ideas. And it gives everyone a chance to both think and speak, helping satisfy both the quiet and the loud participants.

Focus Reflection

In a reflection activity, there may be multiple questions for learners to discuss. Some questions may get more than enough attention while others may get too little attention. We need to balance the amount of focus each question gets in order to help learners discover the valuable insights awaiting them.

One way of doing this is to specify the output of the discussion. That might be a list of 10 things, a definition of a term, or the root cause of a problem. It could be anything, really. But **specific information on exactly what they need to achieve by answering the question**—as opposed to just giving them a question and allowing them to discuss freely—**can greatly enhance the amount of depth they go into.**

I have found this principle to work, time and time again. I give them a question to discuss but, after a short while, they feel they've given it adequate attention by writing one sentence and start playing with their phones. So I go up to them and tell them to list 10 things. This really forces them to reflect deeper on the question, analyse it from a variety of angles, and even drop some assumptions they originally had.

Another way of getting people to focus well is to make the timing transparent. At the very least, let them know how long they have to discuss this particular question. Often, I see trainers give learners a question to discuss and just leave them to it without telling them how much time they have.

The problem of this is that, with no clear time boundaries, people decide on those boundaries themselves. Sometimes, those boundaries will be too long or too short and, as a result, learners pace themselves inappropriately. They may finish the discussion too soon without going into enough depth, or they may even spend too much time on certain areas at the expense of other areas.

Even better than letting them know the time limit is to actually use a timer. I use an app on my MacBook called Alinof TimerPro. It's a countdown timer that can be shown in full screen. I put it up on the projector and, as I start the discussion, I start the timer. This really helps learners pace themselves and get the amount of depth from the discussion that I intended them to.

Designing the Activity

At the end of this section is a template for designing reflection activities to make the above easier for you to use.

- ## Energising Reflection Activities

Another reason learners may not get enough out of a reflection activity is because they find it boring. Discuss this question, write down these answers—even I would find that pretty boring.

Naturally, the solution to this is to jazz it up. Make it fun for everyone. If you can, even go as far as to make reflection more fun than the preceding activity that it's debriefing.

Fun adds energy. It gets the heart pumping. It directs as much cognitive attention to the task as there is to spare. We can add energy and make it fun by using several principles:

- **use more body parts**
- **go large**
- **use props**
- **visualise**
- **make it a task**
- **draw on popular culture**

As a disclaimer, many of these ideas have been inspired by Dr. Roger Greenaway's articles on his website, reviewing.co.uk. He is a fantastic facilitator with many great ideas for enriching this aspect of your training and I strongly recommend you check him out.

Use More Body Parts

I once ran a discussion activity with about 90 participants. It was part of my research for a course I was designing on customer service for a hotel chain. I was fortunate enough to be given the opportunity to spend an hour-and-a-half with these 90 people to hear their viewpoints on what they needed from the course.

One activity I ran in this session was to show a series of statements and ask if they agreed or disagreed with them. At first, I had them all sitting down in groups of 10. I asked them to raise one arm if they agreed and to raise two arms if they disagreed. Nobody raised their arms. They obviously weren't very engaged, and if I was to get the information I wanted out of this activity, I would have to engage them. So, I used this principle.

I told them all to stand up. Then I said that, if they agree with the statement, they should stand to the left of the room, and if they disagree, they should stand to the right of the room. All of a sudden, they all started talking. Everyone had an opinion. The simple act of standing up got their blood flowing. Even more than that, the act of standing somewhere on a line was a representation of their commitment to an opinion.

If they stood in that position, then they had better be prepared to justify why. It turned out to be a very heated debate.

This principle is so simple, yet so effective as well. If you have groups sitting down to discuss a question, then get them to stand up. This is one of the benefits of using flip charts in training—it gives them something to stand around. It also gives them something to write on.

Another easy way of using this is just getting them to move around the room. When I have different questions to discuss, I will write each question on a separate flip chart. I give each group a set time, say 4 minutes, to discuss the question on that flip chart. When the time is up, they move along to the next flip chart, and discuss the question written there for the same amount of time.

The activity I described above is so easy to set up and run, and makes for a really focussed and engaging discussion. Learners are focussed on one question for a set time limit. They get to stand up and move around. Each group gets to spend an equal amount of time on each question. Furthermore, as they move to questions previous groups have already answered, they get to see different ideas the groups before them had. They even get to build on these ideas. It's a simple way of structuring a reflection activity, and very effective.

Go Large

This is an interesting principle. I'm not fully sure why it works so well, but it does. It's simple as well—just make things larger.

For example, if the discussion involves putting things onto a grid, then we might give them the grid on a sheet of A4 paper. If we wanted to go large, then we may take that grid and actually map it out on the classroom floor. Suddenly, they go from sitting down, bent over a piece of paper on their desk, to standing up and wandering around a life-sized grid.

This ties in quite nicely to the previous principle, and is probably one of the reasons why this works so well. By making things larger, they have to use more body parts to participate in the activity. Suddenly, they have to lift and carry things, move things around, and walk around.

I think another part of it is to do with imagination. The discussion goes from something they are engaging with on only an intellectual level to something they are engaging with on a sensory level as well. Instead of just thinking, they are now seeing and touching things. This extra-sensory perspective can give rise to new and valuable ideas.

Use Props

Props add a whole new dimension of fun and meaning to a discussion. They could be anything, such as a mask, some chess pieces, a hammer, maps, markers, and so on. Whatever you can get your hands on, you can use as a prop.

Props also encourage the use of more body parts. Learners now have things to pick up, to move about, to throw in the air, and to fiddle with. This gets the blood flowing.

They also engage the imagination. Props can represent things and may represent different things to different people. A water bottle could represent potential. An umbrella could represent protection. A cuddly teddy bear could represent danger. Engaging the imagination in such creative ways is a really easy way to make reflection activities fun.

Sometimes, props even bring about different mental states. When I put on a black cape, I'm now a villain, and I'll think of ways I could have sabotaged my performance. As I put on a construction builder's hard-hat, I'm now here to fix things that went wrong. As I pick up a magnifying glass, I know I'm supposed to go into more detail.

Props help communicate abstract ideas. Rather than having to take an idea, and find a way of articulating it so that others can instantly understand it, we could just show an object that represents the idea. This helps others get it instantly.

Visualise

Pictures are yet another way of stimulating the imagination and easily communicating abstract ideas. Furthermore, much like props, they represent different things to different people.

Give them pictures, such as cut-outs from magazines, piles of postcards, or printouts of things you found online.

Another advantage of props and pictures is that they can stimulate new ideas. They are a whole other dimension for viewing information from. Maybe the pictures remind them of a feeling they had, or an idea that was on the fringes of their awareness, or maybe it gives them a new way of relating to an old idea.

Make It a Task

Turn the review into a task. The task can include things such as taking surveys, creating a map, drawing pictures, performing a demonstration, and so on.

This completely changes their way of perceiving the reflection. It goes from a boring discussion to an interesting task. If the task is to survey people on their thoughts, then they may anticipate the results of the survey. If they need to create a map, then they may derive enjoyment from discovering new places, ideas, and connections. And if it's to demonstrate an idea, then they may enjoy the whole process of interacting with the audience.

At the very least, it gives people something to do. Making it a task changes the focus from simply discussing to doing, which involves more focus, more effort, and more energy. Overall, it's a great way of making reflection more interesting.

Draw On Popular Culture

This is a great source of inspiration for reviewing activities. Look for famous quiz shows, dating shows, or popular trends.

Maybe there is a game show whose format you can copy directly. Maybe you could use a dating show concept to get learners to make ideas as attractive as possible. Maybe there is a new trend in the news or social media and you can use that as a theme for the activity.

One of the great things about this is that people relate to it instantly. If it's a famous game show, then they already know the rules and may have even rehearsed it in their minds before. It adds more enthusiasm to the activity, and it's great for generating a lot of laughs, too.

Energising Reflection Activities

Use More Body Parts

- Get them to stand up and move about. The more of their body they move, the more energy they will have.

Go Large

- Use life-sized props to represent objects of the discussion. For example, map out a grid on the classroom floor instead of on a sheet of A4 paper.

Use Props

- Give them objects to represent concepts and ideas.

Visualise

- Give them a selection of pictures to choose from. They can choose which picture best represents the idea in their head.

Make it a Task

- Instead of just answering questions, turn it into a task, such as taking a survey, creating a map, drawing pictures and so on.

Draw on Popular Culture

- Structure the reflection activity like a famous TV game show.

- ## Increasing Reflection Throughout

One of the joys of being an instructional designer is that we get to be creative. It's part of the fun of this job.

As I've introduced the Shaping Paths approach, I've introduced it in a structured manner—first Priming, then Guiding, then Practicing, then Reflecting, then Committing. But it doesn't have to be structured. You can change the order, you can combine things, and sometimes you can even skip things altogether. The reason I've introduced it as a structure is so that it gives you something to run with if you don't have much experience. Once you have that experience, though, you can mix it up as you desire.

Every step in the Shaping Paths approach has its own value and, generally speaking, your training should include a certain amount of each step. But when it comes to the Reflect step, this one is a bit special.

Reflection is not just something that happens after practice. It's vital for learning anything. We can use reflection with reading activities, with ice-breakers, with videos, and so on.

A good principle to go by is to use reflection anytime you want your learners to learn something.

For example, maybe you have a technique you want to train for a course on Influencing Skills. You looked earlier at the Guiding section and prepared some guiding questions, a nicely structured explanation, and maybe even a few stories. But why stop there? Add some reflection to that as well.

You could show a video of someone using that influencing technique. You can then ask learners what they thought of that technique (venting). Then ask them what, specifically, that person did to use that technique successfully (analyse). Then ask them what they learnt from watching that video (conclude). Finally, ask them how they could use what they learnt from that video (apply). Maybe by doing this, you decide to scrap your original Guide plan altogether.

As you may be starting to see from the above example, the possibilities are endless. Suddenly you can change content into an activity. Instead of requiring learners to passively absorb content, they are now actively reflecting on it.

Sometimes training is less about skill development and more about problem-solving. If that's the case, then focus on sharing best practices, and then give them lots of room to reflect on that.

Reflection is not just limited to the Practice and Guiding sections. It's even something we can do as a way of priming our learners. At the beginning of a training, it's great to get them to reflect on what they have already learnt about this topic from experience and have them share those lessons with their fellow learners.

You might want to use certain mechanisms to encourage the different steps of reflection to come out all the time. The Parking Lot strategy is a great way of getting people to focus on applying their lessons learnt. Simply tape a piece of paper up on the wall and label it 'The Parking Lot'. Then, every time a learner concludes a lesson learnt that they may want to apply at a later time, they can write it down on a Post-it note and stick it up on the parking lot. Later on, when it comes to practicing again, they can go back to the parking lot and see which lesson they want to apply this time.

The main point I want to make here is to go crazy. This job is fun, so let the creative inner child in you run free. The more you enjoy yourself, the more they will, too.

- ## Reflection Activity Template

To make it easier to design a reflection activity, here is a template for you. Simply answer these questions to help you plan it out:

Shallow Reflection:

What question(s) will you use to help them recall their learning?
What question(s) will you use to help them apply their learning?

Deep Reflection:

Will they need to vent? If so, how will you let them vent and for how long?
What questions will you use to help them analyse the experience?
What questions will you use to help them identify their key learning conclusions?
What questions will you use to help them plan how to apply what they have learnt?

Planning the Activity:

How much time will the reflection take? How will you plan your training so that you have enough time to run the reflection activity?

Do you need to teach them the principles of reflection? If so, when is the most appropriate time to do so? And what is the most efficient way of doing so?

How will you structure the reflection activity to ensure everyone spends enough time on each step of the reflection process?

How will you focus their attention to ensure they go into the right amount of detail?

How will you make sure they don't spend too long on it?

How will you energise the reflection activity?

Reflection Activity Template – Part 1

Shallow Reflection:
What question/s will you use to help them recall their learning?
What question/s will you use to help them apply their learning?

Deep Reflection:
Will they need to vent? If so, how will you let them vent and for how long?
What questions will you use to help them analyse the experience?
What questions will you use to help them identify their key learning conclusions?
What questions will you use to help them plan how to apply what they have learnt?

Reflection Activity Template – Part 2

<table>
<tr><td align="center">Planning the Activity:</td></tr>
<tr><td>How much time will the reflection take? How will you plan your training so that you have enough time to run the reflection activity?</td></tr>
<tr><td>Do you need to teach them the principles of reflection? If so, when is the most appropriate time to do so? And what is the most efficient way of doing so?</td></tr>
<tr><td>How will you structure the reflection activity to ensure everyone spends enough time on each step of the reflection process?</td></tr>
<tr><td>How will you focus their attention to ensure they go into the right amount of detail? How will you make sure they don't spend too long on it?</td></tr>
<tr><td>How will you energise the reflection activity?</td></tr>
</table>

Reflecting Summary

The following flowchart is a summary of everything we have looked at in this section:

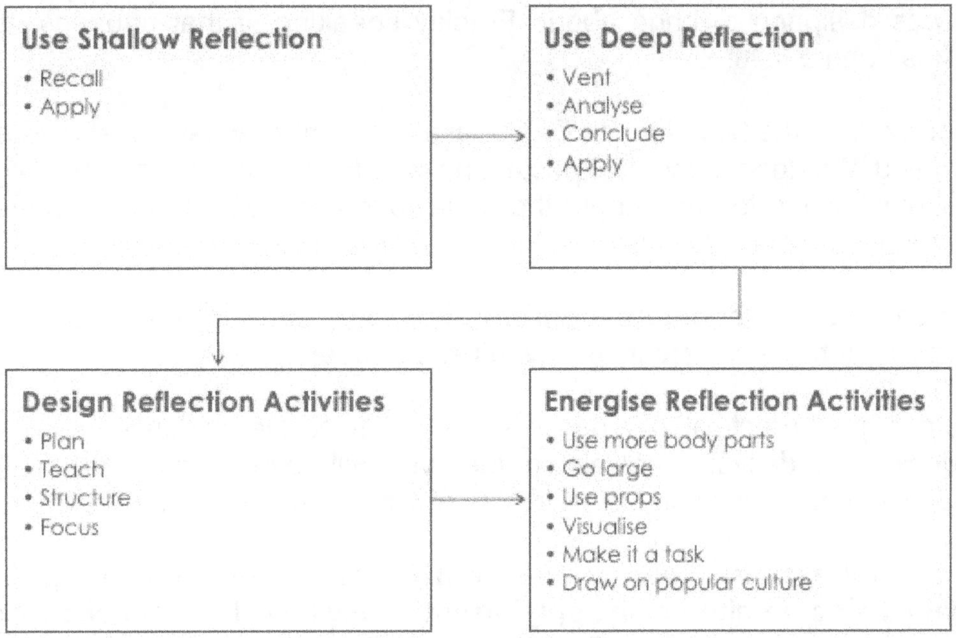

Committing

It ain't over until the stakeholder sings.

It's tempting to think that, once everyone walks out of the training room, our job is done. To some degree, it actually is, because we probably won't be interacting with our learners much beyond that point. But our training's job is far from done.

After the training is when the real change begins. It's when our learners return to their work and start using what they've learnt in a way that matters. At least, that's what we hope happens.

At that point, our learners might not be able to successfully realise the changes our training was designed to bring about. Frankly speaking, if that happens, then our training has been a failure.

Remember, during the Mapping the Gap phase, we clarified what stakeholders expect of our training. We defined these expectations in terms of business outcomes. And we designed our training to bring about the behavioural and performance changes that are required in our learners to satisfy our stakeholders' expectations.

Only when our stakeholders confirm that our training has matched their expectations can we consider our training a success.

If you've designed practical training tools, and followed the guidance in this book on how to design and deliver your training, then you will have done all you can to meet those stakeholder expectations. Now it's out of your hands and in the learners' hands.

But before you pass it all over to the learners, there's one final thing you want to do: gain their commitment in applying what they have learnt back to their jobs to the best of their abilities. The more committed they are, the higher the chances of your training being a success.

In this final section of the training, we want to gain our learners' commitment to enacting this change. So, let's see what we can do to maximise that commitment.

- ## Compliance in the Process of Commitment

There are two ways of making someone do something: commitment and compliance. You can either make someone want to do something or force them to do it.

There is a time and a place for both. If you are looking to an Olympic athlete to break world records, then you will still need a certain amount of commitment, no matter how much compliance you use. It takes great passion, obsession, and a will to push the human body to its absolute limits.

But, then again, throughout the course of history, compliance has forced slaves to push their bodies beyond their limits and work themselves to death.

The thing about compliance is that, when the rule enforcer is not around, the workers run away. Compliance is exhausting for all involved (although normally far more so for the poor workers).

Commitment is what we want from our learners, for the very simple reason that we can't be standing behind every one of our learners with a whip all the time. They are on their own out there in the big, wide world.

Because they're on their own, they need to be self-motivated. **They must feel the need to change, as well as want to change, and have the intention to change.**

The biggest implication of this is that we can't force our learners to commit, so we need to help them discover what they are willing to commit to.

We need to allocate time towards the end of the training where learners sit down and evaluate what they have learnt. We then give them the structure and guidance to help them evaluate by themselves the possible actions they can take after the training. They evaluate which actions are most aligned with their own goals, ambitions, and plans. Then they stand up and share what they have decided they are going to do. Put simply, we guide them through a process of commitment.

Ironically, we want compliance in this commitment process.

We should assume that learners won't go through an adequate commitment process of their own will. Most likely, they will forget to do this. Or they don't realise the importance of doing this. Or maybe they *do* take some time to go through a process of commitment by themselves, but their own process is insufficient.

Have you ever set New Year's resolutions and then given up on them after several weeks? Or set yourself a big goal (like running a marathon), but then failed to achieve it? Or tried losing weight, but failed? I suspect you have, because that's part of human nature.

We frequently overestimate our ability to change ourselves. The reason we fail is because we don't understand human nature. We assume change happens through willpower alone, but it doesn't. Willpower is an extremely useless tool for enacting change.

Thankfully, human nature isn't that difficult to understand. In the following sections, I will share some essential lessons about human nature that will help us change ourselves and, more importantly, **help us help our learners change themselves**. With this knowledge, we can design a commitment process that will help learners commit to something that they can see through to the end. Then all we need to do is gain their compliance in this process of commitment.

- ## The Elephant and The Rider

Training is about helping people change. A great metaphor—or analogy—for understanding change is that of The Elephant and The Rider. I mentioned this earlier, in the section about using analogies, and I'm going into more detail about it here because it is so important.

The metaphor states that there are two parts to our brain:

The Rider—the rational, analytical, long-term part
The Elephant—the emotional, habitual, short-term part

Both of these parts frequently come into conflict, and I am sure you have encountered this conflict plenty of times in your own life.

For example, maybe one evening, after watching a documentary about healthy living, you suddenly decide that you are going to go running every day. So, that night, before you go to bed, you set your alarm for 5:30 a.m. This is The Rider part of your brain, thinking about the long-term benefits of running. It has made a plan to go running tomorrow morning.

The next morning, your alarm goes off at 5:30 a.m. but you quickly hit the snooze button and go back to sleep. This is The Elephant in action. It's thinking about *now*. And *now* it's much more comfortable to lie in bed than to get up, walk over to the wardrobe, try to find something to wear, and then head out the door to go running.

As clever as the Rider is, if he goes against The Elephant, he is always going to lose. The Elephant is strong, and The Rider is weak.

Sometimes, The Rider will try to go against The Elephant and succeed for a short time. Maybe, one morning, you successfully drag yourself out of bed, put your running shoes on, and head out the door. But, by the time you start running, you've already lost the will. This is because you were depending on willpower to go running. Willpower is incredibly limited. Will power is, essentially, the strength of The Rider, and that quickly runs out when he tries to push The Elephant.

In order to successfully bring about change, both The Rider and The Elephant must be aligned. To align them, they both need particular things.

Firstly, The Rider needs direction. If he wants to make The Elephant go in a particular direction, then he needs to be very clear about where he wants to go.

If you successfully wake up at 5:30 a.m., but then stumble over to your wardrobe and can't figure out what to wear, then you are going to spend some time deliberating. Should I wear these pants? Is it too hot for them? Which running shoes should I wear?

When The Rider doesn't have clear direction, he loves to deliberate. Unfortunately, all of this deliberating leads to analysis paralysis (lots of thinking and no doing). The Rider may even exhaust himself with all of this thinking.

So, instead, we need to give The Rider a clear direction. Spend 10 minutes, the night before, checking the weather. Prepare your running clothes and the running route beforehand. Then, when the time comes to run, The Rider doesn't have to deliberate over anything; he can just focus on guiding The Elephant.

Now that we know The Rider needs clear direction, what does The Elephant need?

The Elephant needs motivation. He cares about the *now*. If it's cold outside and warm in bed, then he's going to want to stay in bed. And if you wake up too early and feel sleepy, then The Elephant is going to demand that you go back to sleep.

So, we need to ensure The Elephant has sufficient motivation. One way of doing this is reducing the amount of motivation required. For example, choose a warmer day to go running. Make sure you go to bed at a reasonable time and get a good night's sleep the night before. Maybe even reduce the distance of the run, to make it easier.

You can also increase the motivation. Maybe you arranged to go running with a good friend and so you know they are waiting for you. Or maybe you've just signed up to an app that posts your running results onto social media, and you really want to share it with your friends. Maybe you have arranged to play football this weekend, so you want to go running to get fit before then.

So, clear direction and enough motivation can help align The Rider and The Elephant. But there is also one other thing that can help keep them aligned. And that is The Path (hence the title of this book 'Shaping Paths').

Imagine The Rider and The Elephant are walking through a jungle and, in every direction, there is dense forest. That makes it hard for The Rider to find clear direction, and it also makes it hard for The Elephant to feel motivated enough to keep walking through all those annoying trees.

But if, instead, directly ahead of them, there was a clear path through the forest, they would find it easier to have enough direction and motivation. There would be no need for deliberation or no need for putting up with annoying tree branches. They could just walk forward.

The Path represents the environment. It represents the things in our environment that make it easier for us to realise this change.

So, if we want to go running, then we need to look at what in our environment can encourage us to go running. For example, maybe there is a park right next to our house with a nice running track. Maybe we could go to sleep in our running clothes, and put our running shoes by the foot of our bed so, when we wake up, all we need to do is just get out of bed. Or, even better, we buy a running machine and put it next to the bed. That way we don't even need to go outside! We just roll out of bed and start running!

The Elephant and Rider

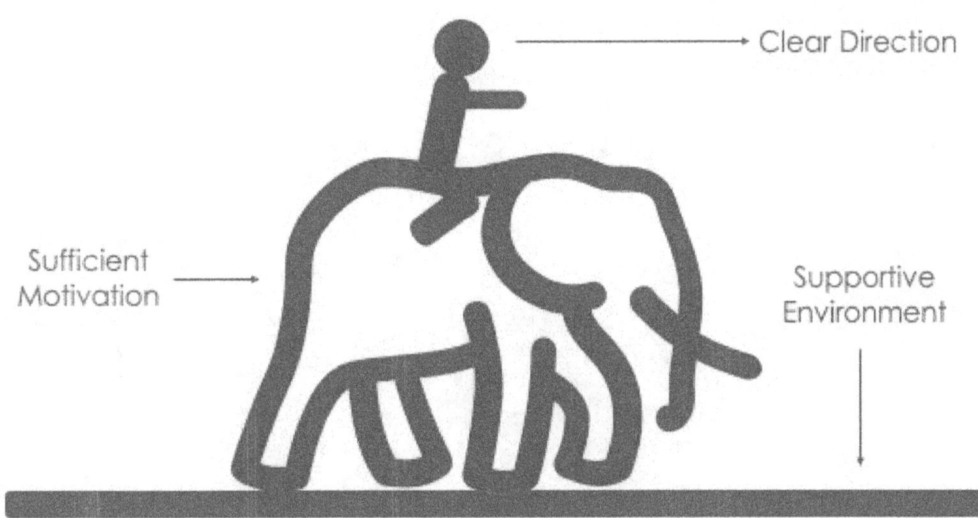

A fantastic book on the subject of change is *Switch* by Chip and Dan Heath (and is actually where I got this metaphor from). This book goes on to say that there are three important implications of this metaphor:

1. What looks like resistance to change is often lack of clarity.
—Maybe we want to go running more. But what does 'go running more' mean, exactly? That lack of clarity will get The Rider deliberating rather than taking action.
2. What looks like laziness is often exhaustion.
– Why would people want to go running in the rain at 5:30 a.m. when they're too tired because they didn't sleep enough? And how would they find the motivation to go running more when they're already so busy and exhausted from their day job?
3. What looks like a people problem is often a situational problem.
– The reason people don't do enough exercise is often because they're too stressed from work and busy with other things. By the time they finally have time to exercise, they're too exhausted and only have enough energy to crash out in front of the TV. It would be much more effective to focus on reducing stress levels first.

So, whatever change we want to bring about, we need to make sure that we have the following three conditions in place:
1. A clear direction
2. Sufficient motivation
3. A supportive environment

- ## The Habit Loop Theory

It is estimated that 45% of our waking behaviour is habitual. This means 45% of our waking behaviour happens with minimal awareness. We wake up and immediately open our phones to check the news. We walk past the bakery and just have to go in and buy a cake. We feel stressed and reach for a cigarette.

Habits are extremely powerful. They represent the unconscious, short-term, elephant side of our mind. They've been ingrained into us through years of conditioning. We no longer need to think to perform a habit; we just act.

How does this relate to training and commitment?

Habits are both the goal and the barrier. Through training, we intend for learners to develop new, good habits. To do that, they will have to overcome bad habits.

How Habits Work

Charles Duhigg's book, *The Power of Habit*, summarises what we know about habits into a simple 3-step process:
1. Cue
2. Routine
3. **Reward**

1. Cue

This is what triggers the habit. Waking up triggers the habit of checking our phones. The sight and smell of the bakery triggers our habit of eating cake. Stress triggers our smoking habit.

Charles Duhigg summarises triggers into 5 different types:

1. Location
2. Time
3. Emotional State
4. Other people
5. Immediately preceding action

A big part of creating or changing habits is identifying the trigger. If you wanted to quit smoking, you would have to identify all the things that trigger that habit in you. For example, a lot of smokers may be able to relate to the following triggers:
1. Location—The office stairwell
2. Time—Morning break, lunch break, and afternoon break

3. Emotional state—Stressed
4. Other People—Other colleagues or friends who are smoking
5. Immediately preceding action—Drinking coffee (or beer)

Once you identify the trigger, you need to decide on the routine you want to take to create or change your habits.

2. Routine

This is the actual behaviour itself (picking up our phones and checking the news, buying and eating the cake, or lighting up and smoking a cigarette) plus all the steps that make up that behaviour. The more specific you can get about each step, the easier it will be to change the habit.

In fact, one of the easiest ways to change habits is to focus on something BJ Fogg calls Tiny Habits (which you can check out at https://www.tinyhabits.com). These are short and simple steps that can be performed in less than 60 seconds. Because they are so small, they require minimal effort to perform, and help us convince our slow, grumpy, stubborn elephants to do them.

The Elephant does not like doing a lot of work. Trying to build a habit that will take an hour to perform every day is really challenging, and nearly impossible for most people. It requires too much willpower, and the Elephant will find too many excuses to override it. But if it takes less than 60 seconds to do, it can be very difficult for the Elephant to override its Rider.

Another great way of using Tiny Habits is by anchoring them to existing habits. As I've already mentioned, existing habits are extremely powerful driving forces of our behaviour. Instead of fighting them, why not use them?

Tiny Habits and anchoring are exactly how I managed to add studying Japanese to my morning routine. I already meditate for 10 minutes every day after I get up—a habit that took me many years to master but is now finally a consistent part of my morning routine. After I meditate, I immediately open up my iPad and study Japanese. I tell myself I only need to do 60 seconds worth of studying. That way, if I don't have the willpower to complete the whole lesson I'm on, then at least I have done 60 seconds of studying. What I find normally happens is that, after the 60 seconds, I've already got into the right frame of mind for studying Japanese, so I continue it and complete the lesson anyway.

But not just any routine will help us achieve our goal of changing habits. The routine must be directly tied into the final part of the habit loop: reward.

3. Reward

According to The habit Loop Theory, habits are driven by a desire for a certain reward. Checking your phone first thing in the morning may satisfy your curiosity for what happened whilst you were sleeping. Buying and eating cake gives you a sugar rush. Smoking a cigarette calms can you down.

One of the tricks to changing habits is to find a routine that gives you the exact reward you crave when your habit is triggered. If you wanted to stop smoking, you would have to find a new routine that gives you the exact same reward smoking gives you. Maybe a nicotine patch will help calm you down, maybe doing exercise will, or maybe smoking an e-cigarette will.

It can sometimes be a challenge to figure out what that reward is when it comes to changing our own personal habits. Maybe smoking isn't for calming us down. Maybe we simply get joy out of lighting up a cigarette and inhaling the smoke. Maybe it helps us feel more social. Maybe it's just the sensation of having that stick in between our fingers. It can take a while to figure out exactly what that reward is.

When it comes to training, we know that our learners have their own goals and problems they are looking to solve. These can be the rewards that will drive their new habits.

If they want their staff to take more ownership over their work, then that could drive their new habit of asking questions instead of telling their staff to do things all the time. If they want their stakeholders to take their opinions more seriously, then that could drive their habit of speaking slower and more baritone every time they give a presentation. And if they want to feel more in control of their time, then that can drive their habit of scheduling all of their tasks at the beginning of the working day.

It's All about Awareness

Successfully changing habits requires a great deal of awareness. Fortunately, The Habit Loop Theory tells us very clearly what we need to be aware of. We know we need to identify the trigger, break down the routine, and link it to a reward.

As trainers, it is our task to raise awareness of those three steps during the process of commitment. The rest is up to the learners.

The Habit Loop Theory

- ## Commitment Plans

Plans are great. The probability of successful change is significantly increased when there is a plan for that change. So, if we want our learners to commit to change, we need them to make a plan of application, or what I call an Application Plan.

This Application Plan should give clear direction, link to their motivations, and identify what support they will need. It should also help our learners raise awareness of the cues, routines, and rewards that will drive these changes.

We can do all of the above by following this process:
1. Revisit the Purpose
2. Clarify the Cue
3. Break Down the Steps
4. **Create Accountability**

Revisit the Purpose

Intrinsic motivation is the driving force for adult learning. Adults learn for a purpose, not because they are told to. Your learners came to your training for a purpose. They have a goal they want to achieve or a problem they need to solve. Now is the time to revisit that purpose because it is that purpose which will drive their new habits. They need to know what's in it for them, what the outcomes of their habits will be, and how those outcomes will benefit them.

The following questions will help learners revisit their purpose:
- **Why did you come to this training?**
- **What do you want to achieve after this training?**
- **What problems can this training help you solve?**
- **What benefits are you looking to gain after this training?**
- **What will happen if you don't change?**

Break Down the Steps

This is where we focus on the behaviour. This is the Rider part of The Elephant and Rider metaphor, where they need to remove all ambiguity and make it as clear and simple as 1, 2, 3.

A challenge for some learners in this part is that they may have too many actions they wish to take. If they plan on taking too many actions, they will be overwhelmed and struggle to implement any of them.

A great question to ask here is: 'What 3 actions will help you the most?' Three is a manageable amount—anything more than that will be too difficult to implement. Another benefit of this question is that it helps them focus on the vital few—the three simplest actions that will help them the most; the 20% of effort that will lead to 80% of results.

If they have more than 3 actions planned and really don't want to give up any of them, that's okay, too. We can just ask them to shelve those actions for now—write them down somewhere and revisit them at a later date. We can encourage them to focus on 3 actions for this month, and then, next month, they can focus on 3 more.

Another thing that can sometimes help is asking them to choose actions that take no longer than 60 seconds to do, like with Tiny Habits (www.tinyhabits.com). They should be focussed on essential first steps, or actions. David Allen, in his famous book *Getting Things Done,* says that we don't complete projects, we complete actions. Framing them in this way avoids any ambiguity.

So, we can use questions like the ones below to help learners break down the steps:
- **What 3 actions will help you the most?**
- **What simple steps can you perform in less than 60 seconds that will help you the most?**
- **If you have more than 3 actions, then where can you save these actions for revisiting them a later time? When will you revisit them? How will you remember to revisit them?**

Clarify the Cue

All habits are triggered by cues. If we want our learners to build new habits, we need to help raise their awareness of the cues that will trigger these habits.

Questions like the ones below will help learners raise awareness of their cues:
- **When do you need to do your new action?**
- **Where will you be at that time?**
- **What emotions will signal the need to use this new action?**
- **What other people will be around you at that time?**
- **What preceding actions can you link to this new action?**

Create Accountability

This final step will close up this application into an unbreakable chain of accountability. Knowing someone else will hold them accountable to this application plan will motivate them. It also adds an extra layer of extrinsic motivation on top of the intrinsic motivation they identified when they revisited their purpose.

They could be accountable to their boss, their colleague, or even a friend or spouse. They could make this commitment to that person face-to-face, by email, by phone, or even via social media.

What's important is that they make this commitment to this person **now**, before the training is over. Laying down this accountability is the very first step in implementing their Application Plan, and is something they can start doing during the training whilst we still have them.

Some good questions to ask for this part:
- **Who can help motivate you to implement your habit plan?**
- **How and when will they measure your success in implementing this habit plan?**
- **How will you communicate with them about your habit plan?**
- **What should you say to them about this? And how can you contact them now?**

Make It Your Own

I use the above process in all of my trainings. Sometimes, I will give them a form to fill in, with a list of questions to answer. Other times, I will put them together with a buddy and display the questions via a PPT slide. Sometimes, I will send them an email template of these questions and ask them to send their plan straight to their boss.

Again, the possibilities are endless here. What matters is making sure you get them to finish this process in any way you can. And if you can get them to take a simple first step before they leave the room, (even something as simple as setting a reminder on their phone), then you have greatly increased the chances of them acting on it.

Commitment Plan

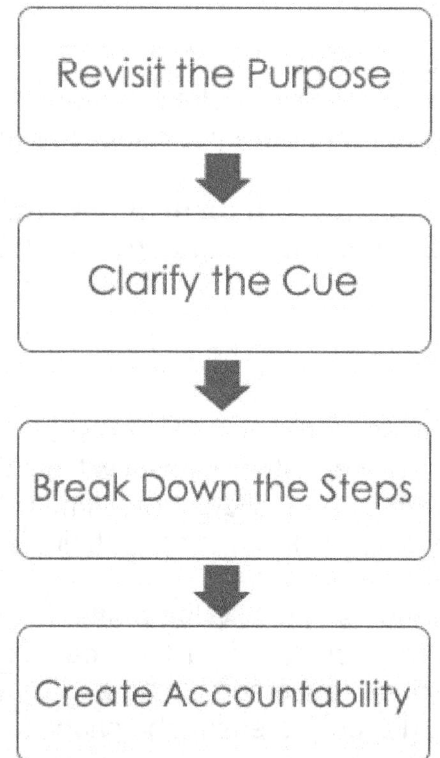

Committing Summary

The following flowchart is a summary of everything we have looked at in this section:

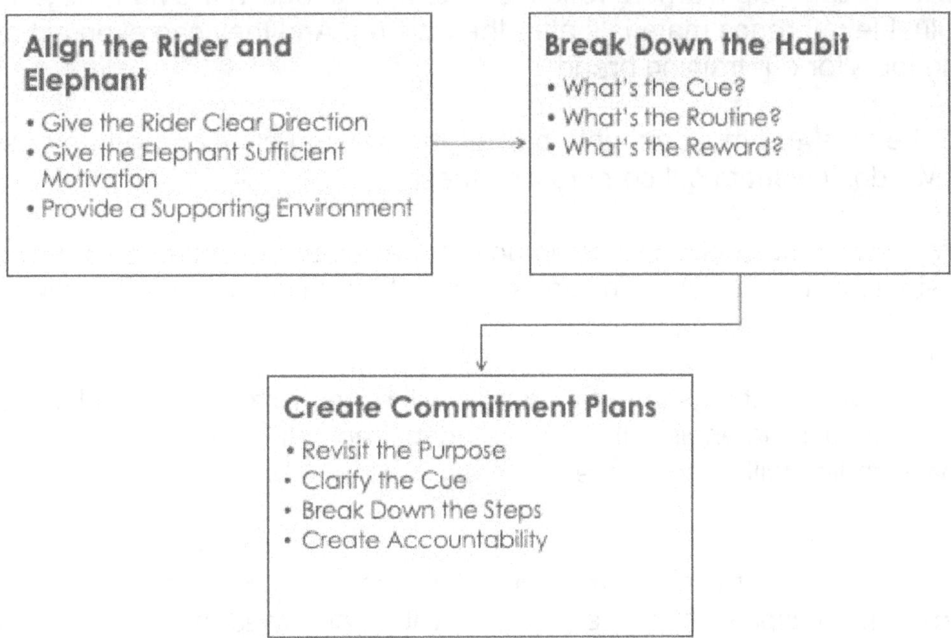

Part 5—Creating Materials

Training is mostly about the experience and what goes on inside our learner's heads. The true value of training is intangible. It's soft and squishy, difficult to see, and difficult to measure. But that doesn't mean it's all intangible.

The training materials we create are going to be the most tangible part of our training solution. They're going to be the things that learners look at, touch, take away and show to other people.

Our training materials will help in so many ways. They can manage expectations on what the course will cover and when. They can help guide learners through knowledge sections. They can help learners reflect on the right things in the right way. They can act as valuable reference materials after the training. And they can even act as useful marketing tools for our training brand.

Because they are the most tangible part of the training solution and have so many benefits, we don't want to cut corners with these.

The way they look and feel communicate a huge amount. Either they look unprofessional or professional, inviting or uninviting, intriguing or off-putting, and so on.

And the way we write things in our materials will have an impact on understanding. If we write poorly, our materials will confuse and distract our learners. If we write clearly, then understanding will be a breeze.

In this section, we are going to look at how to design materials. We'll first look at designing for visual impact, where we'll learn about using visuals and some basic graphic design principles. Then we'll look at writing and readability, where we'll learn how to write in ways that people can understand instantly. Finally, we'll look at how to be productive when designing materials, where we will ensure we make every minute of our effort count.

Designing for Visual Impact

We take in information about the world around us through our five senses. We see, hear, smell, taste, and feel our surroundings. Whilst training is generally more of an intellectual experience, it is still processed through the five senses, so the sensory aspect of our training is going to have a big impact on how it's experienced.

The visual impact of our training materials is one area that we have a lot of control over. We can optimise the look and feel of our materials to make them more appealing, understandable, and memorable.

Poor visual impact creates many challenges for our learners and even sometimes for the person delivering the training. This is where the phrase 'Death by PowerPoint' comes from. Consider the following problems that are created by poor use of PowerPoint:

- Too much information on the slide overwhelms learners. They spend more time focussed on trying to dissect and interpret the slide, distracting them from more important things.
- Childish clip art images lead learners to perceive the materials as childish and beneath their level.
- Text that is too small and poorly contrasts with the background colour means people sitting at the back of the room can't read it.
- Poorly selected images that don't clearly represent the message they should be communicating mislead learners, leading to misunderstandings.
- Poorly selected colour schemes make people feel uneasy.

I could go on and on, but I'm sure you've seen plenty of examples yourself. Of course, slideshows aren't the only area where visual impact is important. You'll probably have a number of handouts, aids, and maybe even tools that you'll be using as well. Poor visual design in these things can also cause similar problems to the aforementioned ones. The key thing to keep in mind when designing for visual impact is that the visual aspect should aid understanding and not distract from it. Anything misleading, unclear, or off-putting takes valuable cognitive resources away from where they should be focussed.

Visual design can be great fun to work on, and incredibly satisfying. But it's also something that we can easily go overboard on. Be cautious of spending more time on visual design than on the design of the training itself. Remember that the goal of visual aids is to simply aid understanding. If they achieve that, then that's enough.

In this section, we will look at a number of easy to use techniques that can optimise visual impact.

• Choosing Your Tool

There are so many visual communication tools out there now that it can be hard to keep track. The most famous one, of course, is PowerPoint, closely followed by its famous rival, Keynote. But there are also many others to consider:

- Prezi
- PowToon
- Prezentit
- SlideRocket
- Haiku Deck
- RawShorts
- Google Slides
- Slidebean

Don't forget the publishing tools available for handouts as well. You can use PowerPoint and Keynote as publishing tools by simply changing the slide dimensions. I have a handout template in PowerPoint that is designed for an A4 portrait layout and I find it very easy to use. But you can also consider the following:

- Word
- Publisher
- Pages
- InDesign
- Scribus
- Serif PagePlus
- iStudio Publisher
- SwiftPublisher

A quick Internet search will reveal many other tools available, but before you choose which ones to use, consider some of the pointers below.

Ease of Use

Tools should be easy to use. Some of them may take a little while to get used to. But once you're used to them, they should make it easier for you to get the job done. If there is a learning curve, then consider how long that will take, and how much time you can allow for it.

Consider the functionality of the tool. Does it do everything you need it to? If it doesn't, are there workarounds available? Are those workarounds convenient?

At the end of the day, the tool should help you, not hinder you. So, make sure it does everything you need without getting in your way.

Enjoyable

You should use a tool you like using. You're going to be spending a lot of time using it, so if you don't enjoy it, then you'll just end up being frustrated.

Some people prefer Macs, others prefer Windows. Some prefer Keynote to PowerPoint. And some prefer tablets to laptops. Find a tool that makes you feel good, and that lets you use it in the way you want to use it.

Shareability

Shareability is probably the number one reason why Microsoft PowerPoint is my tool of choice. If I am working with other trainers, they are almost definitely going to have PowerPoint. If they don't, then pretty much any PowerPoint alternative can convert a PowerPoint file into its format. And if I turn up at my client's office and my computer doesn't work, then I can easily transfer the PowerPoint files to their computer (which 99.99% of the time will have PowerPoint) using a USB.

If you are going to be training in lots of different places, or designing for lots of other trainers, then I strongly recommend sticking to a safe format, such as PowerPoint.

Flexibility

How much can this tool do? Can it be used in all the ways you need it to? Find a tool that gives you the most options, and use that tool.

For example, when I first started designing materials, I would first design the slides in PowerPoint, then the handout materials in Publisher. To do this, I'd have to save the slides first as photos, then put the photos on a USB, then log on to a Windows computer (because I couldn't use Publisher on my Mac), then copy the photos to the Publisher document, and so on.

The whole process was incredibly time-consuming and overly complicated. Since then, I've tried to streamline my material design process as much as I can and minimise the number of tools I use. This has allowed me to reduce the number of steps in my workflow.

In fact, these days, I normally just use my handout template in PowerPoint. I open it up, type everything in there, and add any images I need. Then, I'm done. If I want to add a slideshow to go with it, I can, so, again, I open up PowerPoint. Sometimes, I work using my MacBook. Other times, I'm out and about with my iPad. It doesn't matter which device I am using because I can use PowerPoint on any of them now. Being able to do everything in the same tool, on any device, saves me a lot of time and helps make my life simpler.

Questions to ask yourself when choosing the right tool:

- Is it easy to use?
- Do you enjoy using it?
- Is it easy to share?
- Does it have all the functions you need? If not, are there suitable workarounds?

- ## Designing Templates

In any field of design, there are a lot of decisions to make, and designing for visual impact is no exception. The sheer number of decisions to make can be overwhelming.

This is why we have templates.

Templates allow us to make a certain amount of design decisions *only once*, such as:
- Colour scheme
- Fonts
- Dimensions
- Layout
- Style

Once the template is complete, we don't have to worry about those decisions again. This makes our life much simpler. Every time we want to create new materials, we have a lot less to worry about. We spend less time deliberating, we make faster decisions, and we get more work done in less time.

Another advantage of using templates is that they help with branding. If you are designing training as part of a certain brand, then the template will help represent that. It can display your brand's logo, colours, styles, and so on.

Your template can also help maintain consistency. If you deliver lots of different training, to different people, and even send your materials to different trainers, then a template will help to consistently represent your brand.

When it comes to designing templates, we start to stray away from the field of Training design and verge into the realm of graphic design. If you are not an expert in graphic design, then I strongly recommend that you find someone who is to design your template for you.

There are a number of online platforms that can help you find freelance graphic designers at good prices such as:
- Upwork.com
- Fiverr.com
- Toptal.com
- 99designs.com
- Peopleperhour.com

(Of course, a quick web search will reveal many more sites.)

Some of the things that need to be kept in mind when designing a template:
- Grids
- Background
- Colour
- Fonts

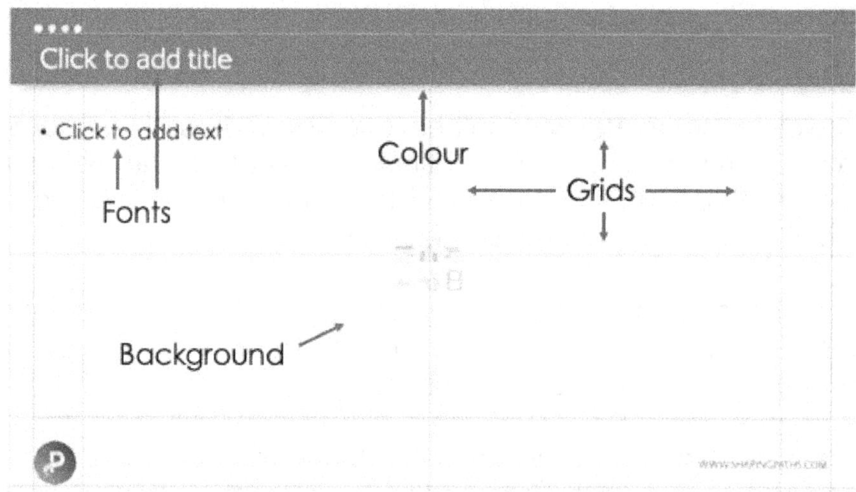

Grids

How many times have you looked at a blank document and struggled to decide where to put something?

You paste a picture into the document, but then decide that's not the right place, so you move it around. Then you add in something else, but now they don't quite seem to fit together. So you keep moving things around, but never quite seem to find the right fit. Grids help with decisions like this.

Grids divide the canvas into a series of lines and boxes. Then once you come to adding in elements, you simply need to align them with those lines and boxes.

Grids don't help just you. They also help your audience. They add a feel of unity and consistency. When elements are aligned by the grid, it looks neater. And when the alignment relationships are similar between each page and/or slide, this helps maintain that consistent feeling.

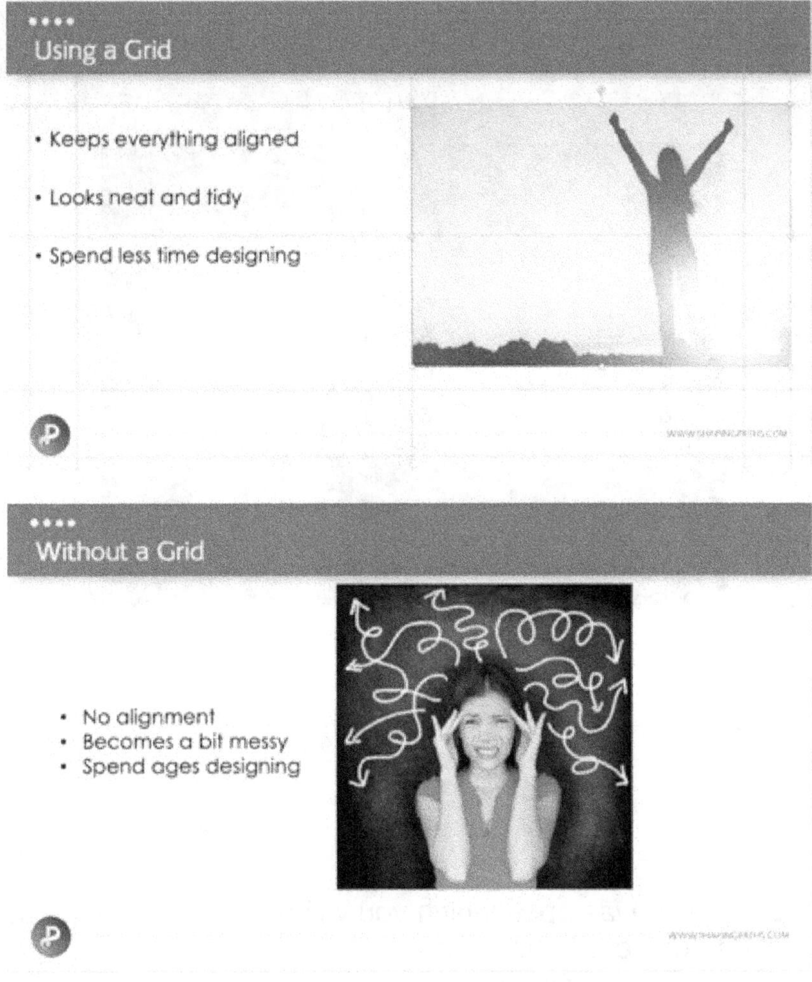

There are lots of different ways of using grids. If you browse any website and analyse the layout, you will see plenty of examples. A very famous example of grids is 'The Rule of Thirds', which is commonly used in photography. This divides the picture up into thirds. Photographers then use this grid of thirds when taking pictures, and try to align the key elements on the points where the different gridlines intersect. This creates a more pleasing effect on the eye when viewing it.

Consider how many elements you are going to be using, on average. The more elements you will use, the more columns and rows in your grid you will need. However, for training materials, we want to avoid overwhelming our learners with too much information, so keep the grids and columns to a minimum. This constrains us later on, helping us avoid adding in too much information when we come to create each individual page and slide.

Background

The background is the canvas upon which you will place and arrange your elements. Here, you will need to make decisions about:
- Size and dimensions of the background
- Colour
- Texture
- Patterns
- Logo placement

Remember, the background is not the key focus point. It is simply there to host your key focus points. So, I generally recommend that you keep the background as simple as possible. The simpler it is, the more options it will give you later on.

Consider how much space the background allows you to work with. If things like borders, frames, and even logos take up too much space, then you won't have anywhere to put things when you actually come to use it. The template I currently use has one header and a smaller footer, leaving me lots of space to work with in the main canvas area.

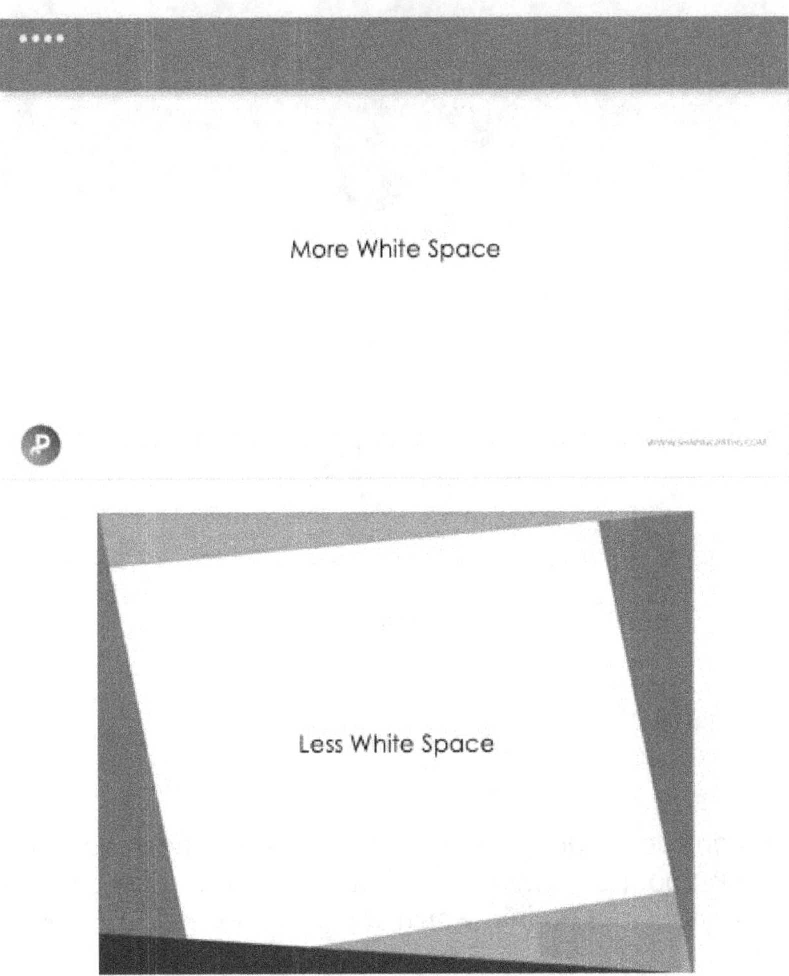

Also, consider the colours, texture, and patterns and how those will relate to the elements you place on the slide. Personally, I like to keep a clean white background with no texture or patterns. I have found, through experience, that a lot of stock photos have some element of a white background to them. When I add them on top of a light grey background, a dark blue background, or a black background, they tend to clash rather than blend in. To get around the clash, I have to use special frames for the pictures, which takes up even more space. So, these days, I stick to a plain white background, which is much easier to work with.

Another thing to consider is how this will affect your printing costs. If every page or slide is black, think about how much ink that is going to take up when it comes to printing! Plain white requires no ink, which will save you money (and ink) in the long run.

Using Colour

Colour communicates the look and feel of your brand and your materials. Different colours, shades, and tones represent different concepts, feelings, and associations.

Colour is not something that should be taken lightly (pun intended). Not only do you need to keep in mind what the colour should represent, but you also need to keep in mind how the different colours you choose relate to each other.

Nature is a great source of inspiration for finding colours and different combinations. For example, orange and blue is a great combination that many different brands use, and it comes from the colour of the sky in combination with the colour of the sun. If you browse through some of your holiday photos and analyse the colour combinations that come from the places of natural beauty that you have been to, then you will find some striking combinations that help create certain feelings.

Another great tool is the colour wheel. The colour wheel takes what we know about colour, and helps us find harmonious combinations of colours. If you want to try it for yourself then I recommend the free tool below:
https://color.adobe.com/create/color-wheel/

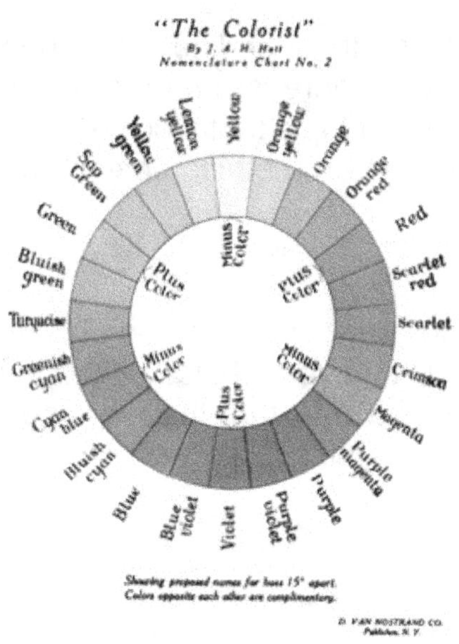

A 1908 color wheel with red, green, and violet "plus colors" and magenta, yellow, and cyan blue "minus colors".

Sourced from:
https://en.wikipedia.org/wiki/Color_wheel#/media/File:RGV_color_wheel_1908.png

When it comes to combining colours, there are several different types of schemes that we can go with. These colour schemes are formulas for creating harmonious colour combinations. Here are 8 different types of a colour scheme:

- **Monochromatic**—A single base colour and different variations of shades or tints of that same colour
- **Polychromatic**—A variety of different colours.
- **Achromatic**—Typically a combination of black, white, and shades of grey.
- **Analogous**—A selection of colours that sit next to each other on the colour wheel
- **Complementary**—A selection of colours that sit opposite each other on the colour wheel
- **Split-Complementary**—One base colour and two colours that sit adjacent to that base colour's opposite on the colour wheel
- **Triadic**—Like the split-complementary, but the split-complements are pushed out a little more so that all three colours are spread evenly on the colour wheel
- **Tetradic**—One complementary colour scheme combined with other complementary colour schemes

Colour is where I really start to draw the line in this book, as we are getting well into the territory of graphic design. There is a lot more to understand about colour than what I have written above. It is a topic that I looked into and experimented with in the past, but quickly decided that it is something best left up to an expert.

Fonts

Fonts also communicate meaning. Fonts can be playful, classy, serious, snazzy, etc. The key thing to remember is that your choice of font communicates the look and feel of your style. You should make sure that the font you choose is consistent with the general style and feel you are aiming for.

I'm Overused

I'm Traditional

I'm Assertive

I'm Playful

I'm a Typewriter

I'm Classy

Another thing to consider is the legibility of the font. Is it easy to read? Does trying to read it give you a headache? Some fonts are designed just for decorative impact (such as fonts that look like handwriting) and so may not be that legible. Others are designed with legibility in mind. We want our fonts to aid understanding, not distract from it, so choose a font that is legible.

Can you read me?

Can you read me?

When choosing a font for legibility you will also need to consider serifs. Serifs are tails that appear on the end of letters. A serif font has these tails, whereas a sans serif font doesn't. These tails tend to lead off horizontally, which actually guides the eye to the next letter. Because of this, in theory, serif fonts are easier to read than sans serif fonts. Typically, sans serif fonts are reserved for short bursts of text like headlines or titles. In practice, however, this is not always the case.

I have Serifs

I don't have Serifs

You will also need to consider font sizes. If it is too large, it looks odd. If it is too small, it's difficult to read. As a rule of thumb, for printing materials, the body text should not be smaller than size 10. For slideshows, around 20 is the size to aim for, so the people at the back of the room will be able to read it.

Some fonts require purchasing. Maybe you see a font you like on some website, but then, when you try to find it, you suddenly discover the entire font will cost you $1000 to license! There are many fonts available for free, so use them.

Also, consider whether or not other people have that font installed on their computers. If you are sharing your training materials with other people, and they don't have that font on their computer, then their computer will automatically replace the font with something it does have. This can create some nasty surprises when you turn up at the training room and take your first glance at the printouts.

This is yet another huge topic that takes us away from the realm of Training design and into the magical kingdom of graphic design. Once again, I strongly recommend you seek advice from an expert on this topic if you are not very familiar with it.

- ## Selecting Visuals

'A picture is worth a thousand words' goes the old saying. As I described earlier, part of the learning experience is the sensory experience, so visuals will have an impact on understanding, retention, and even the general appeal of the training.

Choose well and visuals will aid your training, but choose badly and they will create problems. So how do we make the right choices when it comes to visuals?

Relevance

This is the first thing to keep in mind. Visuals must be relevant. Consider the point you are trying to get across and select the visual that does the best job of representing that. The risk of getting this wrong is that the image confuses our learners. They will either spend too much time trying to interpret the image (thus distracting them from where they need to be focussed), or they will get the wrong message altogether.

Visuals are also great when they demonstrate what you are training. If you are training techniques (for example, active listening), then choose pictures of people performing those techniques (for example, a person listening intently to another person).

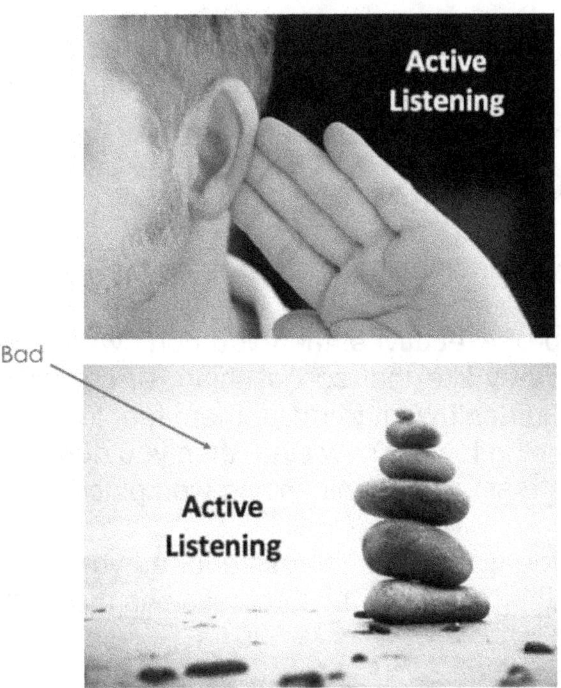

If the pictures are of people your learners respect performing those techniques, this is even better. If you have the time, you can go into their workplace and arrange to take photos of their colleagues and supervisors demonstrating the techniques they will be learning.

If you're not certain whether or not the image you choose is relevant, then ask some of the people around you. Ask them what this picture makes them think of. If their interpretation is along the right lines, then you're in the clear.

Feel

Cartoons feel childish. Pictures of businessmen and businesswomen in suits in a corporate setting feel professional and serious, yet to some people can feel cliché. Pictures of natural scenery feel peaceful. What feeling are you trying to communicate?

Most of the training I deliver is of a corporate nature, so I tend to select images that go with that. I have a lot of pictures of businessmen and businesswomen, dressed in suits, doing business things, in business settings.

If you are training the topic of health and safety, then you will probably want pictures of men and women in potentially hazardous environments, wearing hardhats or other protective gear, and behaving in a generally safe manner.

If you are training people on how to cook for a plant-based diet, then you'll probably want lots of pictures of vegetables, natural settings, and fresh ingredients being prepared in a kitchen setting.

Feeling is important, so don't underestimate it.

Some audiences may have certain expectations of the feeling of your training.

If you are training a group of executives, then you don't want to patronise them with childish cartoons (unless they like that sort of thing, of course). If you are training teenagers, then maybe you don't want to make them feel too serious. And if you are delivering on-boarding training to your new staff, then you don't want them to feel that this is going to be a dull, stressful, and uninspiring workplace.

So, consider the feeling you want to get across and, as you select your visuals, ask people what they think of them to see if their impressions match that feeling.

Cost

Some visuals are free, some cost a bit of money, and others cost a lot of money. When it comes to cost considerations, you need to consider where you get your pictures from.

If you are looking for free pictures, then a quick image search of any search engine will reveal an infinite amount of pictures for you to use. However, not all of these pictures automatically come with permission to use them. In fact, most of them don't.

If you are looking for free images that you have permission to use, then Google has a handy feature. Enter what you are searching for on the image search, then select Tools, then Usage Rights, and you will be given options to filter out images that you don't have permission to use. For more information on the different usage rights filters, try this link here:

https://support.google.com/websearch/answer/29508?hl=en&ref_topic=3180360

Having said that, you may need to provide an attribution for any image you find for free. To learn more about this, I recommend visiting the link below:

https://wiki.creativecommons.org/wiki/Best_practices_for_attribution

To stay on the safe side, I recommend purchasing stock images. For stock images, you basically pay a fee to license them, giving you permission to use them however you want for as long as you want (generally speaking). However, each license may vary somewhat, so be sure to check what permissions the license gives you.

There are a number of sites where you can purchase stock images. These can be costly, though, so you will need to compare and contrast the different payment plans available. Here are some of the bigger stock photo sites where you can purchase a wide selection of high quality images:

- Shutterstock.com
- iStockphoto.com
- Bigstockphoto.com
- Gettyimages.com
- Stock.adobe.com

There are many other sites out there, including some that give you a free selection of images. However, the ones I have listed above tend to have the best selection of images. Some of them have better search options. For example, Stock.adobe.com allows you to search for photos of a certain dimension and colour. As for pricing, they are generally very expensive, but I have found Bigstockphoto.com to have the more favourable pricing options.

Some also give you a free trial, which gives you access to their images for free for a certain period of time. But if you have a few hundred dollars to spare, I strongly recommend you purchase a selection of stock photos from one of the above sites, because they are of great quality and you can use them over and over again.

• Arranging Elements

Now that you have your canvas, your visuals, and your text, it's just a case of arranging them. The arrangement of elements is where A LOT of people slip up, quite simply because they are unaware of the rules that govern the arrangement of elements.

The way elements are arranged communicates a lot about how they relate to each other, how the slide feels, and even what the elements mean. If you get the arrangement wrong, your visuals will communicate the wrong message.

Thankfully, the rules of arranging elements are quite straightforward. According to Nancy Duarte's book, *Slide:ology: The Art and Science of Creating Great Presentations*, there are 6 key rules to remember:
- Contrast
- Flow
- Hierarchy
- Unity
- Proximity
- White Space

Contrast

Amongst all of your elements, SOME may need to stand out more than others. These are the elements that you want your audience to pay MOST attention to. So, first ask yourself: **What is the most important element on this slide?**

We can then use contrast to make this element stand out from all the others. Generally speaking, there are 5 key ways we can use to make something stand out:
- Size
- Shape
- Shade
- Colour
- Proximity

The things that stand out the most grab the most attention.

Flow

Our audience will process these elements in a certain order. Whether or not they process them in the order we intended is up to how we arrange these elements.

Think about how your eyes read text on a slide or piece of paper. Where do they go first? Then where? And then where?

Most Western readers' eyes will start in the top left and work towards the right, then drop down to the left in a Z shape. We should assume any audience will have this habit and will view our elements accordingly.

If you want your elements to be viewed in a different order to the Z shape, then we need the elements to flow in the desired order.

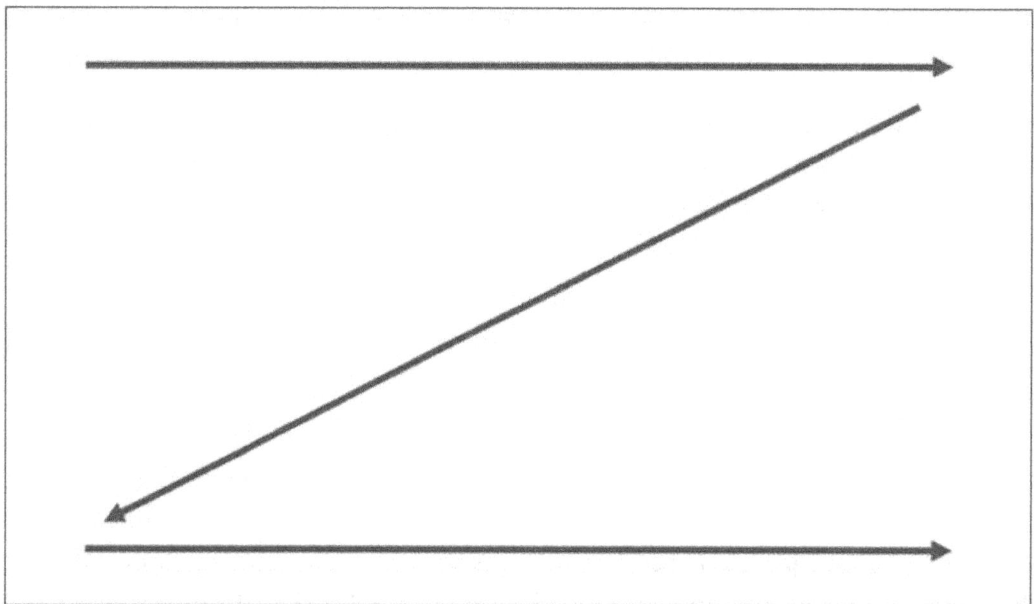

We can use the following methods to manage the flow of our elements:
- Arrows
- Numbers
- Direction of Visuals
- Animations

Arrows and numbers speak for themselves. '1' is the first place they should look, '2' is the second, and so on. Arrows help guide the audience from one element to the next one.

Direction of visuals is something a lot of people overlook. If you have a picture of a person and their eyes are looking towards the left, then that naturally indicates to the audience to look left.

But if you have the next element appearing to the right of that image, then that clashes. Your learners' eyes won't naturally go there. They may be able to guess they should look at that place next, but they will feel uneasy looking at the slide because there is a conflict between where they want to look and where they should look.

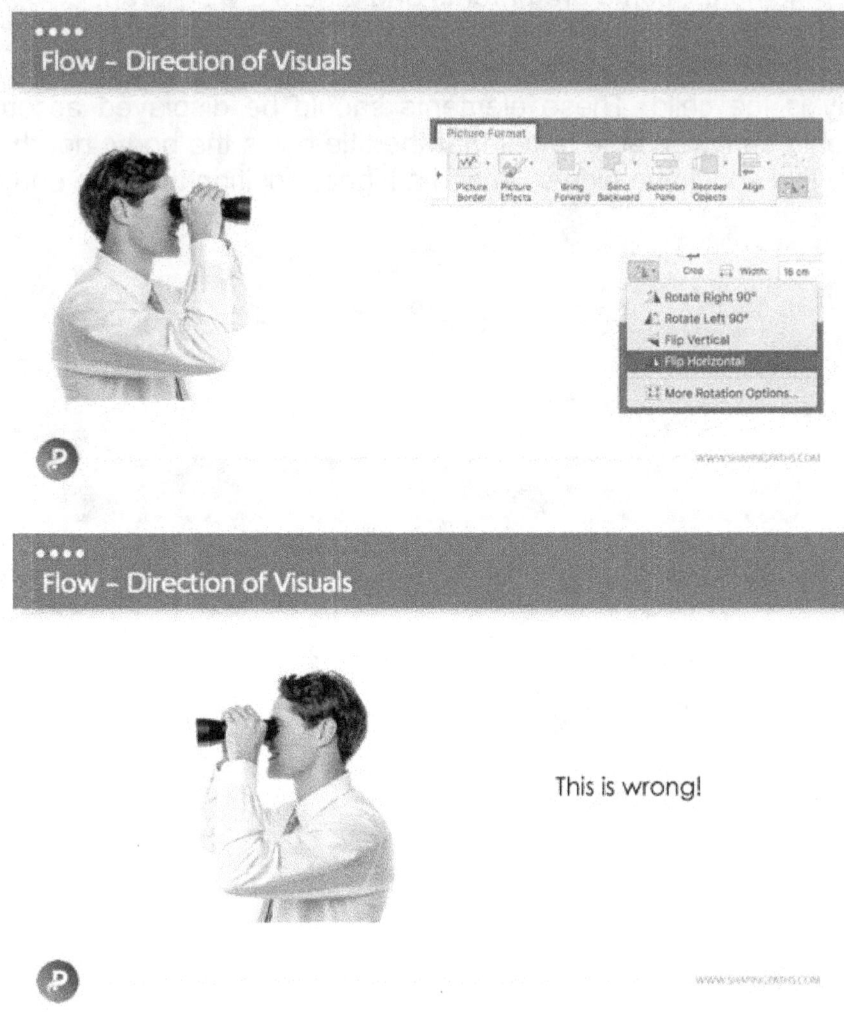

Animations are more useful for slideshows than anything else. Rather than reveal every element all at once, animations reveal them one by one. This creates a natural flow and avoids overwhelming the audience.

However, try to avoid using any overly flashy animations and getting carried away with them in general. As fun as they are to use, they can be overwhelming and distracting to the audience. In some cases, they will even make you look unprofessional.

Hierarchy

The elements on your slide are like a family. In a family, there are parents and children. Amongst your elements, some are parents and others are children.

Consider the relationship between the title and the body text. The title is the parent, and the body is the child. These elements should be displayed accordingly. The audience should easily be able to tell that the title owns the body, not the other way round. So the title should be bigger, and in a higher position than the body.

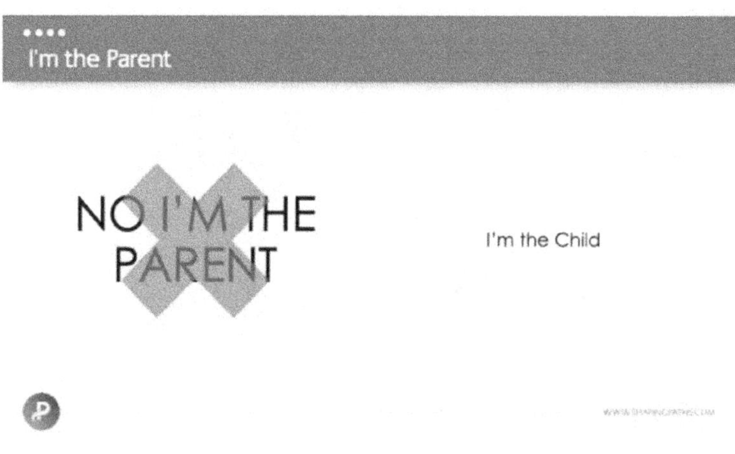

If we suddenly make it the other way round, looking at it makes us feel uneasy. Something about it just doesn't seem right. And for some in the audience, it may even create confusion.

We can also use hierarchy to clarify the relationship between different images. For example, the more important ones should be bigger and stand out more. So, remember to clarify the hierarchy of the different elements and display this accordingly.

Unity

I mentioned this earlier when we looked at designing templates. We can use a grid to decide where to place elements. Because every slide or page uses the same grid, we are able to maintain a feeling of consistency throughout the whole document.

Templates, in general, help achieve unity. Each slide or page has the title and the body in the same place. It may even have the same border, and/or the logo in the same place. This can make it easier for the audience to digest information, as the number of different things to interpret on each slide is reduced.

Another advantage is that when different people use the template, they can design as they please and everyone can keep a consistent style.

One thing to keep in mind when placing elements is that you want to keep them aligned with other elements—either aligned to the left or right, or to the top or bottom. This helps to keep a consistent feeling amongst elements and also helps you decide where to place them. Most tools (such as PowerPoint or Keynote) have an 'Align' function, so simply select the elements you want to align, and then use the Align function to align them as you require.

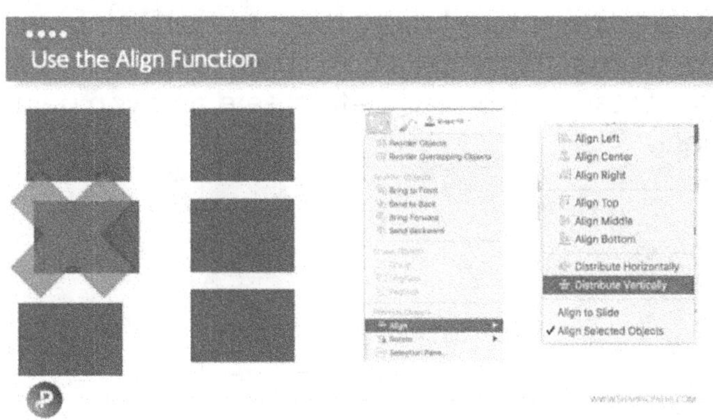

Proximity

The proximity of elements to one another communicates their relationship.

Items that are placed in close proximity and distributed evenly may communicate unity. When dispersed randomly, this may communicate chaos. One standing out from the others may represent inequality.

If things belong together, then place them together. If they belong to separate categories, then show that clearly. Remember that the proximity of your elements communicates their relationship, so place them accordingly.

White Space

This is the blank space remaining on your canvas after all elements have been placed, and there are three ways you can use this white space to your advantage.

1. Use white space as a measure of harmony. If you've placed too many elements, then there will be little white space left. If they've been organised poorly, the white space will be distributed unevenly.

2. Use white space to emphasise and contrast the elements on your slide. For example, if there is just one element, then place it in the centre so the white space can surround it and draw attention to it.

3. Use white space to create clear boundaries between different elements. Similar to the Align function, most tools also have a Distribute function (which is normally found next to the Align function). This function helps evenly distribute elements—either horizontally or vertically—to create an even balance of white space between each element.

Arranging Elements

 Contrast

 Flow

 Hierarchy

 Unity

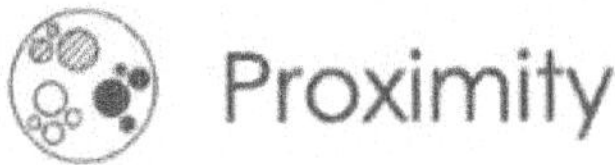 Proximity

White Space

- ## Using Slideshows

There are lots of strong opinions out there about using slideshows. Many trainers vow never to use slideshows in their training, and with good reason. But that doesn't mean they shouldn't be used.

When used appropriately, slideshows can be of great help to you, your learners, and your training. It's just a case of using it right. So, consider the following guidelines if you do wish to use them:

- Gap-Show
- Road Sign Quality
- The Ghost Effect
- Visual Ease
- SmartArt

Gap-Show

The best way to use slides in training is to use slides that actively encourage learners to participate (as opposed to passively sit there and absorb information).

Think of your slide as a Gap-Show. Instead of presenting information, it presents a gap of information. Include some information, but purposefully leave out other information. This then gives you an opportunity to invite your learners to fill in the gaps.

Only write key words, simple summaries, or names. Think of the slide as a What on the Why, What, How Scale. It leaves out the How and the Why, allowing you to invite learners to fill in the details, one by one. If they can't, then invite learners to question you about the details.

Another way of making Gap-Shows is to make each slide a quiz, a puzzle, a test, or an invitation for sharing experiences.

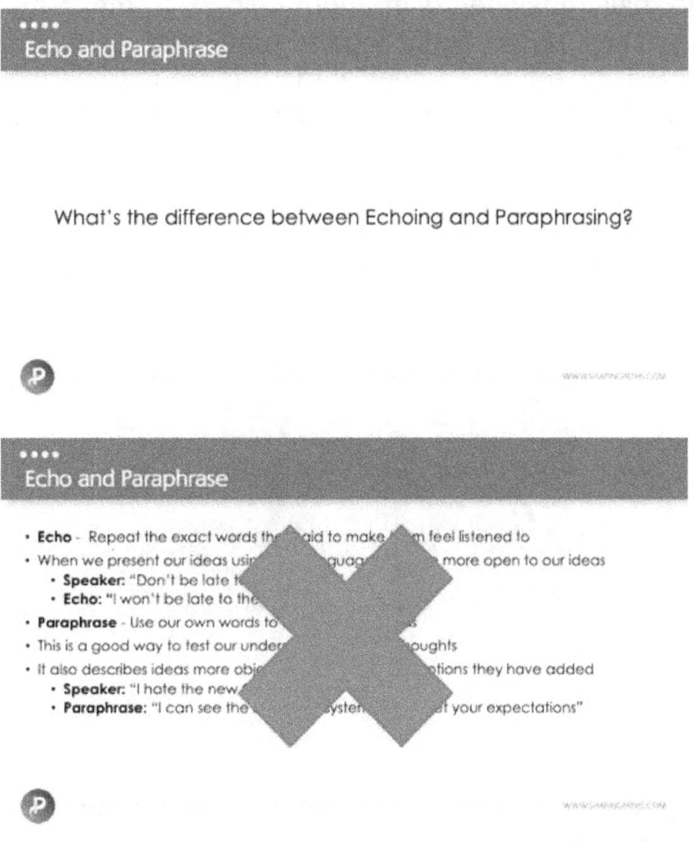

Using Gap-Shows instead of slideshows will even help you to use more questions than lectures when going through any Guiding sections in your training. So, stop thinking of slides as good messengers of information. Think of them as opportunities to invite participation.

Road Sign Quality

If you change your slideshows to Gap-Shows, then you will have created a visual aid that greatly increases participation. But a Gap-Show will still have information on it, and we need to make sure that information can be processed as quickly as possible.

Consider, for a moment, how road signs are designed. The purpose of a road sign is to communicate vital information as quickly as possible. Anyone driving past a sign has barely a split second to look at it and process the information on it. If there is too much information to take in, then the drivers may drive past it before they've finished reading it—or, even worse, find themselves distracted by the sign and end up crashing into something.

Road signs are normally designed with bright colours to make them stand out from their surroundings. They have highly legible fonts that contrast strongly with the background colours. They have very few words. Where they can, they replace words with pictures or symbols. The next time you pass a road sign, take a look and analyse how it's been designed.

Our slides should achieve the same quality of design as a road sign. Slides should not distract learners from other important things, nor should they take too long to process. They should communicate key information as quickly as possible.

The Ghost Effect

Most slideshows are displayed using projectors. This can be a real pain for us, as the projector beams a massive ray of light right where we normally want to stand. When we stand in this light, the beam casts a light on our face, making us look like a ghost.

Not only is this a real pain for us, but it also looks unprofessional. A slide is supposed to be displayed without having anything blocking its way. When you stand in its way, you look weird, you block out information, and the resulting Ghost Effect may distract learners and even cause them to giggle.

To avoid the Ghost Effect, watch where you stand. Stand to the side of the screen whenever you want learners to refer to it.

When you don't want learners to refer to the screen, use the magical 'W' and 'B' buttons on your keyboard. 'W' will cause the screen to whiteout, which actually isn't that useful for avoiding the Ghost Effect. In fact, I only mention this for reference, I don't recommended using the whiteout effect. But 'B' blacks the screen out, which also causes the projector to blackout. This allows you to stand in front of the screen without looking like a ghost.

Be careful of using these functions too often. I once used the blackout effect so often that someone actually called in the IT guy to have a look at the projector!

Visual Ease

Don't break the template!

So many times I have seen people completely ignore their templates. Each slide suddenly has a new font, a new title position, a new colour, even a whole new template!

Keeping a consistent style on each slide will help maintain the feeling of visual ease. Suddenly breaking the template achieves the opposite effect, and can be distracting and even make you look unprofessional, as a result.

So, keep in mind things like colours, fonts, sizes, and positioning—and make sure they are kept consistent between each slide.

SmartArt

SmartArt is yet another reason why I have decided on PowerPoint as my tool of choice. It is a fantastic function that helps you take boring lists and turn them into tables, flow charts, diagrams, and so on.

Simply write a list on the slide, select the list, click the SmartArt button, see the different ways of arranging it that it offers, and then choose one. Not only does SmartArt produce decent looking visuals, it can save you a great deal of time as well.

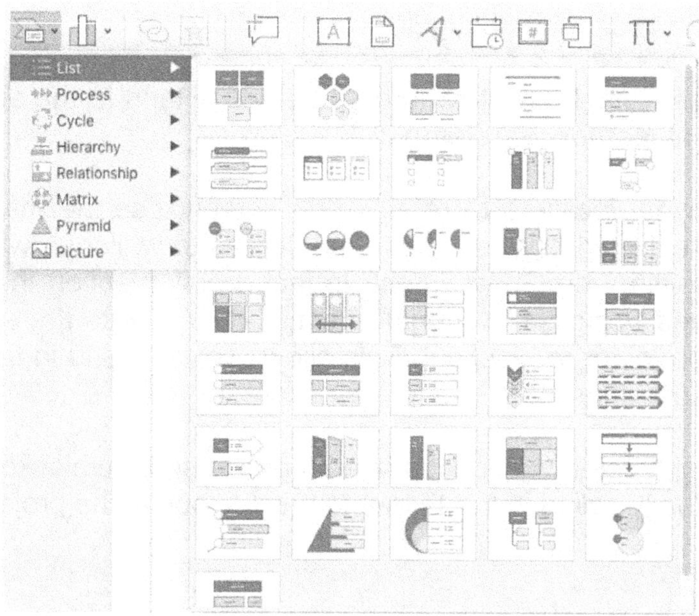

As you are doing this, remember to keep consistent with your template. SmartArt might not automatically do this for you. It might change the fonts and colours, etc., so you may need to manually change these back to match your template.

- ## Using Videos

Videos make for great learning material. They even add a bit of spice by mixing things up. But videos need to be used with caution to get the best result, so consider the following points when using them:
- Relevance
- Copyright
- Clarity
- Logistics

Relevance

This point is obvious, yet very easy to overlook. Make sure that the video is relevant to the training.

One big challenge with using videos is that they can take up a lot of time. If their purpose is to simply get a point across, then consider whether there is a faster way of doing this.

The best reason for using videos is as a reference point for any practice or reflection activities. They can be great tools for showing case studies or for reviewing learner performance in previous practice activities that were filmed. Just make sure that, before you start the video, you clarify what the learners should be focussing on, and then structure the following activity to refer back to points in the video.

One other good reason to use videos is to raise energy levels. There may be some points in the day where the energy is low. Videos can help raise that energy. Again, try to keep videos for these purposes quite short. If you have something longer that you think they may be interested in, then save it for the breaks.

Copyright

Make sure you have permission to use the video. There are lots of great free resources out there for videos, with TED.com being a fantastic one.

Clarity

Learners need to easily understand the video.

Understanding can be hindered by poor video and audio quality, so never just download a video and assume it's all good. Always test the video before training to make sure that both the visual and audio aspects are clear.

When videos consist of mostly dialogue, make sure the dialogue is clear. Strong accents may be difficult for some learners to understand, especially for non-native speakers, so try to add subtitles to help them, if you can. Even better, if you identify any terms in the dialogue that you think will be difficult to understand, then explain these terms to your learners beforehand, so they are prepared for it.

Logistics

Videos don't always work smoothly, for a number of reasons, but most problems can be prevented by being well prepared.

Firstly, ensure you have enough time to run the video and any follow up activities. Remember that videos can eat up a lot of time, and this time is only increased when you add on the time needed for extra activities. So, as you start the day, check what time you need to start showing the video and how long you need for the activities. Then, pace yourself accordingly.

Secondly, check sound and video connections before showing the video. Projectors and speakers are full of unpleasant surprises, and it is better to discover these sooner rather than later. It's always a good idea to check the technology at the start of the day. As a rule of thumb, I always carry my own portable speakers with me as a backup.

Finally, just before you run the video, make sure you have everything ready. Make sure learners are ready and paying attention. Make sure the projectors and speakers are set up. Then dim the lights, draw the curtains, and make sure you stand somewhere that doesn't block the screen and also allows you to quickly turn the lights back on once the video is finished.

• Using Flip Charts

Flip charts are fantastic training tools and should be included in every training. The thing that makes them stand out is that they are always a work in progress. Anyone can add to them at any time, and so are another way of increasing participation.

Flip charts are great for displaying information with your own personal touch. Things like concepts, tools, and even things you have agreed on with the learners can be put up on flip charts, then displayed and referenced throughout the course.

Even better, flip charts can be used to invite information from the learners. Questions invite answers, tables invite data, and a blank canvas invites self-expression.

Best of all, flip charts can be used to display information that has been provided by the learners themselves. Previous activities then serve as reference points for future activities. They take pride and ownership over the information they generated. They can see it is value to everyone else. As a result, it becomes more meaningful and more memorable.

Flip charts can be works of art, but also works of junk. So, consider the following guidelines for designing them:
- Lining, Sketching, and Tracing
- Sticky Stuff
- How and Where to Hang
- Health and Safety
- The Curse of the Pen

Lining, Sketching, and Tracing

I have seen countless examples (many of which have been produced by myself!) of messy flip charts that contain awful sketches, wonky tables, uneven text sizes, and so on. Learners are generally quite forgiving about these issues, but that doesn't mean we shouldn't avoid them. In fact, turning a messy flip chart into a work of art can be done simply through lining, sketching, and tracing.

When you have tables or specific segments on your flip chart, lining can help create clear boundaries. But rather than simply just drawing lines on it (which will likely be uneven), try folding the paper first. For example, if I want to divide my paper into thirds, then I will first fold it into thirds and then draw lines over the folds. I then hang the paper back up underneath stacks of other paper to help flatten the folds out, or fold the folds the other way to counteract the creases of the original folds.

Sketching is also a great way of preparing any visual elements. Simply use a pencil.

Pencil marks can be so light that they don't show up clearly unless you look closely at the flip chart. So, take some time to sketch things out first. If you make a mistake, don't worry because it won't show up. Just rub it out and carry on. When everything is done, simply draw over with a dark-coloured pen or marker.

Tracing helps with more complicated visuals. For example, maybe for some strange reason you want to draw an eagle on your flip chart. First, find a picture of an eagle online. Download it, adjust the size to suit your needs, print it out, stick it behind your paper, and then draw over it. Voilà! You now have an impressive work of art!

Sticky Stuff

Rather than waste time drawing things by hand, just stick stuff on. Simply print things beforehand, bring them to the training, and then use what you can to stick them on the flip chart.

There are lots of adhesives available, such as Blu Tack, tape, glue, and even special adhesive spray. Adhesive spray generally has the same stickiness as the adhesive on a Post-it note, which is perfect for working with flip charts.

Another great idea is to bring a shower curtain (preferably just a single coloured curtain—avoid ones with patterns or stripes!) and stick it on the wall. Then spray it with adhesives spray. This way you can then stick any piece of paper to it throughout the training.

This is great for activities that include brainstorming, voting, or just organising information.

How and Where to Hang

You are probably going to want to hang your flip chart papers somewhere other than on the flip chart stand, especially when they are full, but sometimes there isn't much space available that's easy to hang stuff on, so plan this in advance.

Look for areas on the walls that would be great for hanging things up. Make sure they are easily viewable from where your learners are sitting. Take a look at those areas of the wall and see what you need to hang them up. Drawing pins, Blue Tack, and tape are always good things to carry around.

One other thing to do in advance is to tear the paper cleanly. Flip chart paper can be a nightmare to tear and requires a lot more effort than I normally prefer to use. But doing this in advance means you can do it with more caution.

Health and Safety

Some flip chart stands are dangerous. I have used numerous flip charts that fell over once my pen made contact with the paper.

At the beginning of the day, check the stability of the flip charts and make sure they are not positioned so that they will fall on top of your learners.

If there are any hazards, then make everyone aware of them whenever they use the flip charts.

The Curse of the Pen

Never assume the pens or markers in the room will work, because they probably won't. They might be too old, or someone forgot to put the lid on and they dried out. Or maybe they work great at the beginning of the day, but run out of ink after several hours.

A good idea is to buy your own selection of good quality pens and markers and take them with you to every training. Just make sure you get them back at the end of the day!

Writing and Readability

I am frequently surprised by the poor readability of the training materials I receive. I have worked with various international training companies who send me long-winded case studies with colloquial expressions and rarely-used terminology. It has then been my job to help the non-native English speakers that I work with in Asia to decode exactly what these materials are saying.

When these training companies allocate 20 minutes for a role-play activity, yet it takes the learners 15 minutes to finish reading the case study, there is obviously something very wrong with readability.

The way you write your training materials will have a very big impact on the learning experience. Your writing should be confusion-free. It must require as little brain power as possible. And it must take as little time to understand as possible.

I'm sure you know the basics of English grammar, and can spell reasonably well (albeit with the occasional assistance of a spell-checker). I'm sure you can probably use a keyboard and find your way around a word processor fairly well, too. But there is more to good writing than just those.

In this section, we'll look at what we need to keep in mind when it comes to structuring our materials, writing our materials, and editing our materials. If you follow the guidelines in this section, you'll have writing that looks good and is a breeze to read.

- ## What is Readability?

You can read some text once and immediately get it, whereas other text seems to take a few tries to understand. We don't want to write things that our learners will struggle with, because that struggle is just another unnecessary distraction from more important things as well as a barrier to understanding.

We want our writing to be readable. Actually, a lot of other people want their writing to be readable as well. Magazine editors, copy writers for web sites, and even technical writers writing instruction manuals all need their writing to be as readable as possible.

If a magazine is not readable, then people won't buy it. If a website is not readable, then it'll lose visitors. And if an instruction manual isn't readable, then users may make mistakes—even fatal mistakes, when it comes to operating machinery.

Readability is extremely important. Readability is a measure of how easy your writing is to understand. Simply put, the clearer it is, the more readable it is. And we can use readability measures and guidelines to improve our writing.

There are a number of ways of measuring readability, but it is typically measured using the Flesch Reading Ease Formula, which was developed by a man called Rudolf Flesch. It scores readability on a level of 0 to 100. The higher the score, the better. These scores equate to the education levels generally required to understand the material. A score of 90-100 means an 11-year-old child could read it, whereas a score of 0-30 would be better suited to a university graduate.

The Flesch Readability Ease formula is a very simple calculation involving average sentence length and average syllables per word. I won't bore you with the details of how to calculate this by yourself because you don't need to. Instead, you can use one of the many online tools available to you. Simply copy and paste your text into one of the tools below and see what result you get:
- http://www.readabilityformulas.com/free-readability-formula-tests.php
- http://www.thewriter.com/what-we-think/readability-checker/
- https://readable.io/
- http://www.hemingwayapp.com/

There are, of course, many other tools available, which a simple web search will reveal.

If you have tried one of the above tools, then you may have discovered that Flesch is not the only way of measuring readability. There are also several other formulas that do the job.

What is important here is that you actually measure readability, especially for longer texts. Furthermore, you should also take steps to write in a more readable style. As you may have gathered from the Flesch formula, one way of doing that is by writing shorter sentences and using words with fewer syllables.

Score	School Level	Readability
90 - 100	5th Grade	Very easy to read.
80 - 90	6th Grade	Easy to read.
70 - 80	7th Grade	Fairly easy to read.
60 - 70	8th & 9th Grade	Plain English.
50 - 60	10th – 12th Grade	Fairly difficult to read.
30 - 50	College	Difficult to read.
0 - 30	College Graduate	Very difficult to read.

But there are also some other things we should keep in mind, which we will look at next.

- ## Layout

Before we get into the details of writing, we first need to consider how our learners will navigate our materials. Much like how we use GPS to plot our route before we actually get on the road, our learners will want an easy way of finding what they want to read.

So, we need to keep the following things in mind to get the most out of our layout:
- Contents
- Headings
- Lists
- Consistent Format

Contents

Contents help our learners find what they are looking for much faster, and therefore help turn our training materials into useful reference tools, post-training.

If you're going to have contents, then you need to have page numbers, so make sure to format your document so that it has page numbers.

When it comes to displaying page numbers on each page, I have found that the centre bottom is the easiest place to work with. If you keep them to the left or right, when you print them out, you will find that some pages have the page number close to the edge of the document, whereas others have them close to the next page. This breaks up the feeling of consistency and makes it harder for our learners to navigate.

If you know what you're doing, then you can set your template up as a double page spread and place the page numbers accordingly so that they come out in the right places when printing. My personal preference, though, is to keep things simple, so I avoid double page spreads and just keep page numbers to the bottom centre.

When it comes to the contents page itself (also called the Table of Contents), consider using a dotted line to guide the reader's eye from the section title to its corresponding page number.

Headings

If you have different sections in your document, then start each section with a heading. Big and bold makes the heading stand out from the rest of the text. In fact, eye-tracking studies have shown that people's eyes are drawn to bold text.

The effect of bold text is easily diminished, however, if you write everything in bold, so save bold for only the headings and occasional key words. To make your headings stand out even more, make sure that they are noticeably bigger than other text.

Use Bullet Lists

People's eyes tend to be drawn to bullet lists, probably because they stand out amongst the oceans of text paragraphs. Use bullet lists to layout the different steps and points in your document, but don't overuse them. A good rule of thumb is to use bullet lists for between 3-6 items. Less than 3 is not a list, and more than 6 can become overwhelming.

Furthermore, ensure you use consistent formatting when using bullet lists. If the first item in the list starts with a verb, then all items must also start with a verb.

Consistent Formatting

This is something to get sorted before you start writing anything. Head to the Format section of whichever software you are working with and make sure you have the following set up:
- Font
- Font sizes
- Page size
- Margins
- Header styles

If you are copying and pasting text from another document, then this may mess up your formatting. In most Microsoft Office programs, a clipboard icon will pop up when you do this. Click the clipboard and select 'Match Destination Formatting'. This will keep the formatting consistent with the formatting you defined for this document.

- ## Clear Writing Habits

Writing for readability is actually very easy, especially if you build the right habits, which are, thankfully, very easy to build as well. All you need to do is:
- **Use Short Sentences**
- **Use Verbs**
- **Focus On DO**
- **Use Clear Language**

Clear Writing Habits

Use Short Sentences

Use Verbs

Focus on DO

Use Clear Language

Use Short Sentences

Shorter sentences are easier to read. Not only do long sentences have the opposite effect, they are also intimidating. No one wants to read a massive block of text.

When writing a typical document for printing or emailing, a good rule of thumb is to use less than 25 words per sentence and less than 5 sentences per paragraph. I call this the 25 Rule.

Of course, this is just a general rule. I've used this as a reference throughout my book, but there are plenty of times where I have broken it. When it makes sense, don't be afraid to break the rules.

If you have a longer sentence, then either eliminate certain words, or break it up into multiple sentences.

Use Verbs

Any instructions need to use verbs, not nouns.

For example, we could say 'Performance gap analysis is, generally speaking, a good place to start'. Alternatively, we could say 'Start by analysing the performance gap'.

Which do you think is clearer? The second one (the one that uses verbs), of course!

Using verbs has several advantages. First of all, verbs allows us to use the imperative form, which is what we use for giving instructions.

For example:
1.   Smile at the customer
2.   Introduce yourself using the 'Name > Value > Credibility > Offer' template to build rapport
3.   Ask open questions to uncover their needs
4.   Summarise their needs to check your understanding

These are more direct, and therefore clearer, than for example the following:
1.   Always greet your customer with a nice smile

2.   Talk a little about yourself to get them to know you better and build rapport
3.   Remember to ask open questions, not closed questions
4.   Always finish by summarising your understanding of their needs

If you look a bit more closely, you'll notice that the second set is slightly more ambiguous. Words like 'always' are redundant. What does 'a nice smile' look like? As opposed to what? A 'not nice smile'? And what does 'a little about yourself' mean? And should I be just 'remembering' to use open questions, or actually using open questions?

That probably seems very fussy and, frankly, it is. But if we want to make our writing as clear as possible, we need to eliminate any ambiguity. As much as possible, we want to increase the possibility that any different people reading the same piece of information will understand *exactly* the point we are trying to get across.

Furthermore, we want to minimise the amount of thinking required in order to take action. Ideally, we want our learners to read, then do. We don't want them to read, then re-read, then decipher the meaning, then create a plan of action, and then, finally, take action. We want to reduce the gap between taking in information and using that information.

Another advantage is that using verbs allows us to stay in the active voice, as opposed to the passive voice. The active voice states things in the order of Who Does What, whereas the passive voice uses the order of What is Done by Whom. When we use the passive voice, we are forced to change our verbs into nouns, which means we must add all sorts of extra, useless words.

For example:
Active Voice:
Jamie designed the training.
Passive Voice:
The training was designed by Jamie.

With the passive voice, we have to add two extra words: 'was' and 'by'. If you write using mostly the passive voice, then all of those extra words quickly add up.

Focus on Do, Ignore Don't Do

Don't blink.

What are you thinking of now? Probably blinking, despite the fact that I told you not to blink. So why are you thinking of blinking?

Because I said the word 'blink'. That word is now in your brain and you can't get rid of it. If I didn't want you to think of blinking, then I shouldn't have used the word 'blink'.

So, what do you think might happen if we write the following instructions?
- Never swear at the customer.
- Don't use closed questions; these prevent the customer from sharing more information.
- Try not to look at your watch whilst the customer is talking.

At the very least, your learners are going to have those thoughts in their mind. This greatly increases the chance that they actually do what you *don't* want them to do.

So, only tell your learners what you want them to do.

Furthermore, including the negative adds an extra layer of thinking. For example:

'I'm not available the first two days of the week, I'm busy on Friday morning and probably in the afternoon, too. Thursday I might be out all day. And Wednesday morning I'm not available either.'

When am I available? I'll let you figure it out, but you can probably deduce that it would be much more useful if I just wrote 'I am available on…'.

When you include the negative, they need to think in order to find out what it is they need to do. And the more thinking they have to do, the more effort it takes to start turning these training materials into action. So don't make them think!

Use Clear Language

Any kind of language that does not have an obvious meaning, or that confuses the reader, is unclear.

Words like 'Try to', 'Should', 'If at all possible' imply that they don't have to do these. This adds yet another layer of thinking as our learners debate how much they should actually follow.

Abbreviations, technical terms, acronyms, etc. all increase the chance of misunderstanding.

For example, look at this sentence I once saw in an email:

'Pls send the JD to the AFD by COB Thurs.'

What the hell does this mean? It should have read:

'Please send the Job Description to the Accounting and Finance Department by close of business Thursday.'

OK, maybe that makes a longer sentence. But it makes a clearer sentence. If our learners don't understand what we're talking about, then it's not going to be very useful.

Keep the language you use as simple as possible. Consider whether a 10-year-old could read it. If they can, then your learners will definitely have no problems.

If you are writing training materials that will be viewed by non-native speakers (and the reality is that, if your training is for a multinational company, you most likely are), then spare a thought for them. Their English isn't as good as yours. They don't know all these fancy colloquialisms or cultural references. But if you target your language at the level of a 10-year-old's, then you are not patronising them, you are helping them.

At the end of the day, if you want to help your learners, make your writing as easy to read as possible.

- **Eliminate Fluff**

If you've followed the guidelines from the previous sections, you'll have nice, clear writing that looks good. But the way it looks is just one part of it. There's also the content that your writing is describing, and this needs to be fluff-free.

Fluff is useless. It takes up space. It's completely unnecessary. For example, you walk past a shop selling fish and see the following sign: 'Fresh fish sold here, at our fish shop!'

That is an incredibly fluffy sign. We can get rid of the fluff and make it shorter and sharper by considering three letters, IRO:
- Irrelevant—Words or details that are not related to the key message
- Repeated—The same word or detail appearing more than necessary
- Obvious—Words or details that are made obvious by the context

Consider how we could use IRO to eliminate the fluff from our fluffy sign.

First of all, what is irrelevant? Well, I don't need to know 'here, at our', because I don't really care who I buy my fish from.

Secondly, what is repeated? The words 'sold' and 'shop' imply the same thing (fish sold at a fish shop). So let's get rid of 'sold'. Also, 'fish' appears twice, so let's get rid of the last one.

And, finally, what is obvious? 'Shop.' I can tell that by looking at it. So now I'm left with just 'Fresh Fish'.

But wait… there's something else that's obvious as well. As I walk past, I can both see and smell fish. So let's get rid of that, leaving us with just the word 'Fresh'. To top it off, let's draw a picture of a fish around the word fresh. And there we have it, a fluff-free sign.

You can use IRO to edit any piece of writing, so have a good look through your training materials and use this to eliminate the fluff.

Eliminate Fluff

Irrelevant

Repeated

Obvious

- ## Less Is More

Aside from layout, writing, and content, one final thing to consider is the quantity of documents we give our learners and trainers.

I frequently receive packs of training materials with dozens of documents. Facilitator's notes here, a trainee workbook there, handouts for Activity 1 here, another handout for Activity 13 over here, a recommended reading list, and so on. It confuses the hell out of me, because I have to keep opening and closing different documents, and cross-referencing.

The more documents you use, the greater the risk of confusion.

If you have several tools which are for use in the same task, then put them into one document. Clearly separate each tool within that document to allow the learners to find the parts they are looking for.

The same principle applies for handouts. Try to keep them all together in one document. Only make a document separate when the nature of the task requires it (for example, in some role-plays, when different people have different roles).

Get into the habit of asking yourself 'Do I really need to include this?' And because I can't say this enough, remember: LESS IS MORE.

Keeping Productive

I originally debated about whether or not to include this section. I thought productivity might not be relevant to designing and delivering training but after researching and reflecting more on it, I realised it is completely relevant.

Productivity affects both the quality of your work and the quality of your life. Designing training can be a very mentally taxing task that, if not managed well, can really start to impact the quality of your work and your life.

As much as I enjoy designing training materials, I find it challenging, at times. Design projects can be daunting, time-consuming, and exhausting. In this modern world, we have a constant influx of emails and instant messages to distract us, increasingly tight deadlines to meet, and more and more difficult people to please.

You might not have those same challenges. You might be one of the lucky people with the luxury of time. If you are, you can figure out a process that suits you. You can spend just as much time and as little time as you want on each task you need to do. And if you are a perfectionist with the luxury of time, you can even redo things as much as you want, until you finally get the result you are looking for.

But I'm going to assume you don't have the luxury of time. If that is the case, then you need to make every minute count. You need to produce high quality results in as little time as possible. And you need to do it in as few goes as possible.

So, in this section, we'll look at how we can get the most out of every minute, and maintain a high level of productivity from start to finish.

• Brain Power

There are many tasks involved in designing materials. From start to finish, you are almost definitely going to be doing every one of these:
- Searching for reference materials
- Referencing reference materials
- Brainstorming
- Outlining
- Writing
- Proofreading
- Editing
- Selecting visuals
- Editing visuals
- Arranging visuals
- Reviewing visuals
- Filing materials
- Sharing materials

All of these tasks require concentration, or what I like to think of as 'brain power'. As you do each of these tasks, you will use up some of your brain power. Some require a lot of brain power, whereas others don't require as much brain power. For example:

High Brain Power Tasks:
- Brainstorming
- Writing

Moderate Brain Power Tasks:
- Referencing reference materials
- Outlining
- Proofreading
- Editing
- Selecting visuals
- Editing visuals
- Arranging visuals

Low Brain Power Tasks:
- Searching for reference materials
- Reviewing visuals
- Filing materials
- Sharing materials

The above categorization is based on my experience with these tasks. Your experience may differ, but I imagine it's somewhat similar.

Now, when we come to each of these tasks, we want to make sure we have enough brain power to complete them. If you've had a tough day, you're desperate to go home, and you're sleepy, then you are really going to struggle with brainstorming and writing. At most, you may be able to manage filing the materials and sharing them.

But, if it's the beginning of the day and you roll into the office beaming with energy, then you'll have the right amount of brain power to get through brainstorming and writing. It would be a bit of a waste to use this optimum time of the day to just do filing and sharing, and then leave brainstorming for later in the day, when you've been drained of energy by all the other demands of your work.

There is a little bit more, however, to making the most of our brain power than just doing tasks when we have the right amount of energy.

Brain Modes

Try this simple experiment:
1. Take out a timer, and time how long it takes you to recite the alphabet from A to G.
2. Now time yourself counting from 1 to 7.
3. For the final part, combine both the alphabet and counting. So say A1 first, then B2, and so on until you get to G7. See how long this takes you.

Most likely, the final step took you considerably longer. The first two steps were very easy, because your brain only had to do one task at a time. But the final one involved you doing two tasks simultaneously, which your brain struggled with.

What you just experienced was what I like to call 'brain modes'. Think of your brain like a computer. When it does one task, it needs to load up the application for that task. If you are brainstorming, your brain needs to expand and be open to all ideas that come up. If you are writing, it needs to be laser-focussed on one train of thought. That takes time and a bit of energy. And when it does another task, it needs to load up another application, which also takes time and energy.

The challenge comes when you keep zigzagging between each task. Your brain needs time to get into the right operating mode to take on that task. If you keep jumping between each of those tasks, your brain needs to keep loading and closing the different applications, which is an incredibly inefficient use of energy.

In fact, some tasks take a considerable amount of time to get into. If I am writing, it can sometimes take me about 10 minutes to get into the flow of things. If an email suddenly pops up and I open that, I then need to take another 10 minutes to get back into the flow of my original writing task.

The biggest implication of this is that we need to tackle one task at a time. Zigzagging wastes valuable brain power and time.

No Distractions

The modern world is full of distractions. As I write this, I have put my phone on the Do Not Disturb mode because the last time I checked it I had missed calls, instant messages, emails, news headlines, and low battery notifications coming in. If I didn't switch on the Do Not Disturb mode, these would be distracting me every few seconds.

Distractions are like leeches. They literally suck away energy, time, and productivity. Every time you get distracted from a task, you need to reload that application. It's like a computer rebooting every time an email comes in.

So, to get the most out of your brain power, make sure that you have nothing to unnecessarily take you out of the brain mode you are in (at least, not until you have finished the task you need to do).

Pacing Your Brain

If you've ever tried any physical activity that involves running, you know that you can't just go all-out all of the time.

The last time I checked, the world record for running 5 km was around 13 minutes. My record is 26 minutes. I was quite pleased with myself until I compared it to that time.

Of course, I could try to match the 13-minute record by running at a pace of about 1 km every 2.6 minutes. But I'm not sure if I have the physical strength to run that fast. And even if I did have the strength, I would also need the endurance to keep going for that length of time. I doubt I even have the genetics to achieve such a feat.

Brain power is exactly the same. If we overdo it, we get exhausted. When I am playing football and I get exhausted, my reaction time gets slower, my movements get sloppy, and I start to make mistakes. It's the same with brain power. When we get exhausted, we can't focus very well, we miss things, and we make mistakes. And what I find is that, when my brain power is low and I continue working anyway, I just stare at the screen like a vegetable.

So, what this means is that we need to take breaks and give our brains time to recover. I do exactly the same when I am running. I'll walk first, to warm up, then do a light jog for a few minutes, then sprint for a few seconds. Then I take a rest by walking for a few more minutes before I start the same cycle over again. When we are using significant brain power, we want to do the same thing.

Generally speaking, we can concentrate on any one task for a maximum of 90 minutes before our brain power stores start to get depleted. The reality is probably quite different and varies for everyone, but the 90-minute rule is a reliable one to go by.

Once you go past 90 minutes, you will probably lose the ability to concentrate. You can push yourself past the 90-minute mark, but there's probably not much point. Your brain will switch off and you'll end up in the vegetable state. It's the equivalent of trying to push a boulder up a hill. It's exhausting and futile.

So, make sure you only work when you have enough brain power to do so, and take regular breaks to help pace yourself. You will be more productive as a result!

You could also take measures to enhance your brain power. Making sure you get a good night's sleep will ensure you start the day with your brain power at its maximum capacity. Practicing concentrating on single tasks for increasing lengths of time may gradually increase your brain power's endurance. And stimulants, such as caffeine, can also help take you beyond your brain's natural limits (although you may pay for it afterwards).

Auto Mode

Remember, not every task requires a lot of brain power. Some are quite routine. For example, I find doing the ironing quite a routine task. In fact, it is so routine that I am able to listen to audio books when I do it.

For most experienced drivers, driving is also a fairly routine task, especially if it's driving the same route you drive every day. That's is why most people can carry on perfectly normal conversations, or even listen to audio books, whilst driving.

However, sometimes these tasks suddenly stop being routine. If my iron catches on fire, or a lorry suddenly appears directly ahead of us in the wrong lane, then these tasks no longer become routine and we must now divert a lot more brain power to the task. Most of the time this doesn't happen, but it is still a possibility.

Make it Routine

So, some tasks happen on auto mode, whereas others happen in manual mode. An implication of this is that we can gradually turn some tasks into auto-mode tasks.

For example, selecting visuals is something that originally took a lot of concentration for me. However, now it is an auto-mode task. The way I turned it into an auto-mode task was by keeping a big folder of the same pictures. In total, I have several hundred stock photos to browse through (on my computer). But I've browsed through this folder hundreds (if not thousands) of times over the years, I have become so familiar with them that I don't even need to think about it. In fact, sometimes I don't even need to browse; I just need to type in the keyword for the picture I want and it automatically comes up.

The more tasks you can turn into routine, auto-mode tasks, the more productive you will be. This means doing these tasks in exactly the same way each time you approach them, essentially making them a habit. So, keep a stockpile of the same resources, use the same tools, and use the same workflow over and over to make it routine.

Of course, you will never make some tasks routine. For example, brainstorming and writing will be different every time. They will always require a lot of brain power.

But maybe you can still simplify them somewhat. For example, you could always use the same software and follow the same steps each time you do it, or even use a template for writing. The key is to make as much of your work as routine as possible.

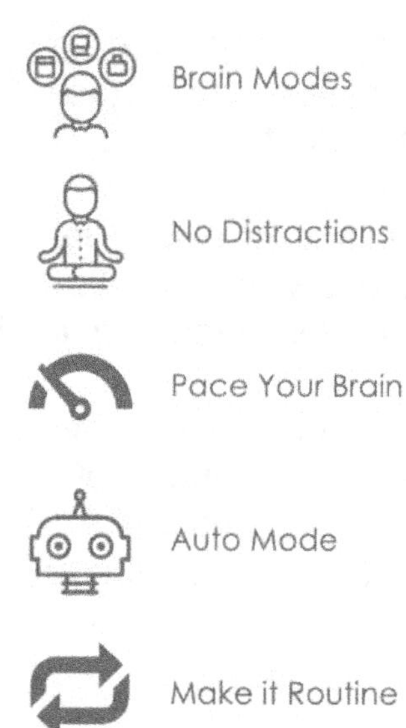

Use the Principles of Brain Power to Your Advantage

The above principles are well worth keeping in mind when it comes to planning your work flow. They will help you get the most out of your time, and help you avoid getting exhausted.

Now, let's have a look at how to make the most of these principles in a bit more detail, by beating procrastination and dealing with stumbling blocks.

- ## Beating Procrastination

One of the biggest causes of procrastination is the prospect of a daunting task. When something seems big and unmanageable, our brains naturally want to avoid it. It's at this point that we start scrolling through social media, playing games, or chatting with our colleagues.

Our brains are like tunnels with light at the end. A tunnel that is dark is incredibly daunting and signals to our brain 'AVOID!', so we need to show our brains the light at the end of this tunnel to make it more willing to take on the task.

The key to doing this is to break the task down into actionable steps. An actionable step is something that we can easily complete. Because they are so easy, and they come with the reward of completing important work, our brains start to become more attracted to the task.

For example, compare the two statements below and think about which one you are more likely to procrastinate on:
1. Design the productivity course
2. Research strategies for overcoming procrastination

I would procrastinate on the first one, because it is a mammoth task that straight away sets my brain into 'avoid' mode. The second one is much easier to visualise (I just need to Google it) and I can see the end point more easily.

An important prerequisite to the above is actually being aware of when you are procrastinating, and using that as a cue to start analysing the task and breaking it down.

Recognise that you may be procrastinating for other reasons as well. Maybe you don't have the motivation because your brain doesn't see the point of doing the task. I have had numerous times where I sat down to design a module and my brain just didn't want to. Rather than push through this resistance, I always take the time to listen to my brain and find out why it is resisting. When I do so, sometimes I find that I don't actually need to design that module because it doesn't fully fit with the aims of the course. Other times, I find that I need to be designing a different module altogether.

• Beating Blocks

Every so often we hit a stumbling block that takes us out of our zone and into the realm of confusion. Maybe we start debating whether we need to include this section or not. Maybe we think it needs to be organised in a different way. Maybe we're not sure how to word things. Not to worry. There are several ways of overcoming blocks.

Background Processing

First of all, recognise that what goes on in the background of your brain is actually very powerful. When you stop consciously thinking about a task, that doesn't mean your brain stops thinking on it. In fact, your brain continues processing it in the background, and does a lot of work.

Sometimes, the best thing to do is to just stop working, and let your brain figure it out in the background. Once you come back to the task a few hours later, your brain will surprise you with the answers you were looking for.

I think of it like this: the background part of my brain is actually the universe. All great ideas don't come from me consciously thinking them up; they are gifts from the universe that emerge from my unconscious. The more relaxed I am, the more my unconscious connects with the universe to receive its powerful gifts. But once I start stressing out, my conscious mind takes over, my unconscious mind closes down, and I lose touch with the universe.

Of course, there is no science to suggest that our unconscious minds are actually magical gateways to the universe, but it's a nice way of thinking about it!

One other implication of background processing is to plan downtime for thinking about complex issues. Sometimes, the night before I am going to start work on something complicated, I'll have a look through the task and identify areas that may create confusion. I'll write down some questions that I want my mind to ponder on and then I'll just leave it. I consider this a process of inputting the issue to my brain for background processing. My brain can process it overnight, whilst I sleep. The morning after, when I come to do my work, I already have fresh insights on how to deal with this potentially confusing area… all before I even start the task.

You can use this tactic, too, whenever you are faced with challenges or tasks that may cause confusion.

Go for a Walk

Every so often, we stumble across a problem that we just can't think of a good solution for, no matter how hard we try. We might sit for ages, trying to think of something but struggle to do so. And then, as we give up and walk to the kitchen to pour a cup of coffee, the solution suddenly comes to mind. It's as if walking unleashed a new thinking process in our brains that led to a better idea.

In fact, that is exactly what happens. Studies have proven that walking makes us more creative. Not sitting down, not running, but *walking*. The science suggests that, when we walk, our heart pumps a little bit faster, sending more blood and oxygen to all organs throughout the body, including the brain.

Furthermore, the pace of walking is effortless for us to perform. Wandering freely requires no conscious attention and frees up our minds. Running requires a bit more attention (because it is harder than walking), so our minds won't wander quite as much when running.

Where we walk will also have an impact on our thinking.

When taking an urban stroll, we will be bombarded with stimuli. Bright lights, the sounds of passers-by chatting in foreign languages, and even the numerous advertisements around us all bombard our senses. Our minds won't wander as freely in such an environment, but the stimuli around us may inspire our mind with new ideas. Conversely, if we walk in the countryside, the relaxing environment will not overstimulate our mind, leaving it free to ponder over whatever it wants to.

So, the next time you have a tricky issue to think through, try going for a walk. If you need new ideas, then go for a walk in the city. If you need to just think something through, then go for a pleasant countryside stroll. Hopefully—probably, actually— you'll stumble upon a solution.

Seek Fresh Input

Find new ideas. These can come from different people or by looking in different places.

Ask other people what they think. Sometimes we get stuck when viewing the issue from one particular angle or thinking about it in one particular brain mode. Other people use different brain modes, view things from different angles, and have different insights to share with us. Their input can help us think of our problem or issue in new ways.

You can also find new resources to get input from, such as a different book, a different author, or even a different format. For example, a lot of my areas of research are in psychology, and I read books about psychology from a variety of angles. Sometimes, they are from a marketing angle, or a design angle, or a productivity angle.

I normally come across the same concepts, but presented from different angles.

For example, one concept I've seen from multiple angles is how our brains have two main modes ('Approach' and 'Avoid', which I talked about already). Seeing it from a design perspective helps me consider the implications of designing things that get people into those modes. Seeing it from a productivity perspective helps me consider how our own work gets us into these modes and affects our working quality. And so on.

Articulate It

Help your brain articulate the issue. Sometimes, a feeling of confusion goes around and around in our minds because we haven't quite figured out what the confusion actually is. But the act of articulating the issue forces us to put it into words, which adds clarity to the issue, and sometimes even helps us find a solution.

We can either articulate it by talking to people or by writing it down.

Talking to people forces us to frame it in a way that they can understand. This really helps us think through the issue and find the words that describe it most clearly. Sometimes, it all becomes so much clearer once we've chosen those words.

Writing helps us get these thoughts out of our mind. We aren't as focussed on finding the right words when writing; we are more focussed on just getting it out of our minds. Just keep writing until it's all out and clear.

If you do try writing, try actually handwriting it rather than typing it. Writing is an art, whereas typing is merely a technical skill. Using our hand to write actually helps us express ourselves more. The look and feel of pen on paper, using different colours, and writing and drawing these issues can really help stimulate the brain.

Creating Materials Summary

The following flowchart is a summary of everything we have looked at in this section:

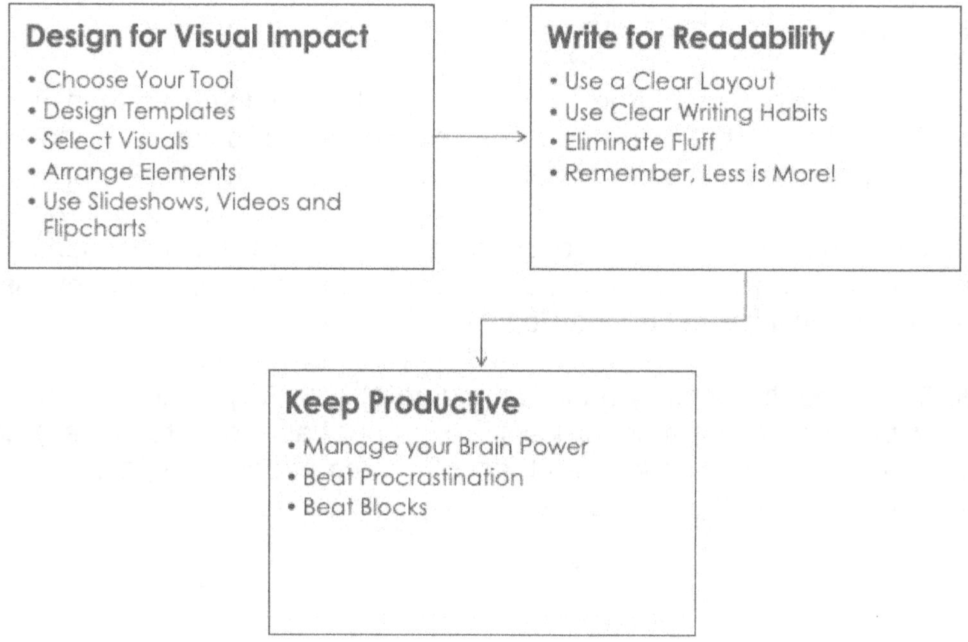

Conclusion

I sincerely hope this book has been useful for you and that:
- It gave you new ideas
- It provided you with answers in your times of need
- It bridged the gaps you needed to cover
- It helped you develop or enhance your own philosophy
- It gave you more confidence and more purpose

I'm a big believer in 'stealing like an artist', and you'll probably have noticed that I have 'stolen' a lot of ideas from various places (and attributed them). It is my hope that you will steal some of the ideas from this book and make them even better. If you'd like to learn more about where I 'stole' my ideas from, then you can check out the 'Books that Inspired Me' section.

There are certain key messages in each section that I hope you can take away and use to help you in the pursuit of designing and delivering a practical learning solution. Here are those key messages:

Part 1: Training Doesn't Work

Training is a lot like dieting. Its success is dependent on certain conditions being present. So, make sure those conditions are present before agreeing to design or deliver training.

Part 2: Mapping the Gap

Performance Gaps—Training is a way of bridging performance gaps that are impacting the business. But not every performance gap can be helped by training. So, make sure you are targeting the right performance gaps through your training.

Defining Outcomes—The most effective way of evaluating training impact is to measure stakeholder satisfaction because, after all, it's the stakeholders who decide if our training will go ahead or not. So, learn the expectations of all of your stakeholders and design your training to satisfy them.

Part 3: Designing for Lasting Impact

Researching a Solution—The goal of research is to answer the 4 Key Questions: What, Why, How and When. Choose the most efficient and effective resources for answering those questions.

Design for Application—People forget things too easily. So, design your training around tools that focus on applying learning back where it counts: the workplace.

Designing for Emotion—We can design training to intentionally impact our learners on an emotional level. We should do that because emotion can also drive their use of tools back at work. Furthermore, through emotional design, we can increase the value of our training.

Part 4—The Five Elements of Delivery

Priming—People need to be in the right mental state to learn. So, start your training by priming them, and take action to keep them primed throughout the whole training.

Guiding—Learners need to understand certain things before they can take action. Choose the most efficient and effective way of helping them achieve that understanding so they can move to acting as soon as possible.

Practice—There's limited time in the training room, so every minute counts! Design your training and practice activities so they can spend as much time as they can practicing the fastest right version of the behaviours we want them to master.

Reflection—Reflection is the brain's way of forming the mental connections that are required to learn, and is ultimately the only way people do learn! Structure shallow and deep reflection activities throughout the training as frequently as possible to strengthen the learning impact.

Committing—It takes commitment to apply learning back to the workplace. But it's easy to overestimate the power of our commitment. So, help learners make realistic commitments to application before finishing the training.

Part 5—Creating Materials

Designing for Visual Impact—Visuals impact the feel of our training. How do learners need to feel if we want them to learn? Choose a visual feel that helps them feel the way we want them to.

Writing for Readability—Training materials should help (and not hinder) learning. So, avoid complexity. Instead, write so clear that even a young child could understand. The less time our learners spend trying to understand, the more time they can spend learning.

Keeping Productive—Designing training requires a lot of creativity and a lot of brain power. So, take steps to manage your brain power so maximise your enjoyment, and optimise your productivity.

Books that Inspired Me

- *Barnga: A Simulation Game on Cultural Clashes* by Sivasailam Thiagarajan
- *Brain Rules: 12 Principles for Surviving and Thriving at work, Home, and School* by John Medina
- *Brilliant Business Writing 2e: How to inspire, engage and persuade through words* by Neil Taylor
- *Business Storytelling for Dummies* by Karen Dietz and Lori L. Silverman
- *Coaching for Performance: The Principles and Practices of Coaching and Leadership* by John Whitmore
- *Design for How People Learn* by Julie Dirksen
- *Drive: The Surprising Truth About What Motivates Us* by Daniel H. Pink
- *Emotional Design: Why We Love (or Hate) Everyday Things* by Don Norman
- *Evolutionary Psychology: A Beginner's Guide* by Robin Dunbar and Louise Barrett
- *Facilitator's and Trainer's Toolkit: Engage and Energize Participants for Success in Meetings, Classes, and Workshops* by Artie Mahal
- *Flow: The Psychology of Happiness* by Mihaly Csikszentmihalyi
- *Gamestorming: A Playbook for Innovators, Rulebreakers and Changemakers* by Dave Gray and Sunni Brown
- *Getting Things Done: The Art of Stress-Free Productivity* by David Allen
- *How to Design and Deliver Great Training* by Alan Matthews
- *How to Get People to Do Stuff: Master the art and science of persuasion and motivation* by Susan Weinschenk
- *How to Have a Good Day: The Essential Toolkit for a Productive Day at Work and Beyond* by Caroline Webb
- *How to Make Sense of Any Mess: Information Architecture for Everybody* by Abby Covert
- *Influence: The Psychology of Persuasion* by Robert B. Cialdini
- *Informal Learning at Work: How to Boost Performance in Tough Times* by Paul Matthews
- *Made to Stick: Why Some Ideas Take Hold and Others Come Unstuck* by Chip Heath and Dan Heath
- *Make it Stick: The Science of Successful Learning* by Peter C. Brown and Henry L. Roediger
- *Maximum Willpower: How to Master the New Science of Self-Control* by Kelly McGonigal
- *NLP at Work: The Essence of Excellence* by Sue Knight
- *Practice Perfect: 42 Rules for Getting Better at Getting Better* by Doug Lemov and Erica Woolway
- *Rapid Instructional Design: Learning ID Fast and Right* by George M. Piskurich
- *Rapid Training Development: Developing Training Courses Fast and Right* by George M. Piskurich

- *Seductive Interaction Design: Creating Playful, Fun, and Effective User Experiences* by Stephen P. Anderson
- *Simple and Usable Web, Mobile, and Interaction Design* by Giles Colborne
- *Steal Like an Artist: 10 Things Nobody Told You About Being Creative* by Austin Kleon
- *Sully: My Search for What Really Matter* by Chesley B. Sullenberger by Jeffrey Zaslow
- *Switch: How to Change Things When Change Is Hard* by Chip Heath and Dan Heath
- *The 7 Habits of Highly Effective People: Powerful Lessons in Personal Change* by Stephen R. Covey
- *The Art of Explanation: Making Your Ideas, Products, and Services Easier to Understand* by Lee LeFever
- *The Charisma Myth: Master the Art of Personal Magnetism* by Olivia Fox Cabane
- *The Coaching Habit: Say Less, Ask More & Change the Way You Lead Forever* by Michael Bungay Stanier
- *The Design of Everyday Things* by Don Norman
- *The Happiness Hypothesis: Putting Ancient Wisdom to the Test of Modern Science* by Jonathan Haidt
- *The Insider's Guide to Technical Writing* by Krista Van Laan and JoAnn T Hackos
- *The Power of Habit: Why We Do What We Do* by and How to Change, Charles Duhigg
- *The Presentation Coach—Bare Knuckle Brilliance for Every Presenter* by Graham Davies
- *The Quick and Easy Guide to Memory Improvement: 45 Practical Tips You Can Use to Boost Your Memory* by Thomas C. Randall
- *The Quick and Easy Guide to Mnemonics: Improve Your Memory Instantly with 15 Powerful Memory AIDS* by Thomas C. Randall
- *The Six Disciplines of Breakthrough Learning: How to Turn Training and Development into Business Results* by Calhoun W. Wick and Roy V.H. Pollock
- *Training and Development for Dummies* by Elaine Biech
- *Wired for Story: The Writer's Guide to Using Brain Science to Hook Readers from the Very First Sentence* by Lisa Cron
- *Write to Sell* by Andy Maslen
- *You Can Have an Amazing Memory: Learn Life-Changing Techniques and Tips from the Memory Maestro* by Dominic O'Brien

About the Author

Jamie Dixon did not enjoy being in classrooms at school. Those early experiences drive his passion for designing and delivering practical learning solutions today.

Originally born in West Sussex, England, Jamie moved to China at the age of 21, to seek new adventures. He planned to stay for just one year, but fell in love with the country, got married, and settled down. He's had a home in Shanghai now for more than a decade.

Jamie started his career in HR before deciding to focus on training so that he could spend less time sitting in an office and more time doing something fun. He quickly found out it was not that easy! From engaging people to actually helping people, there were many challenges along the way.

Furthermore, the experiences of working in a culture so different from his home country—and in a foreign language as well—caused Jamie to question his assumptions about the way things should be done. By building this habit of constantly questioning his reasoning for doing things, Jamie gradually discovered a way of designing and delivering training that leaves everyone happy.

His desire to find a way of designing and delivering training that left everyone happy led to obsessions with mastering every aspect of training. From conducting efficient and effective needs analysis to starting the training in the right way, all the way through to delivering clear explanations and helping learners apply learning back to work, and so on, Jamie has spent many years trying to figure out the best ways of doing these things. He's sought answers from sources far and wide, and taken design lessons from other fields (such as user experience design) and experimented with applying those back into the classroom. The end result is his book *Shaping Paths: How to Design and Deliver PRACTICAL Training.*

In his spare time, Jamie enjoys spending time with his wife, his son, and pet Cockatiel. He also enjoys meditating, reading, and learning other languages. These days, Jamie splits his time between China and the UK, where he helps his clients by designing and delivering training to help people connect with others.

A Note from the Author (and Contact Information)

Thank you so much for taking the time to read through *Shaping Paths*.

This book has been designed as a reference aid for you when designing and delivering your training. Its purpose has been to help you make your training more practical so your learners can start to realise the full value of your training. I sincerely hope you have found it useful.

If you have any questions or would like to get in touch then feel free to email me or check out my website.

My email address is jamie.dixon@shapingpaths.com.
My website is at www.shapingpaths.com.

I wish you the best of luck in shaping paths for your learners!

Shaping Paths

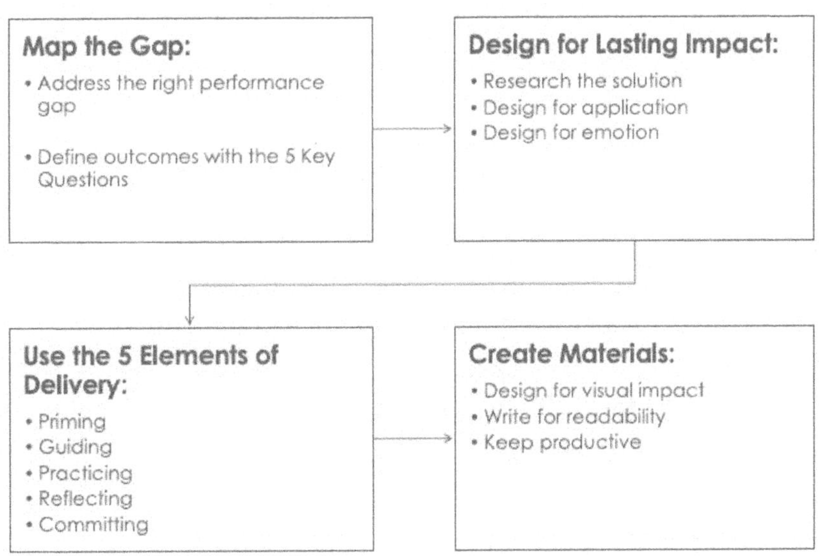

www.ingramcontent.com/pod-product-compliance
Lightning Source LLC
Chambersburg PA
CBHW080249030726
47593CB00009B/2420